THE PSYCHOANALYTIC STUDY
OF SOCIETY

Volume 12

THE PSYCHOANALYTIC STUDY OF SOCIETY

Volume 12

Essays in honor of George Devereux

Edited by
L. BRYCE BOYER
SIMON A. GROLNICK

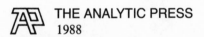 THE ANALYTIC PRESS
1988

Distributed by
LAWRENCE ERLBAUM ASSOCIATES, PUBLISHERS
Hillsdale, New Jersey   London

Distributed solely by

Lawrence Erlbaum Associates, Inc., Publishers
365 Broadway
Hillsdale, New Jersey 07642

ISBN 0-88163-069-1
ISSN 0079-7294

Printed in the United States of America
10 9 8 7 6 5 4 3 2 1

Editors

Robert A. Paul, Ph.D., Atlanta, GA
Fitz John P. Poole, Ph.D., La Jolla, CA
Gilbert J. Rose, M.D., Rowayton, CT
Richard Sennet, Ph.D., New York, NY
Bennett Simon, M.D., Boston, MA
Melford E. Spiro, Ph.D., La Jolla, CA
H.U.E. Thoden van Velsen, Ph.D., Utrecht
Donald F. Tuzin, Ph.D., La Jolla, CA
Vamık D. Volkan, M.D., Charlottesville, VA
Aaron Wildavsky, Ph.D., Berkeley, CA

Contributors

Steven Bauer, M.D. Associate Professor of Clinical Psychiatry, Cornell University Medical College.

Edward F. Foulks, M.D., Ph.D. Sellars-Polchow Professor of Psychiatry, Tulane University Medical School.

Benjamin Kilbòrne, Ph.D. Lecturer, Department of Anthropology, UCLA.

William W. Meissner, M.D. Clinical Professor of Psychiatry, Harvard Medical School. Training and Supervising Analyst, Boston Psychoanalytic Institute.

Daniel Merkur, Ph.D. Assistant Professor, Department of Religion, Syracuse University.

Paul Parin, M.D. Psychotherapeuticher Mitarbeiter an der Psychiatrischen Universitäts Klinik, Burghözli, Zurich.

Leora Rosen, Ph.D. Anthropological Consultant, Walter Reed Army Institute of Research. Washington, D.C.

H.U.E. Thoden Van Velsen, Ph.D. Professor, Instituut Voor Culturele Antropologie van de Rijksuniversiteit, Utrecht.

Contents

George Devereux: In Memoriam[1]

1

George Devereux slipped beyond the Great Divide on May 28, 1985. His death marks a substantial loss to psychoanalysis and psychological anthropology. An astonishingly erudite, brilliant, creative, and difficult man, Devereux has invited stories that often make him appear comical and quixotic. Certainly for those who knew him, Saint George did have his dragons, whether in the form of wives, enemies, critics, or internal demons. However, beneath the stories—his own or those about him—one encounters both tragedy and genius.

George Devereux went through two names, two religions, five disciplines, and many marriages. Yet he never felt he had found his place in the sun. His quest was at once physical, intellectual, and spiritual. Driven by a sense of homelessness, he took considerable trouble in his last years to arrange for his cremated remains to be transported from France to the Mohave burial grounds in Parker, Arizona, where he was given a ritual Mohave funeral.

A Hungarian whose family lands were invaded by the Rumanians in his childhood, he first envisioned a career as a concert pianist, later studying composition with Walter Piston. He left Hungary (then Rumania) while in his late teens to go to Paris, where he studied physics under Marie Curie. His first cousin, Edward Teller, was to become well known as a physicist. Devereux's was not to be a career in physics, however, although the influence of theoretical physics in his work runs very deep. He fell seriously ill in Paris. After months of hospitalization and convalescence, he began work with a publishing house and, when he was well enough, cast about for a way of pursuing a university career. Then, one Saturday afternoon in winter he met Marcel Mauss at the Ecole Pratique des Hautes Etudes and persuaded him to accept

---

1. This paper has been immeasurably improved by the generous criticism of several friends and colleagues to whom I am most grateful: Bryce Boyer, Melford Spiro, and Robert J. Stoller.

one more student. Some time in 1932 Devereux, who had been born into a Jewish family, was baptized a Catholic and changed his name from Dobo to Devereux, becoming French in name as well.

In Paris, Devereux studied under both Mauss and Lucien Levy-Bruhl, the latter a much underestimated figure whose work in philosophy, epistemology, and the history of the social sciences deserves as much re-evaluation as do his books on non-European forms of thinking, belief, and logic (primitive mentality). Both these mentors profoundly influenced Devereux; both encouraged him to the United States. Arrangements were made for him to do his doctoral work under Kroeber at Berkeley. The fieldwork among the Mohave, which he began under Kroeber's guidance, led to lasting attachments with the Mohave, even though he did not get along with Kroeber. That he had his remains buried in Parker in the Mohave tradition attests to the depth of these bonds.

Partly because he was not being heard in anthropology, Devereux sought psychoanalytic training. Karl Menninger brought him to Topeka in the days when the Menninger Clinic was one of the liveliest places in the world for creative explorations in psychoanalysis and psychoanalytically oriented research. In the fifties and sixties, George practiced psychoanalysis in New York City.

Devereux had written roughly 150 articles and at least half a dozen books and had emerged as one of the great pioneers of psychological anthropology when he decided to return to France and begin yet another career, this time as a classicist. He studied Greek and moved to Paris, where he occupied his first permanent university position, at the Ecole Pratique. Thus Devereux's quest led him back to the same university where Mauss had taught; and having returned home he met his seminars on Saturday afternoons, the same day and time that Mauss had chosen. Moreover, for his "homecoming" he decided to learn ancient Greek, the subject Mauss had mastered but of which Devereux was ignorant at the time of their meeting. Several years after beginning ancient Greek, he was invited to All Souls College at Oxford by E. R. Dodds and others as an All Souls scholar for a year, all expenses paid.

2

In the pages that follow I shall piece together what I see to be the relationship between the man and his achievements, endeavoring to be faithful to Devereux's ideas concerning the importance of anxiety—individual, cultural, and universal—in all scientific work. Devereux realized that he was able to write what he did because he was a Hungarian who sojourned in France and lived in the United States; he knew that what he did was a testament to what he was—and could not be.

Much can be said about the nature of Devereux's curiosity; much can be made of the kinds of specific problems that he addressed in his hundreds of papers. I shall concentrate here on *From Anxiety to Method in Behavioral Science* (1967), the work that best establishes Devereux's lasting reputation in the social sciences, anthropology, and psychoanalysis. An adequate understanding of this book—more than anything else he wrote—encourages, and indeed requires, some acquaintance with George's world. Significantly, the book is dedicated to Marcel Mauss, his mentor at the Ecole Pratique.

The central argument of this volume is simple: The sciences of man will never become even reasonably reliable until those who practice them recognize the part played in their theories and their scholarly activities by their own anxieties and fantasies. Unconscious processes affect the scientific endeavor, Devereux argued, in the framing of the materials selected for observation and in the assessment of those interactions on which fieldwork is based. He is quite plain: ". . . behavioral science data arouse anxieties, which are warded off by a countertransference inspired pseudomethodology; this maneuver is responsible for nearly all the defects of behavioral science." The only way of founding the behavioral sciences more firmly is to "attack the greatest complexities frontally, by means of the extremely practical device of treating the difficulty per se as a fundamental datum not to be evaded, but to be exploited to the utmost—not to be explained, but to be used as an explanation of seemingly simpler data" (p. xvii).

In other words, if the sciences of man arouse anxiety, one must not compulsively attempt to alleviate the anxiety, but rather understand what it means. This is especially so because the more anxiety a phenomenon arouses, the "less man seems capable of observing it correctly, of thinking about it objectively and of evolving adequate methods for its description, understanding, control and prediction" (p. 2).

If this is the case—and Devereux presents convincing evidence that it is—then the primary task facing the behavioral sciences is the appropriate and rigorous analysis of the observer's anxieties. For until these are clarified, holds Devereux, we cannot know what it is we are observing; because so much energy goes into distorting and allaying the anxiety itself, we cannot clearly see the object of our investigations or adequately analyze the process of our explorations.

Before proceeding, let us step back and examine the thesis together with what we know of Devereux's life. A Hungarian who left his Rumanian-occupied home, lived in France, and then came to the United States talks about the importance of the observer's feelings. "Look at me, the observer! What I think as an observer is of value to science; I do not have to become just like the stereotypical observers who do not matter for the descriptions of what they are observing!" And if this "Look, Mom, no hands" analysis of anxiety seems extraneous, consider the life that Devereux led. His life finds a place as a background to his book, which he felt the best thing he ever did. Furthermore, let us assume that the anxiety is real, however it chooses to express itself.

As Freud noted in his *Interpretation of Dreams,* the dream of a fire which awakens the dreamer is to be taken seriously, for even if the fire is imaginary, the fear is real. Given this assumption, let us consider the links Devereux makes between his own anxieties as an individual (the Hungarian who went to Paris, changed name and religion, went through five professions, and so on), and the anxieties he claimed must be understood as the basis on which to found future social science.

By placing the observer's anxieties at the center of the behavioral sciences, of course, Devereux is arguing for the importance of the observer qua individual. Logically, such an argument is the counterpart of the idea that the informant is also an individual, who must be assumed to manifest not only the modal personality he is purported to share with other members of his culture, but also his own idiosyncratic individuality. As a result, his accounts of cultural life are necessarily distorted by purpose, context, and defenses. But by making both informant and observer of significance as individuals. Devereux necessarily raises the specter of relativism.

Thus, one must necessarily conclude that the data *are* skewed in different ways by the observer as an individual as well as by the informants; the very difficulties of the observer are to be used, as are the frustrations and reactions to which these difficulties give rise. In this respect, Devereux questions the assumptions about culture as a system, perceived independently of the observer's blind spots and purposes, his or her background and psychodyamics. He explicitly refutes claims of cultural relativism.[2] Cultural relativism, he believes,

---

2. Cultural relativism is a term whose full elucidation would require a monograph on American cultural anthropology. Franz Boas and his students are frequently associated with cultural relativism, which in many ways has defined the major developments in American anthropology since the beginning of the century. Two implications

makes individuals of any given culture pawns of what are construed by the observer to be the rules of the cultural system. For cultural relativists there may be differences between cultures, but within each culture, members abide by what they see to be the desirable values and goals; there is little disagreement or difference in the ways these are perceived or desired, or in the efforts made to achieve goals recognized as worthwhile. Thus the perceptual relativism advocated by Devereux is quite distinct from the cultural relativism of anthropologists like Leslie White, Marvin Opler, and others.

Not until the observer's understanding of himself as observer, and his recognition of his differences with the informants, become part of the data to be analyzed, can the behavioral sciences be set on firmer ground. Thus, Devereux's stand opposes cultural relativism, according to which the doings of people are "only observed," not reacted to, and the observer's judgments have no place whatsoever in the understanding of this material. There is, in fact, a modern cult of psychoanalytic thinking that holds that observers will have no anxieties to overcome if only they can manage to empathize adequately with the patient. Such positions imply a psychological relativism analagous to the cultural relativism against which Devereux argued so cogently.

In the light of Devereux's background as a Hungarian Jew *cum* French Catholic in the United States, why he might have insisted so strenuously on individual differences becomes a matter worth considering. He is speaking about the value of his own individualism; he is not simply an American anthropologist talking about how individuals conform or do not conform to what society holds to be the model of conduct and "normal" behavior about which no observer can make any value judgments. He is a Hungarian who lives and works in

of the doctrine of cultural relativism are useful in this context. The first deals with the extent to which the observer is believed to be capable of abstracting himself or herself from the values of the culture to which he or she belongs, in order to be "objective" and "nonjudgmental" about the values of the culture studied. What the Bonga-Bonga do is ipso facto good for the Bonga-Bonga. Thus, in this sense, cultural relativism implies that the observer be in a state of innocence and grace unequalled even by the newborn. The observer "just observes and collects"; he does not theorize even about what he is doing, let alone about what he thinks he is doing. The second implication of cultural relativism useful in this context pertains to the hostility against claims that a concept of universal human nature has any relevance for anthropology or sociology. Thus, questions of how Mohave beliefs in dreamed creation myths respond to human needs for cultural values, for example, are never asked by cultural relativists. Nor are questions pertaining to any judgments about the "health" or "illness" of the culture studied. Devereux sought to define criteria of normality and abnormality in pan-human terms, such that cultural values could then be understood in a larger context of a theory of human nature.

America at a time when Boasian (i.e., German-American) models dominate the field. He is a gadfly reminding American cultural relativists that their relativism is itself relative to their own discipline and culture.

When he says that the Sedang are wretchedly cruel people and the Mohave are delightful and sexually creative, he is expressing something of his own human and subjective (and Hungarian) reactions, which are part of the picture to be seen and understood. One possible explanation for his publishing virtually nothing on the Sedang (about which he had reams of notes) was that he hated them and did not want to delve into what they represented for him. Clearly, he idealized the Mohave, in whom he had found a good mother in the Winnicottian sense. Like Freud, he needed both a sweet friend and a bitter enemy. Many times I tried to persuade him to publish Sedang materials. He responded either with indifference, saying he had more important things to do, or with vituperation, stating unambiguously that he violently hated the Sedang. Committed as he was to the principles enunciated in *From Anxiety to Method,* he could not have dealt with the Sedang without also dealing with his own reactions to them, without dealing with his own anxieties as observer in that field situation. That he was disinclined to do. Perhaps because he needed to idealize the Mohave he needed also to vilify the Sedang.

3

Let us return now to Devereux's conceptions of data and of the scientific method. He writes:

A phenomenon becomes a datum for a particular science only through being explained in terms of the characteristic intervening variables of that science. No phenomenon, no matter how limited and specific, belongs a priori to any particular discipline. It is *assigned* to a particular discipline *through* the manner in which it is explained and it is this 'assigning' which transforms a phenomenon (event) into a datum, and, specifically, into the datum of a particular discipline. Just as there exist no *pre*-assigned *phenomenon,* so there exist no *un*assigned *data* [p. 16].

Or, to say roughly the same thing, Devereux relies on Poincaré's principle that "method is the choice of facts," adding that "it is simply a matter of agreeing on what one considers *relevant* in a given context" (p. 16).

Of course, one can disagree with Devereux's claims, but what remains of importance in his valiant attempt to construct a theory of evidence based on ideas about method, an attempt he continued in his work on the principle of complimentarity in the sciences of man (*Ethnopsychanalyse complimentariste*). These efforts to develop an epistemology for the sciences of man are a mainstay of *From Anxiety to Method* (1967). In fact, he says clearly that the theoretical problems raised by Sapir's discussions of the "Two-Crows denies this" [informants can disagree] are the very ones to which the second part of the book is dedicated. "I not only propose to recognize the existence and scientific import of divergences between the reports of two behavioral scientists, but also to correlate them with their respective personalities, with the structural and functional complexities of their own cultural background and also with that of the culture which they studied" (p. 43). This remark again points up Devereux's insistence on a theoretical framework allowing for individual differences, both in informants and observers.

Individual differences in observers—such as those in shamans ("Individual Ritual Differences in Mohave Shamanism")—cannot be understood in terms of conscious ideation alone. The very notion of anxiety used by Devereux implies *unconscious* dimensions of which the observers may well not be aware, either because their professional defenses screen these from them, or because they themselves are unaware of the inevitability of anxiety reactions to behavioral science data.

Because "man acts with panic to the unresponsiveness of matter" (p. 32), he needs to deny unresponsiveness and "to control his panic." This need induces him "to interpret physical occurrences animistically, and to impute to them "meanings" which they do not possess, so as to be able to experience them as 'responses.' When such perceived 'responses' cannot be elicited, man imagines (hallucinates) them" (p. 33).

Anxiety is crucial for child development (animism), the prototype of all panic being the child's inevitable experience of the unresponsiveness of the mother to his needs. Therefore a tendency toward animism is present in *all* adults as the product of the human family (p. 32). Were the unresponsiveness of matter not a trauma for all human beings, then "meanings" would not be imputed to events, activities, feelings, and the like, and human understanding, communication, and experience as we know them could not exist. Hence, the very conditions under which there would be no distortion in the behavioral sciences are at best hypothetical.

In short, basic hypotheses about the nature of anxiety, of the human family, of the individuality of the observer all contribute to Devereux's ideas about the foundations of the behavioral sciences. In other words, the human need to deal with the trauma of the unresponsiveness of matter underlies the imputation of meaning to our various worlds: physical, social, and psychological. If this proposition be admitted, then it follows that a behavioral science without anxiety is one without meaning. Seen this way, the anxiety of the behavioral scientist represents a source of distortion *and* meaning, and meaning in distortion.

4

Devereux reminds us that the concern of the book is "the limited problem of the distinctive nature of behavioral data and of the theoretical framework which treats life-phenomena as life-phenomena and not as something else" (p. 96). Thus he is not concerned with the anxieties that may or may not enter into the data of the physical sciences. Every method, every theoretical construction grows up in the context of and in response to the reactions and anxieties of the observer. Therefore, argues Devereux, "a great many professional defenses are simply varieties of the isolation defense which 'decontaminates' anxiety-arousing material by repressing or negating its affective content and human as well as personal relevance" (p. 83). Thus the affective reactions that behavioral science data produce are specifically linked to questions of theory and method in the behavioral sciences and are not necessarily the same as those encountered in the physical sciences.

To illustrate these anxieties Devereux mentions both the irrational in sexual research and the failure of anthropologists to take seriously the "sciences" of non-European (primitive) peoples. Nonoccidental psychiatric theories do have something to contribute to the understanding of psychiatric disorders (p. 122). Among other things they prompt us to see the cultural frameworks used by observers in the behavioral sciences, it being inconceivable that any observer should command his ethnic character to hover in midair. Moreover, ethnic character, "which implies the adoption of a culturally determined point of view or frame of reference for the appraisal of reality, is a major source of distortions" (p. 135). Furthermore, the status of being human confers importance on the self-relevance of research in the behavioral sciences, such that self-models affect purportedly objective theories as various as those of "race," "adaptation," and "psychiatric diagnoses."

The imputation of meaning to the social and cultural environment is, holds Devereux, a basic expression of the tendency of the human mind to alleviate the panic engendered by the unresponsiveness of matter. Man needs "to deny physical occurrences animistically, and to impute to them 'meanings' which they do not possess, so as to be able to experience them as 'responses'." This human need emerges as perhaps the most fundamental trait of the human mind. "If stimuli interpretable as 'response' are not forthcoming, man tends to substitute an illusory response for the (inappropriately) expected response which is not forthcoming" (p. 33). As there are inevitably individual and cultural, as well as human, factors in the so-called animistic ideas of primitives and in the so-called scientific ideas of behavioral scientists, Devereux proposes that these factors be assessed and used in both theory and method. There is no reason a priori to believe that non-European ideas about psychiatric disorders are necessarily more heavily laden with hallucinatory distortions than are our own. Furthermore, since it is an essential feature of the human mind to respond to the perceived (and unconsciously fantasized) unresponsiveness of matter, any behavioral science that pretends to truth—but fails to take anxiety reactions into account—is necessarily built on sand.

5

If human beings react to the unresponsiveness of matter with anxiety, and if such anxiety constitutes an essential part of the data (and therefore of the methods) of the behavioral sciences, it follows that the eliciting of data from informants is necessarily "disturbance," which must be understood in terms not only of the informant's, but also of the observer's, reactions (countertransference) to the situation thereby created. This means, explains Devereux, that both transference and countertransference are elicited. The task at hand in extending psychoanalytic epistemology to the other behavioral sciences entails the exploitation of disturbances recognized to have been produced by observation. We must "find out what positive insights—not obtainable by other means—we can derive from the fact that the presence of an observer (who is of the same order of magnitude as that which he observes) disturbs the observed event" (p. 270).

Furthermore, the data thus obtained are particularly useful because they indicate the living reactions to disturbance. "Any unprecedented situation tests the range, scope and adaptability of a system" (p. 272) and of the people who create such systems. In the case of anthropology, for example, much can be learned by analyzing the disturbance caused by the presence, personality, and activities of the anthropologist, a disturbance specific to that kind of situation. The kind of situation is, of course, influenced by the expectations, perceptions, training and motivations of the anthropologist, as well as by the uses to which he intends to put his fieldwork (for example, the writing of an ethnography). Because only the statements the observer makes about his own statements can be assessed by readers, only when the observer is both the observer *and* observed can he intelligibly make the statement, "And this I observe." This is so particularly because, as Devereux remarks "the disturbance occurs 'within' the observer, and it is this disturbance which is then experienced as the real stimulus and treated as the relevant datum" (p. 301).

In other words, the analysis of any disturbance (whether one encountered by a psychoanalyst, an anthropologist, or a sociologist) requires that the observer be capable of describing that disturbance in terms not only of cultural categories (collective representations and sentiments) but also of idiosyncratic differences. Such an analysis of a disturbance cannot be complete without an assessment of the *psychological* dynamics of what Devereux, departing from standard psychoanalytic usage, calls "transference" and "countertransference." Disturbances may be understood in terms of Fromm's distinction between healthy adjustment and sadomasochistic conformism, in terms of the ethnic unconscious or unconscious conflicts on which a particular culture capitalizes, in terms of neuroses of sanity or the neurotic compulsion to seem normal, or indeed in terms of antisocial social ideals.

The second book of Devereux's that I shall treat here, *Basic Problems of Ethnopsychiatry,* (also dedicated to the memory of Marcel Mauss) can be seen to elaborate the arguments he lays out in *From Anxiety to Method.* In this work he asks how studying characteristic patterns of neurosis and psychosis can contribute to anthropology. There are, Devereux notes, ethnic disorders in *all* cultures (for example, amok in Malaysia, arctic hysteria in the Arctic, schizophrenia in Western Europe and the U.S.). Jung (1928) observed: "We always find in the patient a conflict that at a certain point is connected with the great problems of society. . . . Neurosis is thus, strictly speaking, nothing less than an individual attempt, however unsuccessful, at the solution of a universal problem". In the attempt at the solution of a universal, human problem it is necessary and inevitable that cultural models will be used (for instance, models of misconduct in Linton's sense or antisocial social ideals). Furthermore, no analysis of what causes the psychosis of John Doe can be complete without an explanation of why Richard Roe, beset with similar problems and conflicts, has

become neither antisocial nor psychotic. What links John Doe to
Richard Roe thus implies a cultural matrix. Once this is admitted, then,
for example, the series surgeon, anatomist, butcher, assassin, homici-
dal maniac appears as a continuum to be analyzed in terms of cultural
meanings and cultural context: For us, the anatomist is a valued
member of society; in the Middle Ages he was perceived as a mad
vampire.

Such problems are disturbing for the behavioral scientist, whose
reactions and defenses are inevitably going to be affected by cultural
values, models and patterns. For example, in "The Cannibalistic
Impulses of Parents" (1980:122–137), Devereux plainly states that the
"singular lack" of psychoanalytic interest in the entire question of the
cannibalistic impulses of adults toward children is a significant datum,
an explanation of which requires the analysis of "both psychologically
and culturally determined scotomizations" (p. 122). Or consider a
second example, Devereux's study, "Female Sexual Juvenile Delinquency in a Puritanical Society" (p. 155–184). In this paper he discusses female juvenile sex delinquency "from the viewpoint of psychoanalytically oriented social science." Because "the
anxiety-arousing nature of this problem has deeply affected current
theoretical and therapeutic views," his first task will have to be a
careful scrutiny of the "scientific definition and treatment of such girls
from the viewpoint of the *Wissensoziologie* of psychiatry" (p. 156).
Devereux also reminds us that human beings can be destructive in
many ways, only a few of which are labeled "delinquent," "antisocial," or "abnormal," and that such labeling is a *selective* process
profoundly influenced by culture. He criticizes the labeling of theorists
who emphasize epidemiology and do not lend credence to the discrep-
ancies between language and thought. Because they are too preoccupied with linguistic analysis and categories, they are too preoccupied
with linguistic analysis and categories, they cannot allow themselves to
be disturbed by questions concerning the specific cultural meanings of
the disease entities they claim to be studying.

But there is more here. One begins to expect that Devereux will
provide us with an analysis of 1) what he sees to be the cultural
disorders of our own society; 2) the ways in which our own cultural
values, scotomizations, and models influence the process by which
certain persons acquire the status of being "mad"; and 3) the cultural
dimensions of all successful psychoanalyses. And, indeed, one can find
his contributions to all of these problems.

If signal symptoms are culturally conventionalized signals used to
communicate about insane status, and if every signal symptom entails

an attack on major social values, then one dimension of diagnosis is the transformation of an idiosyncratic singularity of behavior into a form in which it can be communicated about, a process of reinforcement in the learning-theory sense of the word. Such a process allows for the use by individuals of cultural materials. Thus, Devereux argues, schizophrenia (or, some might say, narcissistic disorders) is both as prevalent as it is the United States and Europe and as relatively intractable to treatment precisely because of its cultural supports, which practicing psychiatrists and psychotherapists and psychoanalysts have a personal stake in not seeing. "I believe schizophrenia to be almost incurable not only because it has an organic basis but because its principal symptoms are systematically encouraged by some of the most characteristic and powerful—but also most senseless and useless (dysfunctional)—"values" in our civilization."[3] Therefore, schizophrenia is important in our understanding of our culture. And the converse is equally true: our culture is important in understanding schizophrenia. Moreover, it is equally pertinent in enabling the therapist to recognize in himself or herself those persona or introjects cast in one of culture's plays.

As Devereux observes, the therapist's effectiveness "can be hampered quite as much by his ethnocentric and cultural blindnesses and blind spots as by his unconscious idiosyncratic counter-transference reactions." (1980:214) From this it follows that the training of any psychotherapist is incomplete unless it is analytic, unless "the future therapist ceases to scotomize *not only* his subjective conflicts *but also* the objective ones of the society into which he was born and in which he functions as a psychotherapist" (p. 215). One hears in these lines not only the Hungarian practicing in New York, but also the Hungarian who values the independence and intellectual freedom that his position in a "different" culture gives him. He, as a therapist, has two sets of cultural scotomizations to sort out and recognize. In fact, having a dual cultural background is valuable for the therapist; it obliges him to examine his own cultural scotomizations *as well as* those of the culture (or rather of the members of the culture) in which he practices.

---

3. While it could certainly be objected that the WHO surveys have demonstrated that schizophrenia is universally prevalent in nearly equal proportions, such as epidemiological approach does not necessarily invalidate the thrust of Devereux's argument. What he is arguing is that cultural values contribute to the *mise en scène* of psychopathology and that, just as therapeutic action depends on interpersonal interactions and social values, so does the pathology itself. He also says that not all disorders pose threats of the same gravity to the social body. One wishes that his diagnosis of social ills and his evaluation of psychiatric disorders had been integrated in a theoretically more compelling fashion. In this instance, as in others, Devereux's bald claims obscure the value of his insights.

Therefore, we might expect that in some respects immigrants practicing psychotherapy in this country (or anywhere else) can ipso facto be more aware than are we Americans of the ways cultural values support both what psychotherapists and psychoanalysts do and do not do. In that sense, the "Americanization" of psychoanalysis has perhaps impoverished the discipline because it has not been accompanied by an adequate understanding of the cultural dimensions of psychoanalytic practice, one that can be made part of psychoanalytic education.

Devereux's argument extends to what makes psychoanalysis effective in *our* society. The invention of psychoanalysis by Freud would not have been possible everywhere. "Only members of a society in which segmental and impersonal relations are the *main* fabric of society could have devised the psychoanalytic method" (p. 226). Obviously, this is not to say that psychoanalysis cannot be effective in other cultures also. It is rather to emphasize that *our* here-and-now understanding of how psychoanalysis functions in *our* culture requires that we examine, probe, and tolerate all dimensions of our anxieties—the cultural, the idiosyncratic, and the human.

Simply because the Greeks, who bequeathed to us so much, happened to have been among the first peoples to differentiate between the *categories* of reality and imagination does not mean that issues behind these categories are any less problematic and anxiety arousing for us than they are for other societies in which there is no such distinction in categories. Ancient Greece had no prevalent mental illness of the gravity of schizophrenia or the narcissistic disorders and was therefore able to produce the Parthenon and Aeschylus, Thucydides and Plato. Indeed, what makes psychoanalysis effective can be related to what makes schizophrenia or the affective or narcissistic disorders pernicious. In our culture the ethnic neurosis (or psychosis) happens to be a condition more serious than hysteria. Therefore, implies Devereux, our culture is ailing, a point made by Durkheim and others. While anomie and suicide were treated by Durkheim as symptoms of a social ill, schizophrenia is analyzed by Devereux as at once an individual and a cultural (social) fact.

It appears then that Devereux and Durkheim had similar missions: to diagnose social ills, to describe to us what is wrong with the social body. Moreover, both men pursued their ambitions by drawing on the European tradition of a science of man, a global epistemology that seeks to restore wholeness to a fragmented world. Unlike Durkheim, whose epistemology, idealism, and theories of social sentiments and collective representations resemble a magnificent theological system, Devereux writes no book that is aesthetically pleasing; his arguments are often tough and hardgoing; he loads his articles with cases and often loses that sense of style and proportion, of flow and movement which we enjoy in Freud, Frazer or Durkheim. Nonetheless, it is Devereux's genius to make his own anxieties speak and by so doing enable us to hear things in ourselves. In an increasingly dehumanized world, such efforts are enormously important.

Perhaps more than any other scholar of his generation—and some might say of this century—Devereux intuitively sensed the limitations of both Freud and Durkheim and tried to elaborate a comprehensive epistemology embracing complimentary psychological and sociological perspectives in which unconscious forces and anxieties on both individual and cultural levels can be discerned, analyzed and made part of the behavioral sciences. Although he was often unsuccessful in his herculean effort and did not achieve in his lifetime recognition for his contributions to the epistemology of the social sciences, he certainly deserves our admiration and respect for having devoted his life to so monumentally important a task.

BIBLIOGRAPHY

DEVEREUX, G. (1967). *From Anxiety to Method in the Behavioral Sciences*. The Hague: Mouton.

—— (1972). *Ethnopsychanalyse Complimentariste*. Paris: Flammarion.

—— (1980). *Basic Problems in Ethnopsychiatry*. Chicago: University of Chicago Press.

FREUD, S. (1900–1901). *The Interpretation of Dreams*. Standard Edition, 4 & 5. London: Hogarth Press.

JUNG, C. G. (1928). *Two Essays on Analytical Psychology*. (Trans. from the German by H. C. & C. F. Baynes). London: Balliere, Tindall & Cox.

BIBLIOGRAPHY OF GEORGE DEVEREUX

1933

Guillaume de Hevesy's Publications, *American Anthropologist*, 35:552–554. Reprinted in *Journal of the Polynesian Society*, 42:327–329.

Recent anthropological reports of the government of Papua, *American Anthropologist*, 35:792–794

*Courtesy of Drs. Weston La Barre and Ilona Cernat

1935

A note on the mechanical principle of the outrigger, *American Anthropologist*, 35:207–209

1937

Mohave Soul Concepts, *American Anthropologist*, 39:417–422.
Functioning Units in Hǎ(rhn)de:an(ng) Society, *Primitive Man*, 10:1–7.
Der Begriff der Vaterschaft bei den Mohave Indianern, *Zeitschrift für Ethnologie*, 69:72–78.
Institutionalized homosexuality of the Mohave Indians, *Human Biology*, 9:498–527. Excerpted in M. Mead and N. Calas (ed.), *Primitive Heritage: An Anthropological Anthology*, New York, 1953. Revised and expanded in H. M. Ruitenbeek, *The Problem of Homosexuality in Modern Society*, New York, 1963. Also reprinted in R. C. Owen et al., (ed.), *The North American Indians*, New York, 1967. Excerpted and translated in R. Italiaander, *Weder Krankeit noch Verbrechen*, Hamburg, 1969.
L' envoûtement chez les Indiens Mohave. *Journal de la Société des Américanistes de Paris*, 29:405–412.

1938

Social Time: A Methodological and Functional Analysis, *American Journal of Sociology*, 43:967–969.
Principles of Hǎ(rhn)de:a (ng) divination, *Man*, 38:125–127.

1939

A Sociological Theory of Schizophrenia, *Psychoanalytic Review*, 26:315–342.
Maladjustment and Social Neurosis, *American Sociological Review*, 4:844–851.
Mohave Culture and Personality, *Character and Personality*, 8:91–109.
The Social and Cultural Implications of Incest Among the Mohave Indians, *Psychoanalytic Quarterly*, 8:510–533.

1940

A Conceptual Scheme of Society, *American Journal of Sociology*, 54:687–706.
Social Negativism and Criminal Psychopathology, *Journal of Criminal Psychopathology*, 1:325–338.
Primitive Psychiatry (part 1), *Bulletin of the History of Medicine*, 8:1194–1213 & 11:522–542.
Religious Attitudes of the Sedang. In W. F. Ogburn & M. T. Nimkoff (ed.) *Sociology*, Cambridge, MA.

1941

Mohave Beliefs Concerning Twins, *American Anthropologist*, 43:573–592.

1942

Motivation and Control of Crime, *Journal of Criminal Psychopathology*, 3:553–584.
Funeral Suicide and the Mohave Social Structure, *Bulletin of the History of Medicine*, 11 (5):552–542.

Social Structure and the Economy of Affective Bonds, *Psychoanalytic Review,* 29:303–314.

The Mental Hygiene of the American Indian, *Mental Hygiene,* 26:71–84.

Primitive Psychiatry (Part 2), *Bulletin of the History of Medicine,* 11:522–542.

The Social Structure of the Prisons and the Organic Tensions (with M. C. Moos), *Journal of Criminal Psychopathology,* 4:306–324.

1943

Antagonistic Acculturation (with E. M. Loeb), *American Sociological Review,* 7:133–147.

Some Notes on Apache Criminality (with E. M. Loeb), *Journal of Criminal Psychopathology,* 4:424–430.

Letter to the Editor, *American Journal of Sociology,* 48:767.

1944

A Note on Classical Chinese Penological Thought, *Journal of Criminal Psychopathology,* 5:734–744.

The Social Structure of a Schizophrenia Ward and Its Therapeutic Fitness, *Journal of Clinical Psychopathology,* 6:231–265

1945

The Logical Foundations of Culture and Personality Studies, *Transactions of the New York Academy of Sciences,* Series II, 7:110–130.

The Convergence between Delusion and Motor Behavior in Schizophrenia, *Journal of Clinical Psychopathology,* 7:89–96.

1946

Au Musée de l'Homme, *Off Limits,* 5(1).

Preface in Louis Mars, *La Vodou et la Psychiatrie Comparée,* Port-au-Prince, Haiti.

Quelques Aspects de la Psychanalyse aux Etats-Unis, *Les Temps Modernes,* 1:229–315.

La Chasse Collective au Lapin chez les Hopi, Oraibi, Arizona, *Journal de la Société des Américanistes de Paris,* 33:63–90.

1947

The Potential Contributions of the Moi to the Cultural Landscape of Indo-china, *Far Eastern Quarterly,* 6:390–395.

Mohave Orality: An Analysis of Nursing and Weaning Customs, *Psychoanalytic Quarterly,* 16:519–546. Reprinted (abridged) in W. Muensterberger (ed.) *Man and His Culture,* London, 1969.

1948

Mohave Etiquette, *Southwest Museum Leaflets,* 22.

Mohave Pregnancy, *Acta Americana,* 6:89–116.

The Mohave Neonate and Its Cradle, *Primitive Man,* 21:1–18.

Mohave Indian Infanticide, *Psychoanalytic Review,* 35:126–139.
Mohave Indian Obstetrics, *American Imago,* 5:95–139.
Mohave Indian Kamalo:y, *Journal of Clinical Psychopathology,* 9:433–457.
Mohave Zoophilia, *Samiksa, Journal of the Indian Psycho-Analytical Society,* 2:227–245.
Mohave Coyote Tales, *Journal of American Folklore,* 61:233–255.
The Function of Alcohol in Mohave Society, *Quarterly Journal of Studies on Alcohol,* 9:207–251. Reprinted in G. Devereux, *Mohave Ethnopsychiatry and Suicide,* 1961.
Smith Ely Jelliffe—Father of Psychosomatic Medicine in America, (with K. A. Menninger), *Psychoanalytic Review,* 35:350–363.

1949

The Mohave Male Puberty Rite, *Samiksa, Journal of the Indian Psycho-Analytical Society,* 3:11–25.
The Psychological "Date" of Dreams, *Psychiatric Quarterly Supplement,* 23:127–130.
Some Mohave Gestures, *American Anthropologist,* 51:325–326.
Mohave Paternity, *Samiksa, Journal of the Indian Psycho-Analytical Society,* 3:162–194
A Note on Nyctophobia and Peripheral Vision, *Bulletin on the Menninger Clinic,* 13:83–93.
The Social Structure of the Hospital as a Factor in Total Therapy, *American Journal of Orthopsychiatry,* 19:492–500.
Post-partum Parental Observances of the Mohave Indians, *Transactions of the Kansas Academy of Science,* 52:458–465.
Mohave Voice and Speech Mannerisms, *Word,* 5:268–272. Reprinted in D. H. Hymes (ed.), *Language in Culture and Society,* New York, Harper & Row, 1964.

Magic Substances and Narcotics of the Mohave Indians, *British Journal Medical Psychology,* 22:110–116. Reprinted in *Mohave Ethnopsychiatry and Suicide,* Washington, DC: Smithsonian Institution.

1950

Heterosexual Behavior of the Mohave Indians. In G. Róheim (ed.), *Psychoanalysis and the Social Sciences,* 2:85–128, New York.
Notes on the Developmental Pattern and Organic Needs of Mohave Indian Children, *Transactions of the Kansas Academy of Science,* 53:178–185.
Mohave Indian Autoerotic Behavior, *Psychoanalytic Review,* 37:201–220.
Psychodynamics of Mohave Gambling, *Psychoanalytic Review,* 37:201–220.
Psychodynamics of Mohave Gambling, *American Imago,* 7:55–65.
A Guide to Psychiatric Books (with K. Menninger), New York.
Catastrophic Reactions in Normals, *American Imago,* 7:343–349.
Amusements and Sports of Mohave Children, *The Masterkey,* 24:143–152.
The Occupational Status of Nurses, (with F. R. Wiener), *American Sociological Review,* 15:628–634. Reprinted (abridged) in W. H. Form W. H. and Stone, G. P. *The Social Significance of Clothing in Occupational Life,* East Lansing, MI, 1955,
Some Unconscious Determinants of the Use of Technical Terms in Psychoanalytic Writings, *Samiksa, Journal of the Indian Psychoanalytical Society,* 4:1–6. Reprinted the same year in *Bulletin of the Menninger Clinic,* 14:202–206.
Status, Socialization and Interpersonal Relations of Mohave Children, *Psychiatry,* 13:489–502.

The Psychology of Feminine Genital Bleeding: An Analysis of Mohave Indian Puberty and Menstrual Rites, *International Journal of Psycho-Analysis*, 31:237–257.
Education and Discipline in Mohave Society, *Primitive Man*, 23:85–102.
Size, Diet and Standard, *Popular Dogs*, 23:60–61.
The Validity of Psychoanalysis, *Bulletin of the American Psychoanalytic Association*, 6:30–31.
Mohave Indian Personality, *Bulletin of the American Psychoanalytic Association*, 6:33–35.

1951

Reality and Dream: The Psychotherapy of a Plains Indian (Preface by K. Menninger & R. H. Lowie), New York, International Universities Press, new edition 1969. Translated into German and French, 1981.
Mohave Chieftainship in Action, *Plateau*, 23:33–43.
Some Criteria for the Timing of Confrontations and Interpretations, *International Journal of Psycho-Analysis*, 32:19–24. Reprinted in L. Paul, *Psychoanalytic Clinical Interpretation*, London, 1963.
Mohave Indian Verbal and Motor Profanity. In G. Róheim (ed.) *Psychoanalysis and the Social Sciences*, 3:99–127, New York.
Neurotic Crime vs. Criminal Behavior, *Psychiatric Quarterly*, 25:73–80.
The Primal Scene and Juvenile Heterosexuality in Mohave Society (in) G. B. Wilbur & W. Muensterberger (ed.), *Psychoanalysis and Culture* (Róheim Festschrift), 90–107, New York, International Universities Press.
Cultural and Characterological Traits of the Mohave Related to the Anal Stage of Psychosexual Development, *Psychoanalytic Quarterly*, 20:398–422.
Haitian Voodoo and the Ritualization of the Nightmare (with L. Mars), *Psychoanalytic Review*, 38:334–342.
Three Technical Problems in the Psychotherapy of Plains Indian Patients, *American Journal of Psychotherapy*, 5:411–423.
Atypical and Deviant Mohave Marriages, *Samiksa, Journal of the Indian Psycho-Analytical Society*, 4:200–215.
The Oedipal Situation and Its Consequences in the Epics of Ancient India, *Samiksa, Journal of the Indian Psycho-Analytical Society*, 5:5–13.
Logical Status and Methodological Problems of Research in Clinical *Psychiatry*, 14:327–330.

1952

Pratical Problems of Conceptual Psychiatric Research, *Psychiatry*, 15:189–192.
Sociology 1950, (in) Frosch, John (ed.), *Annual Survey of Psychoanalysis*, vol. 1, New York.
Psychiatry and Anthropology: Some Research Objectives, *Bulletin of the Menninger Clinic*, 16:167–177.

1953

Obituary: Géza Róheim 1891–1953, *American Anthropologist*, 55:420.
Psychoanalysis and the Occult (an anthology, edited by G. Devereux, and containing 3 chapters by him), New York, International Universities Press, 2nd ed., 1970.

Psychological Factors in the Production of Paraesthesias Following the Self-Administration of Codeine, *Psychiatric Quarterly Supplement*, 27:43-54.

Why Oedipus Killed Laius: Note on the Complementary Oedipus Complex, *International Journal of Psychoanalysis*, 34:132–141, 1953. Unauthorized reprinting in H. M. Ruitenbeek, *Psychoanalysis and Literature*, (New York, 1964. In E. Lowells & A. Dundes (ed.), *Oedipus, A Folklore Case Book*, New York, Garland, 1983; tr. Italian in E. Starace (ed.), *Los Paternita*, Milano: Angeli, 1983.

Cultural Factors in Psychoanalytic Therapy, *Journal of the American Psychoanalytic Association*, 1:629–655. Reprinted in D. G. Haring (ed.) *Personal Character and Cultural Milieu*, 1956.

1954

Primitive Genital Mutilations in a Neurotic's Dream, *Journal of the American Psychoanalytic Association*, 2:483–492.

The Denial of the Anus in Neurosis and Culture, *Bulletin of the Philadelphia Association for Psychoanalysis*, 4:24–27

A Typological Study of Abortion in 350 Primitive, Ancient and Pre-industrial Societies. In H. Rosen, *Therapeutic Abortion*, New York.

Belief, Superstition and Sympton, *Samiksa, Journal of the Indian Psychoanalytical Society*, 8:210–215.

Social Sciences 1951 in J. Frosch, (ed.), *Annual Survey of Psychoanalysis*, vol. 2, New York: International Universities Press.

1955

The Human Animal: A Rejoinder, *Man*, 55:111–112.

Anthropological Data Suggesting Unexplored Unconscious Attitudes Toward and in Unwed Mothers, *Archives of Criminal Psychodynamics*, 1:564–576.

A Study of Abortion in Primitive Societies, New York, Julian Press. 2nd edition, 1976.

Charismatic Leadership and Crisis. In W. Muensterberger, *Psychoanalysis and the Social Sciences*, vol. 4, New York, International Universities Press.

A Counteroedipal Episode in Homer's Iliad, *Bulletin of the Philadelphia Association for Psychoanalysis*, 4:90–97.

Indochina's Moi Medicine Man, *Tomorrow*, 4(1):95–104. Reprinted in E. Garrett, *Beyond the Five Senses*, Philadelphia: Lippincott, 1957.

Notes on the Dynamics of Post-Traumatic Epileptic Seizures, *Bulletin of the Philadelphia Association for Psychoanalysis*, 5:61–73.

Acting out in Dreams, *American Journal of Psychotherapy*, 9:657–660.

Some Aspects of Transference in a Brain-Injured Patient with Borderline Intelligence, *Bulletin of the Philadelphia Association for Psychoanalysis*, 5(3-4):63–68.

Therapeutic Education, New York, Harper.

Mohave Dreams of Omen and Power, *Tomorrow*, 4(3):17–24.

Bridey Murphy, A Psychoanalytic View, *Tomorrow*, 4(4):15–23.

(The Origins of Shamanistic Powers as Reflected in a Neurosis,) *Revue Internationale d'Ethnopsychologie Normale et Pathologique*, 1:19–28.

A Note on the Feminine Significance of the Eyes, *Bulletin of the Philadelphia Association for Psychoanalysis*, 6:21–24.

Normal and Abnormal: The Key Problem of Psychiatric Anthropology. In W. Muenstenberger. (ed.) *Man and His Culture*, London: Rapp & Whiting, 1969.

Comment on Lessa's Review, *American Sociological Review*, 21:88-89.
Funcion Complementaria de la Psicoterapia y de la Education, *Criminalia*, 22(2):90–94.

1957

Social and Cultural Studies 1953. In J. Frosch. (ed.) *Annual Survey of Psychoanalysis*, IV.
Psychoanalysis as Anthropological Field Work, Data and Theoretical Implications, *Transactions of the New York Academy of Sciences*, Series II, 19:457–472.
The Criteria of Dual Competence in Psychiatric-Anthropological Studies, *Journal of the Hillside Hospital*, 6: 87–90.
A Primitive Slip of the Tongue, *Anthropological Quarterly*, 30:27–29
Penelope's Character, *Psychoanalytic Quarterly*, 26:378–386. Translated into Greek: O Xarakter tes Penelopes, *Platon*, I, A-B:3–9.
Dream Learning and Individual Ritual Differences in Mohave Shamanism, *American Anthropologist*, 59:1036–1045.
The Awarding of a Penis as Compensation for Rape, *International Journal of Psycho-Analysis*, 38:398–401.
Letter to Editor, *Newsletter: Transcultural Research in Mental Health Problems*, No. 2, Feb., pp. 33–35.

1958

The Significance of the External Female Genitalia and of Female Orgasm for the Male, *Journal of the American Psychoanalytic Association*, 6:278–286.
Finger Nails, *Bulletin of the Philadelphia Association for Psychoanalysis*, 8:94-96. Trans. into Japanese: *Tokyo Journal of Psychoanalysis*, 18(6):1–3. 1960.
A Regressively Determined Parapraxis, *Bulletin of the Philadelphia Association for Psychoanalysis*, 8:126–131. Trans. into Japanese: *Tokyo Journal of Psychoanalysis*, 18(7):1–5. 1960.
Cultural Thought Models in Primitive and Modern Psychiatric Theories, *Psychiatry*, 21:359–374.
The Anthropological Roots of Psychoanalysis. In J. H. Masserman (ed.): *Science and Psychoanalysis*, vol. 1, New York.
Reply to Kardiner. In J. H. Masserman (ed.), *Science and Psychoanalysis*, vol. 1, New York.

1959

A Psychoanalytic Scrutiny of Certain Characteristic Techniques of Direct Analysis, *Psychoanalysis and Psychoanalytic Review*, 46:45–65.
The Nature of the Bizarre, *Journal of the Hillside Hospital*, 8:266–278.
Social and Cultural Studies 1954. In J. Frosch (ed.), *Annual Survey of Psychoanalysis*, vol. 5.
The Posthumous Voices, Contemporary Psychology, 4:253–254.
Adultery, *Sexology*, 26:84–85.

1960

The Female Castration Complex and its Repercussions in Modesty, Appearance and Courtship Etiquette, *American Imago*, 17:1–19.

Discussion, *Psychosomatic Medicine,* 32:65–67.

Psychoanalytic Reflections on Experiences of "Levitation", *International Journal of Parapsychology,* 2:39–60.

Obessive Doubt, *Bulletin of the Philadelphia Association for Psychoanalysis,* 10:50–55.

The Lifting of a Refractory Amnesia through a Startle Reaction to an Unpredictable Stimulus, *Journal of the Hillside Hospital,* 9:218–223.

Retaliatory Homosexual Trimuph over the Father, *International Journal of Psycho-Analysis,* 41:157–161.

Schizophrenia vs Neurosis and the Use of "Premature" Deep Interpretations as Confrontations in Classical and in Direct Analysis, *Psychiatric Quarterly,* 34:710–721.

A Psychoanalytic Study of Contraception, *Journal of Sex Research,* 1:105–134, 1965.

1961

Mohave Ethnopsychiatry and Suicide, Smithsonian Institution, Bureau of American Ethnology (Bulletin No. 175), Washington D. C. Augmented edition 1969. Unauthorized reprint of the first edition, St. Clair Shores, Michigan, 1976.

Two Types of Modal Personality Models. In B. Kaplan (ed.), *Studying Personality Cross-Culturally,* I. Evanston, IL. Reprinted in W. H. Kelly (ed.), *Culture & the Individual: A Selection of Readings,* 1969.

Art and Mythology: A General Theory. In B. Kaplan, Bert (ed.), *Studying Personality Cross-Culturally:* Evanston, IL.

Shamans as Neurotics, *American Anthropologist,* 63:1088–1090.

The Non-Recognition of the Patient by the Therapist (with F. H. Hoffman), *Psychoanalysis and Psychoanalytic Review,* 48(3):41–61.

A Heuristic Measure of Cultural Affinity, *Anthropological Quarterly,* 35:24–28.

1963

Primitive Psychiatric Diagnosis. In I. Galdston (ed.), *Man's Image in Medicine and Anthropology,* New York. International Universities Press.

Sociopolitical Functions of the Oedipus Myth in Early Greece, *Psychoanalytic Quarterly,* 32:205–214. Trans. into Greek: Koinikopolitikes Leitourgies tou Oidipoudeiou Mythou, *Epoches,* 17:18–22. 1964.

1964

Rejoinder to Parsons and Wintrob, *Transcultural Psychiatric Research,* 1:167–169.

Chapter 5 in L. Freeman & M. Theodores (eds.), *The Why Report,* Purchase, NY.

An Ethnopsychiatric Note on Property Destruction in Cargo-Cults, *Man,* 64:184–185.

Ethnopsychological Aspects of the Terms "Deaf" and "Dumb," *Anthropological Quarterly,* 37:68–71.

Los Sueños Patogenos en las Sociedades no Occidentales. In G. E. von Grunebaum & R. Caillois (eds.), *Los Sueños y las Sociedades Humanas,* Buenos Aires, Ed. Sudamericana. Trans. into English: *Pathogenic Dreams in Non-Western Societies.* In Grunebaum & Caillois.

La Délinquance Sexuelle des Jeunes Filles dans une Société "Puritaine," *Les Temps Modernes,* 29:621-659.

The Enetian Horses of Hippolytos, *Antiquité Classique,* 33:375–383.

Compte-Rendu d'Enseignement, *Annuaire 1963/64, Ecole Pratique des Hautes Etudes* (VIème Section).

1965

Une Science de la Sexualite:Pourquoi? Preface to F. Henriquez, *La Sexualité Sauvage*, Paris.

La Psychanalyse et l'Histoire: Une Application à l'Histoire de Sparte, *Annales: Economies, Sociétés, Civilisations*, 20:18–44.

The Voices of Children, *American Journal of Psychotherapy*, 19:4–19.

Laws to Live By - Not Under, *Community Education*, 1:299-312.

The Perception of Motion in Infancy, *Bulletin of the Menninger Clinic*, 29:143–147.

Weeping, Urination and Grand Mal, *Journal of the Hillside Hospital*, 14:97–107.

Une Théorie Ethnopsychiatrique de l'Adaption. In R. Bastide & F. Raveau (eds.), *Table Ronde sur l'Adaptation des Africains en France*, Paris (mimeographed volume).

Considérations Ethnopsychanalytiques sur la Notion de Parenté, *L'Homme*, 5:224–247.

Les Origines Sociales de la Schizophrénie, *L'Information Psychiatrique*, 41:783–799.

The Displacement of Modesty from Pubis to Face, *Psychoanalytic Review*, 52:391–399.

Neurotic Downward Identification, *American Imago*, 22:77–95.

Homer's Wild She-Mules, *Journal of Hellenic Studies*, 85:29–32.

The Kolaxian Horse of Alkman's Partheneion, *Classical Quarterly*, 15:176–184.

The Abduction of Hippodameia as 'Aition' of a Greek Animal Husbandry Rite, *Studi e Materiali di Storia delle Religioni*, 36:3–25.

Intervention, *Revue Française de Psychanalyse*, 29:378.

Intervention, *Revue Française de Psychanalyse*, 29:392–393.

Compte-Rendu d'Enseignement, *Annuaire 1964/65, Ecole Pratique des Hautes Etudes* (VIème section), pp. 251–252.

1966

The Cannibalistic Impulses of Parents, *Psychoanalytic Forum*, 1:114–124.

Author's Response, *Psychoanalytic Forum*, 1:129-130.

Loss of Identity, Impairment of Relationships, Reading Disability, *Psychoanalytic Quarterly*, 35:18–39.

Mumbling, *Journal of the American Psychoanalytic Association*, 14:478–484.

An Unusual Audio-Motor Synesthesia in an Adolescent, *Psychiatric Quarterly*, 40:459–471.

Cultural Factors in Hypnosis and Suggestion: An Examination of Primitive Data, *International Journal of Clinical and Experimental Hypnosis*, 14:273–291.

La Nature du Stress, *Revue de Médecine Psychosomatique*, 8:103–113.

Réflexions Ethno-psychanalytiques sur la Fatigue névrotique, *Revue de Médecine Psychosomatique*, 8:235–241. Reprinted in *Travaux du 3eme Congres International de Médecine Psychosomatique*, Toulouse. Ed. Privat, pp. 159–165.

Intervention, *L'Evolution Psychiatrique*, 3:507–512.

Rapports Cliniques et Phylogénétiques entre les Odeurs et les Emotions dan la Névrose Caractérielle d'un Hottentot Griqua, *Psychopathologie Africaine*, 2(1):65–76.

Transference, Screen Memory and the Temporal Ego, *Journal of Nervous and Mental Disease*, 143:318–323.

The Enetian Horse of Alkman's Partheneion, *Hermes*, 94:129–134.

The Exploitation of Ambiguity in Pindaros *O*. 3.27, *Rheinisches Museum für Philologie*, 109:289-298.

Intervention, *Revue Française de Psychanalyse*, 30:187-188.

Compte-Rendu d'Enseignement, *Annuaire 1965/66, Ecole Pratique des Hautes Etudes* (VIème section), pp. 206–208.

1967

Fausse Non-Reconnaissance, *Bulletin of the Menninger Clinic*, 31:69–78.

La Renonciation à l'Identité: Défense contre l'Anéantissement, *Revue Française de Psychanalyse*, 31:101–142.

Greek Pseudo-Homosexuality, *Symbolae Osloenses*, 42:69–92. Trans. into French: Pseudo-Homosexualité Grecque, *Ethnopsychiatrica*, vol. 2(2):pp. 211–241, 1979.

From Anxiety to Method in the Behavioral Sciences, Paris, The Hague, Mouton. Trans. into German: *Angst und Methode* (Taschenbuch), Berlin: Ullstein. Trans. into Spanish: *De la Ansiedad al Metodo*, Mexico D. F., Siglo XXI (1977). Trans. into French: *De l'Angoisse à la Méthode*, Paris: Flammarion (1980).

Notes sur une "Introduction à l'Ethnologie," *Ethnologia Europaea*, 1:232–237.

Preface to special issue in honor of Prof. D. Kouretas, *Psychotherapy and Psychosomatics*, 15:vi–vii.

Observation and Belief in Aischylos' Accounts of Dreams, *Psychotherapy and Psychosomatics*, 15:114–134.

Maladie mentale et Société in *L'Aventure Humaine*, 4:115–118, Paris (Grange Bateliere) et Geneve (Kister).

Compte-Rendu d'Enseignement, *Annuaire 1966/67, Ecole Pratique des Hautes Etudes* (VIème section), pp. 183–184.

1968

L'Image de l'Enfant dans deux Tribus, Mohave et Sedang, et son importance pour la psychiatrie Infantile, *Revue de Neuropsychiatrie Infantile*, 16:375–390.

Considération Psychanalytiques sur la Divination, particulièrement en Grèce. In A. Caquot et M. Leibovici (eds.), *La Divination*, Paris, PUF, vol. II, pp. 449–471.

The Realistic Basis of Fantasy, *Journal of the Hillside Hospital*, 17:13–20.

L'Etat Dépressif et le Rêve de Ménélaos (Eschyle, *Agamemnon*, 410–419), *Revue des Etudes Grecques*, 81:xii–xv.

Orthopraxis, *Psychiatric Quarterly*, 42:726–737.

Compte-Rendu d'Enseignement, *Annuaire 1967/68, Ecole Pratique des Hautes Etudes* (VIème section), pp. 183–184.

1969

Compte-Rendu d'enseignement,, *Annuaire 1968/69, Ecole Pratique des Hautes Etudes* (VIème section). Mohave Ethenopsycpsychiatry and Suicide (2nd augmented ed.), Washington, DC: Smithsonian Institution Press.

1970

The Nature of Sappho's Seizure in *Fr.* 31 LP, *Classical Quarterly*, 20:17–31.

La Naissance d'Aphrodite. In J. Pouillon et P. Maranda (eds.), *Echanges et Communications* (Melanges Levi-Strauss), Paris, The Hague, Mouton, pp. 1229–1252.

The Psychotherapy Scene in Euripides' Bacchae, *Journal of Hellenic Studies*, 90:35–48.

The *Equus October* Ritual Reconsidered, *Mnemosyne*, 23:297–301.

The Structure of Tragedy and the Structure of the Psyche in Aristotle's *Poetics* in C. Haniy and M. Lazerowitz (eds.), *Psychoanalysis and Philosophy*, New York, International Universities Press.

Preface (to the reprinted ed.) in J. S. Lincoln: *The Dream in Primitive Culture*, New York, Johnson Reprint Corp.
Compte-Rendu d'Enseignement, *Annuaire 1968/69, Ecole Pratique des Hautes Etudes*.
Essais d'Ethnopsychiatrie Générale, Paris, Gallimard. 4ème édition 1977. Trans. into English, Spanish, German, Italian.

1971

The Psychosomatic Miracle of Iolaos, *La Parola del Passato*, 138:167–195.
Table Ronde: Conduite à Tenir à l'Egard des Toxicomanes, *Information Psychiatrique*, 47:627–635.
Table Ronde: Thérapie du Couple, *Annales de Psychothérapie* 2, Supplement to 3:17–21, 35–36.
Compte-Rendu d'Enseignement, *Annuaire de l'Ecole Pratique des Hautes Etudes* (VIème section), pp. 214–216.

1972

Ethnopsychanalyse Complémentariste, Paris, Flammarion. Trans. into Spanish, Italian, German, English. Argument reprinted in *Psychiatrie d'Aujourd'hui*, 15:1–12.
Drogues, Dieux, Idéologies, *Medica*, 103:13–20.
Ethnopsychiatria, *Italian Encyclopaedia*, Fabbri, Roma.
Compte-Rendu d'Enseignement, *Annuaire de l'Ecole Pratique des Hautes Etudes* (VIème section), pp. 265–266.
Review of Besançon, Alain: *Histoire et Expérience du Moi* in *La Quinzaine Littéraire*, 145, 15 juillet 1972. Reprinted in *L'Année Littéraire*, Paris, 1972.
Quelques Traces de la Succession par Ultimogéniture en Scythis, *Inter-Nord*, 12:262–270.

1973

(with J. W. Devereux), Manifestations de l'Inconscient dans Sophokles *Trachiniai* 923 sqq. In *Psychanalyse et Sociologie*, Bruxelles: University Press, pp. 121–152.
Le Fragment d'Eschyle 62 Nauck: Ce qu'y signifie ΧΛΟΥΝΗΕ, *Revue des Etudes Grecques*, 86:277–284.
Stesichoros' Palinodes: Two Further Testimonia and Some Comments, *Rheinisches Museum für Philologie*, 116:206–209.
The Self-Blinding of Oidipous in Sophokles *Oidipous Tyrannos*, *Journal of Hellenic Studies*, 93:36–49. Reprinted in Dodds Festschrift.
Compte-Rendu d'Enseignement, *Annuaire 1972/73 de l'Ecole Pratique des Hautes Etudes* (VIème section) pp. 275–277.

1974

Trance and Orgasm in Euripides *Bakchai*. In A. Angoff & D. Barth (eds.), *Parapsychology and Anthropology*, New York: Parapsychology Foundation. Trans. & rep. in Mélieux, Michel and Rossignol (eds.) *Corps a Prodiges*, Paris, 1977.
Compte-Rendu d'Enseignement, *Annuaire 1973/74 de l'Ecole Pratique des Hautes Etudes* (VIème section).

1975

Tragédie et Poésie Grecques, Paris, Flammarion.
Les Chevaux Anthropophages dans les Mythes Grecs, *Revue des Etudes Grecques*, 98:203–205.
Preface (special issue on Ethnopsychiatry) to *Perspectives psychiatriques*, 13:251–253.
Compte-Rendu D'Enseignement, *Annuaire 1974/75 de l'Ecole Pratique des Hautes Etudes* (VIème section), pp. 325–327.

1976

Dreams in Greek Tragedy, Oxford; Blackwell; Berkeley: University of California Press.
Autocaractérisations de Quatre Sedang. In *L'Autre et l'Ailleurs* (Volume for Roger Bastide), Paris: Berger-Levrault, pp. 454–468.
Compte-Rendu d'Enseignement, *Annuaire 1975/76 de l'Ecole Pratique des Hautes Etudes* (VIème section).

1977

Preface to Tobie Nathan, *Sexualite Ideologigue et Névrose*, Claix: La Pensée Sauvage.
Compte-Rendu d'Enseignement, *Annuaire 1976/77 de l'Ecole Pratique* des Hautes Etudes (VIème section).

1978

Preface to Ben Kilborne, *Interprétations du Rêve au Maroc*, Claix: La Pensée Sauvage.
Culture et Symptomatologie, *Actualités Psychiatriques*, 2:12–17. Trans. into English: *Ethnopsychiatrica*, 1:201–212.
L'Ethnopsychiatrie, *Ethnopsychiatrica*, 1:7–13.
The Cultural Implementation of Defense mechanisms, *Ethnopsychiatrica*, 1:79–116.
The Works of George Devereux. In G. D. Spindler (ed.), *The Making of Psychological Anthropology*, Berkeley: University of California Press, pp. 364–406.
Mythodiagnosis, *Curare*, 2:70–72.
Trois Rêves en Série et une Double Parapraxie, *Ethnopsychiatrica*, 1:243–251.

1979

The Nursing of the Aged in Classical China, *Journal of Psychological Anthropology*, 2:1–10.
The Suicide of Achilles in the Iliad, *Helios*, 49:5–15.
Fantasy and Symbol as Dimensions of Reality. In R. H. Hook (ed.), *Fantasy and Symbol* (Devereux Festschrift), London: Academic Press.
Rêve, Grossesse et Régression, *La Psychologie des Peuples*, 34:5–12.
Die Verunsicherung der Geisteskranken, *Curare*, 2:215–220.
Interpretation as Catheterization, *Bulletin of the Menninger Clinic*, 43:540–546.
Breath, Sleep and Dream (Aischylos *Fragment* 287 Mette). *Ethnopsychiatrica*, 2:89–115.
Preface to E. R. Dodds, *Pagens et Chrétiens dans un Age d'Angoisse*, Claix: La Pensée Sauvage
Fantasy vs Schizophrenic Delusion, *Psychocultural Review*, 3:231–237.
Preface to J. M. Masson, *The Indian Mind*, Dordrecht: Reider.

La pseudo-homosexualité grecque et le "miracle grec," *Ethnopsychiatrica*, 2:211–241.
An Undetected Absurdity in Lucian's *A True Story* 2.26, *Helios*, 7:63–68.
Compte-Rendu d'Enseignement, *Annuaire 1978/79 de l'E.H.E.S.S.*, Paris.

Preface to the German translation of Tobie Nathan, *Sexualite, Idéologie et Névrose*,
Frankfort am/Main: Suhrkamp.

1980

Author's rejoinder to a book review, *Social Science and Medicine*, 148:125.
The Family Historical Function, Dysfunction, Lack of Function and Schizophrenia, *The
Journal of Psychohistory*, 8(2):183–193.
Freud, Discoverer of the Principle of Complementarity, *International Review of Psycho-
analysis*, 7:521.
Interview with George Devereux, *Le Monde Dimanche*, June 1980.
Psychanalyse et Homosexualité (reply to readers), *Le Monde Dimanche*, 27 July.
Compte-Rendu d'Enseignement, *Annuaire 1979/80 de l'E.H.E.S.S.*, Paris.

1981

Cultural Lag and Survivals. In B. Boyer & W. Muensterberger (eds.), *The Psychoana-
lytic Study of Society*, New York.
Sadism, Superego and the Organizational Mores, *Journal of Psychoanalytic Anthropol-
ogy*, 3(4).
Argos et la Castration d'Indra et de Zeus, *Ethnopsychiatrica*, 3:183–193.
Preface to Philippe Jeanne, *Classes Sociales et Maladies Mentales a Haïti*, 3rd ed., Port-
au-Prince.
Baubo, die Mythische Vulva. Frankfurt am/Main: Syndikat Verlag.

1982

Femme et Mythe, Flammarion, Paris.
An Alternative Interpretation of Homeostasis with special Reference to Schizophrenia.
" In W. Schmied-Kowarzick & G. Heinemann (eds.), *Sabotage des Schicksals*, Tu-
bingen; Konkurs buch Verlag, pp. 225–235.
Socio-Cultural and Reality Factors in Displaced Pubertal Oedipality, *Journal of Psy-
choanalytic Anthropology*, 5(4); 379–384.
Anxieties of the Castrator, *Ethos*, 10(3): 279–297.
Mourning and Self-degradation. In V. Lanternaxi, M. Massenzio & D. Sabattucci (eds.),
Religione & Civilta, vol. III, pp. 163–169.

1983

The Subjective and the Objective in Freud's Conception of the Oedipus Complex,
Journal of Psychoanalytic Anthropology, 6(1): pp. 17–23.
Les blessures d'Hekto & les Messagers vers l'autre Monde, *L'Homme*, 23(1): 135–137.
Sur-moi et Liberté, *Premier Colloque d'Athènes* (Athènes 25–28 juin 1980), Athènes, pp.
289–291.
Weltzerstörung in Wahn und Wirklichtkeit. In H. von Rolf Gehlen & B. Wolf (eds.), *Der
Gläserne Zaun*. Frankfurt am Main: Syndikat Verlag.
Die Phantasie der Selbstkastration, *Psychoanalyse*, 1:21–31.

REVIEWS

Grau, R: Die Gruppenehe, *American Anthropologist*, 35, pp. 173–4, 1933.

Te Rangi Hiron: Ethnology of Tongareva, *American Anthropologist*, 35: 189–90, 1933.

Nooteboom, C.: De boomstamkano in Indonesie, *American Anthropologist*, 35: 383–4, 1933.

Hoffet, J. H.: Les Moîs de la Chaîne annamitique, *Bulletin de la Société des Etudes Indonésiennes*, 8:47–49, 1933.

Vanoverbergh, M.: The Isne Life Cycle III, *American Anthropologist*, 41: 631, 1939.

Meier, J.: Illegitimate Births among the Gunantuna, *American Anthropologist*, 41: 632, 1939.

Meigs, Peveril III: The Kiliwa Indians, *American Anthropologist*, 42:501–2, 1940.

Fortune, R. F.: Yao Society, *American Anthropologist*, 42:683–4, 1940.

Kardiner, A.: The Individual and His Society, *Character and Personality*, 8, 1940.

Faris, R. E. L. & Durham, H. W.: *Psychoanalytic Review*, 27:251–2, 1940.

Money-Kyrle, R.: Superstition and Society, *Psychoanalytic Review*, 27:251–2, 1940.

Yaskin, J. C.: The Psychobiology of Anxiety, *Journal of Criminal Psychopathology*, 2:592–3, 1941.

Elliott, M. A. & Merrill, F. E.: Social Disorganization, *Journal of Criminal Psychopathology*, 3:165–7, 1941.

Drucker, Ph.: Culture Element Distributions XVII, Yuman Piman, *American Anthropologist*, 44:480–1, 1942.

Whiting, J. W. H.: Becoming a Kwoma, *American Anthropologist*, 44:497–499, 1942.

Sorokin, P. A.: Social and Cultural Dynamics IV, *American Anthropologist*, 44:507–510, 1942.

Merton, R. K. & Ashley-Montagu, M. F.: Crime and the Anthropologist, *Journal of Criminal Psychopathology*, 3:745–747, 1942.

Sorokin, P. A.: The Crisis of Our Age, *Journal of Criminal Psychopathology*, 3:766–8, 1942.

Priest, L. B.: Uncle Sam's Stepchildren, *American Sociological Review*, 8:114–5, 1943.

Simmons, L. W.: Sun Chief, *Mental Hygiene*, 27:313–4, 1943.

Henry , J.: Doll Play of Pilaga Indian Children, *Journal of Clinical Psychopathology*, 7:202–3, 1945.

Mayor's Committee on Marihuana, The Marihuana Problem in the City of New-York, *Journal of Abnormal and Social Psychology*, 40:417–19, 1955.

Morgenstern, S.: La Structure de la Personnalité et ses Déviations, *Journal of Clinical Psychopathology*, 7:848–9, 1946.

Delay, J.: Les Dissolutions de la Mémoire, *Journal of Clinical Psychopathology*, 7:862–3, 1946.

Delay, J.: L'Electroshock et la Psychophysiologie, *Journal of Clinical Psychopathology*, 7:863–5, 1946.

Allendy, R.: Journal d'un Médecin Malade, *Journal of Clinical Psychopathology*, 7:865–6, 1946.

Delay, J.: La Psychophysiologie Humaine, *Journal of Clinical Psychopathology*, 7:867–8, 1946.

Baudouin, C.: La Psychanalyse, *Journal of Clinical Psychopathology*, 7:868, 1946.

Cavé, M.: L'oeuvre paradoxale de Freud, *Journal of Clinical Psychopathology*, 7:869–87, 1946.

Elwin, V.: The Agaria, *American Anthropologist*, 48:110–111, 1946.

Du Bois, C.: The People of Alor, *Journal of Abnormal and Social Psychology*, 41:372–4, 1946.

Elwin, V.: Maria Murder and Suicide, *Journal of Abnormal and Social Psychology*, 42:494–5, 1947.

Delay, J.: Les Ondes Cérébrales et la Psychologie, *Journal of Clinical Psychopathology*, 8:752–3, 1947.

Palmer, M.: Les Méthodes du choc et autres traitements dans meledies mentoler, *Journal of Clinical Psychopathology*, 8:760–1, 1947.

Deshaies, G.: L'Esthétique de Pathologique, *Journal of Clinical Psychopathology*, 8:887–8, 1947.

Róheim, G.: The Eternal Ones of the Dream, *Journal of Clinical Psychopathology*, 8:900–902.

Wallon, M.: Les origines de la Pensée chez l'Enfant, *Journal of Clinical Psychopathology*, 8:902–3, 1947.

Desoille, R.: Le Rêve Eveillé en Psychothérapie, *Journal of Clinical Psychopathology*, 8:903–4, 1947.

Róheim, G.: The Origin and Function of Culture, *Bulletin of the Menninger Clinic*, p. 137, 1947.

Borel, J.: Les Déséquilibres Psychiques, *Journal of Clinical Psychopathology*, 9:509–10, 1948.

Boutonnier, J.: Les Défaillances de la Volonté, *Journal of Clinical Psychopathology*, 9:510, 1948.

Dumas, G.: Le Surnaturel et les Dieux d'après les Maladies Mentales, *Journal of Clinical Psychopathology*, 9:511, 1948.

Delay, J.: Les Dérèglements de l'Humeur, *Journal of Clinical Psychopathology*, 9:608–9, 1948.

Kluckhohn, C. & Leighton D.: The Navaho, *Mental Hygiene*, 33:114–6, 1948.

Leighton, D. & Kluckhohn, C.: Children of the People, *Mental Hygiene*, 32:485–8, 1948.

Róheim, G. (éd.), Psychoanalysis and the Social Sciences, *American Anthropologist*, 50:535–40, 1948.

Fromm, E.: Man for Himself, *Bulletin of the Menninger Clinic*, 13:107–8, 1949.

Mars, L.: La Lutte contre la Folie, *Bulletin of the Menninger Clinic*, 14:147, 1950.

Montagu, A.: On being Human, *Complex*, 3:51–5, 1950.

Róheim, G.: Psychoanalysis and Anthropology, *American Journal of Orthopsychiatry*, 21:847–9, 1951.

Róheim, G.: Psychoanalysis and Anthropology, *Psychoanalytic Quarterly*, 20:453–457, 1951.

Bailey, F. L.: Some Sex Beliefs and Practices in a Navaho Community, *Psychoanalytic Quarterly*, 21:121–123, 1952.

Róheim, G.: Psychoanalysis and Anthropology, *Bulletin of the Menninger Clinic*, 16:34–5, 1952.

Dodds, R. R.: The Greeks and the Irrational, *American Anthropologist*, 55:136, 1953.

Wormhoudt, A.: The Nurse at Length, *Bulletin of the Menninger Clinic*, 18:121, 1954.

Bettelheim, B.: Symbolic Wounds, *Science*, 120:488, 1954.

Henry, G. W.: All the Sexes, *Guide to Psychiatric and Psychological Literature*, 2:5–6, 1955.

Cressey, D. R.: Other People's Money, *Explorations in Entre-preneurial History*, 7:184–6, 1955.

The Search for Bridey Murphy (Record), *To-morrow*, 4:57–9, 1956.

Eaton J. W. & Weil, R. J.: Culture and Mental Disorder, *American Anthropologist*, 58:211–2, 1956.

Moufang, W.: Magier Machts und Mysterien, *Tomorrow*, 5:71–2, 1957.

Anxiety distortion, *Saturday Review,* May 31, 1958, p.3.

Condominas, G.: Nous Avons Mangé la Forêt, *American Anthropologist,* 60:400–1, 1958.

Longworth, C. T.: The Gods of Love, *Journal of Nervous and Mental Disease,* 133:276, 1961.

Bastide, R.: Sociologie des Maladies mentales, *Annales E.S.C.,* 3:657–59, 1967.

Besançon, A.: Histoire et Expérience du moi, *Quinzaine Littéraire,* 143. 19–20, 1972.

La Barre, W.: The Ghost Dance, *L'Homme,* 12:147–151.

1

Irma's Rape: The Hermeneutics of Structuralism and Psychoanalysis Compared[1]

H.U.E. THODEN VAN VELZEN

The relationship between structuralism and psychoanalysis has always been an uncertain one. Prominent structuralists such as Lévi-Strauss (1955, p. 37–47) and Lacan (see Kurzweil, 1980), ch. 6) have repeatedly stressed the similarities between these two approaches to the study of humankind. What Lévi-Strauss and Freud had in common was a belief in the key role of the unconscious. Both men, however, held quite different views about the nature and functioning of this agency. For Lévi-Strauss the unconscious was the product of brain physiology; for Freud, it was fathered by the body and its instincts. The unconscious of the structuralist may be compared with a "thinking machine"; the unconscious of psychoanalysis can be likened to a battlefield of warring forces, hidden deep in the psyche, sometimes betraying itself by inducing somatic changes and emitting coded messages. In Badcock's (1975) apt phrase: "the latent content of Lévi-Strauss' structuralism [is] a de-libidinized Freudianism, a Cartesian psychoanalysis" (p. 111). For Freud's libido Lévi-Strauss substituted Descartes' *cogito* (p. 110).

1. I am indebted to my colleagues Rob Kroes, Arie de Ruijter, and Peter van der Veer for various corrections and useful suggestions. Peter van Koningsbruggen and Geert Mommersteeg have patiently gone over the Kuper and Stone article (1982) to help me with the difficult task of finding the materials on which the structuralists' model was based. The late Jaap Spanjaard generously shared with me his great knowledge of psychoanalysis in general and classical Freudian dream interpretation in particular. Titia Wippler has been extremely helpful in providing me with the classic texts for the Irma dream. Finally, I gratefully acknowledge Bill Epstein's many suggestions for improving this paper and also his editorial exertions in my behalf. I think it highly appropriate to add the standard phrase: None of these persons should be held responsible for the interpretations presented here.

Such pronounced divergencies are bound to come into the open sooner or later. The attempt by the anthropologist Kuper and the psychiatrist Stone (1982) to restudy Freud's (1900) specimen dream ("the dream of Irma's injection") reveals how irreconcilable psychoanalysis and structuralism are.

Kuper and Stone consider the structuralist approach superior to psychoanalysis, even for the study of dreams. After reopening the Irma case, the authors present a tightly knit argument purporting to demonstrate the greater analytical value of their methods over Freudian tools. "Our method," they observe "revealed not only the structure of the dream but also its central message. Both were hidden to investigations that relied on association and symbolism" (p. 1233).

The purpose of this paper is to present a case study of structuralists Kuper and Stone at work: about procedures adopted when constructing arguments and when handling empirical data. These procedures, and the results, are then compared with the work of depth psychologists. The testing ground is provided by the specimen dream of psychoanalysis, "the dream of Irma's injection."

The "Thinking Machine" and the Underworld

Kuper and Stone's position appears to be that Freudian dream analysis fails where structuralist interpretation brilliantly and unexpectedly succeeds. Before assessing these claims, let us first examine the main differences between the two approaches. Freudian dream theory is familiar ground. In psychoanalysis, dreams, like neurotic symptoms, jokes, and parapraxes ("Freudian slips"), are considered compromises between wishes striving for expression and a repressing agency, a censor or a superego. During sleep, a time of lowered vigilance, impermissible impulses may present themselves for fulfillment in the imaginatory and hallucinatory language of the dream. Daytime events, by serving as catalysts, usually decide which wishes will thrust themselves forward. To allow these forbidden longings to be expressed and fulfilled, the censor camouflages or distorts them. Once masked through the mechanisms of condensation, displacement, and representation (the dream work), the dream thoughts containing the repressed materials form the elements of a dream. Together these elements constitute the manifest dream. Free association, Freud argued, enables the dreamer to decode the elements of the manifest dream and thereby gain insight into the underlying unconscious wishes and conflicts. Dreams are the royal road to the unconscious.

Structuralists also recognize a distinction between surface and underlying phenomena. They, like psychoanalysts, insist that outward appearances are often misleading. Or, in Lévi-Strauss' (1955) words: "True reality is never the most visible one; and the nature of the real becomes transparent through the care taken to camouflage itself" (p. 44). But that is where the correspondence with psychoanalysis ends. For the structuralists, what is concealed from direct view are the principles of thinking, predetermined by the brain's structure and physiology. Opposition and correlation characterize mental functioning. From a dynamic point of view, thinking develops according to dialectical principles moving from one point to its opposite and then again to a mediation or reconciliation that supersedes both earlier positions. In due time the synthesis thus formed will generate a new oppositionary entity (term, concept). The results of mental activity reveal numerous binary structures, levels dominated by paired terms or other forms of opposition. Each of these levels refers to other levels, its basic structure being isomorphic with oppositionary structures in other fields or on other levels. Thus, a multilayered structure emerges.[2]

The structuralists' view of the psyche therefore is radically different from the one found in Freud's writings. Structuralists do not base their understanding of the mind on a distinction between an ego as the seat of reason, and an underworld where different mental processes dominate. The principles of thinking, the structuralists' "thinking machine," holds full sway throughout the psyche. There is no need for the ego to be on its guard against unwelcome "volcanic" activity originating in the unconscious. Hence no lessons are to be learned from the malfunctioning of the body (symptoms) or the malfunctioning of the mind (slips of the tongue, for instance). And neither need inadmissible longings and impulses be kept from view.

Kuper and Stone have summarized their approach in the following passage:

> The analysis as it is here applied to dreams proceeds on the basis of three assumptions. The first is that two concepts or terms are in conflict or opposition in the manifest content of the dream and

---

2. Geertz (1973) has summarized the demanding task of a structuralist with the following words: ". . . once certain of these schemas, or structures, are determined, they can be related to one another—that is, reduced to a more general, and 'deeper' structure embracing them both. They are shown to be mutually derivable from each other by logical operations—inversions, transposition, substitution: all sorts of systematic permutations—just as one transforms an English sentence into the dots and dashes of Morse code or turns a mathematical expression into its complement by changing all the signs" (p. 355).

that the manifest dream will work toward a mediation of these conflicting concepts or terms. A second or correlative assumption is that the manifest dream will follow a pattern or sequence of steps or stages working toward the mediation or solution. The third and final assumption is that the move from one stage to the next can be described as a coherent progression. In sum, the dream is a kind of argument, which proceeds from step to step by a quasi-logical dialectic [p. 1226].

When they have approached the end of their reanalysis, the authors feel justified in concluding:

The Freudian assumption is that the unconscious mind works by making associations, which are idiosyncratic in nature. We proceed on the assumption that even in dreams the mind works by applying quasi-logical rules to scenes, sentences or premises in order to proceed beyond them. This is borne out by the dream analysis, while the associations produced by Freud do not radically change our view of the dream. Thus the analysis suggests a very different conclusion about mental processes from that favored by Freud [p. 1233].

STRUCTURALIST ASSUMPTIONS

The Cognitive Perspective

The key metaphysical notion in Kuper and Stone's work is Cartesian: People are primarily thinking creatures, with a natural tendency to follow the rules of logic. As a motto for their article, they chose Descartes' saying: "I see light. To Dream is to think, and to think is to Dream." The mind of the dreamer relies on the same " 'quasi-logical transformations' and 'logical operations' as does the mind of the scientist. (p. 1226). Hence their insistence that the decisive processes of the mind are logical and adaptive.

The Structuralist Perspective

The key concepts that characterize the workings of the mind are structure and transformation. The structure, the conceptual framework of myth or dream, is built up of a series of oppositions: ". . . they always trace down to an underlying opposition of paired terms—high and low, right and left, peace and war, . . . (Geertz, 1973, p. 354). In the Irma dream, as we will soon learn from their reanalysis, the oppositions are between organic illness and hysterical affliction, between a patient's responsibility and a doctor's negligence, between catharsis and infiltration. Transformation is the other key concept. When two ideas or concepts are in conflict, the manifest dream will work toward a mediation of these oppositionary terms (Kuper and Stone, p. 1226). After mentioning their debt to Lévi-Strauss, Kuper and Stone explain the core of their method with the following words: "Myths develop in a much less arbitrary and irrational manner than had often been supposed. They follow coherent rules of development, moving in a dialectical fashion from an initial problem to a resolution. . . . dreams are comparable artifacts of the mind, governed by the same rules of internal development . . ." (p. 1225). This development, this transformation, "occurs through a distinct process of contrasts and reconciliations (p. 1229). In brief, "the dream makes a dialectical argument" (p. 1229).

A Positivistic Perspective

One expects structuralists to be on their guard against the misleading effects of outward appearances, always searching for the "hidden logic" underneath, yet there are moments in the essay when the reader feels unsure about the direction the authors take. Kuper and Stone appear to limit their attention to data that are (almost) observable, registered directly after the dream, arranged in a neat sequence and with minimum interference by the processes of introspection. They seem unconcerned about the processes of secondary revision (Nagera, 1969, pp. 88–92) that take place whenever dreamers put their confused recollections on paper. Dream analysts, they appear to say, should steer clear of the dream thoughts—the latent content of the dream—where interpreters can easily become lost in a labyrinth of idiosyncratic and subjective associations. 'The logic of the manifest sequence' should be our panacea for all those who are disturbed by the dizzying and floating feelings resulting from an avalanche of personal and strongly emotional associations.

The Ordinariness of Dreams

Dreams reflect the day-to-day thinking of the dreamer. Day residues dominate the manifest content, to rephrase this point in Freudian jargon. This perspective is perhaps the most productive of all. As

Schur (1966, 1972) has demonstrated, the events preceding the Irma dream influenced the dream's manifest content. Kuper and Stone (p. 1228) convincingly show that Freud's scientific ideas of the early 1890s return in his dreams.

THE FLIESS OPERATION

For their reinterpretation of the Irma dream, Kuper and Stone make use of two sources: Freud's own preamble to the dream and Schur's (1966) reconstruction of the dramatic events of the months preceding the night of the dream (July 24, 1895). As each account appears essential both for our understanding of Freud's dream and for an assessment of Kuper and Stone's critique, they will be related here. The occurrences revolve around Freud's friend in Berlin, Wilhelm Fliess, and his patient (and later assistant) Emma Eckstein. This new background to the dream was given by Max Schur, Freud's personal physician during the last 11 years of his life. For many years, Fliess, a Berlin rhinologist, was Freud's confidant and adviser. In Schur's words: "He was also the only one who not only believed in Freud's theories but also took the repeated changes of Freud's tentative formulations for granted, encouraged any new discovery, however revolutionary, and provided Freud's only 'audience,' his only protection from isolation" (p. 70). During 1894, severe cardiac distress led Freud to turn to Fliess for support and treatment. Around this time, the friendship between the two men deepened. Freud came to put Fliess in an exalted position. He idolized him, addressing him in letters, for example, as "Dear Magician." In 1950, a selection from Freud's letters to Fliess (the letters Fliess wrote in return are lost, probably destroyed by Freud) was published under the title *The Origins of Psychoanalysis* (Bonaparte, Freud, & Kris, 1954). The correspondence covers the period between 1887, shortly after they first met, and 1902, the year of their final breakup.

When in the early 1960s Schur was working on a paper about Freud's death fears, he received permission to read all of Freud's letters to

---

3. During the 1930s, Freud's letters to Fliess were sold to Marie Bonaparte at an auction. She apprised Freud of her findings; he urged her to destroy them (Clark 1980, p. 154). In 1950 a selection made by Marie Bonaparte, Anna Freud, and Ernst Kris was published under the title *Aus den Anfängen der Psychoanalyse*. An English translation followed in 1954 (*The Origins of Psycho-Analysis*). From a total of 284 documents, 168 were published, some of these with substantial deletions. Unfortunately, as the editor of the *Standard Edition* wrote: "Fliess's side of the correspondence has not survived, having no doubt been destroyed long since" (Strachey, 1966).

Fliess that had been preserved. Schur (1966) discovered that the editors of *The Origins* had excluded valuable material from publication. Schur devoted special attention to a number of letters dealing with the fate of Emma Eckstein, Freud's patient whom he had handed over to Fliess for a nasal operation (probably on one of her sinuses). The operation was performed in February 1895 in Vienna. Fliess returned to Berlin a few days later. As a result of gross negligence on Fliess' part, complications arose that nearly killed Eckstein. Schur's paper strongly suggests[4] that the Irma of Freud's dream is Emma Eckstein and that these dramatic events influenced the manifest contents of the dream. As we will soon see, little of this is to be found in Freud's own preamble to the Irma dream or in the dream report itself. It seems that Freud had constructed his analysis in such a way that Fliess, to whom he sent drafts and proofs of all chapters of *The Interpretation of Dreams*, could not take umbrage. This meant that Freud had to delete almost anything that could link the Irma dream with the Emma episode.

Freud's (1900) preamble to the Irma dream reads as follows:

During the summer of 1895 I had been giving psychoanalytic treatment to a young lady who was on very friendly terms with me and my family. It will be readily understood that a mixed relationship such as this may be a source of many disturbed feelings in a physician and particularly in a psychotherapist. While the physician's personal interest is greater, his authority is less; any failure would bring a threat to the old-established friendship with the patient's family. This treatment had ended in a partial success; the patient was relieved of her hysterical anxiety but did not lose all her somatic symptoms. At that time I was not yet quite clear in my mind as to the criteria indicating that a hysterical case history was finally closed, and I proposed a solution to the patient which she seemed unwilling to accept. While we were thus at variance, we had broken off the treatment for the summer vacation.

One day I had a visit from a junior colleague, one of my oldest friends, who had been staying with my patient, Irma, and her

---

4. As far as I know, Schur has never said in so many words that Irma was Emma Eckstein. But for most scholars who used Schur's 1966 paper there could be no other conclusion.

Later, Shurr (1972) was even more explicit: "I have discussed at length the striking relationship between the details of the Emma episode, the manifest content, associations, associations and interpretations of the Irma dream . . ." (pp. 86–87). For dissenting views, see Swales (1983) and Hartman (1983).

family at their country resort. I asked him how he had found her
and he answered: "She's better, but not quite well." I was
conscious that my friend Otto's words, or the tone in which he
spoke them, annoyed me. I fancied I detected a reproof in them,
such as to the effect that I had promised the patient too much;
and, whether rightly or wrongly, I attributed the supposed fact of
Otto's siding against me to the influence of my patient's relatives,
who, as it seemed to me, had never looked with favour on the
treatment. However, my disagreeable impression was not clear to
me and I gave no outward sign of it. The same evening I wrote out
Irma's case history, with the idea of giving it to Dr. M., a common
friend who was at that time the leading figure in our circle, in order
to justify myself. That night (or more probably the next morning) I
had the following dream, which I noted down immediately after
waking [p. 106].

Schur (1966) offers a quite different version of the events preceding the
Irma dream. With tact and a feeling for diplomacy, he presents his
contribution as an account of "some additional day-residues" and as
"supplementary background material for the Irma dream which will
constitute, so to speak, a preamble to Freud's preamble." Here follows
a summary of Schur's findings:

At the end of February 1895, Fliess, a nose and throat specialist,
visited Vienna. He stated that surgery on the turbinate bones and nasal
sinuses could cure a wide variety of afflictions such as gastrointestinal
disorders and, above all, disturbances of sexual functions. Fliess was
not only Freud's friend, but also his exalted intellectual mentor, his
confidant, and his personal physician, who had earlier treated him for
two severe cardiac illnesses (Schur, 1972, pp. 40–65). Freud asked
Fliess to examine Emma, a patient Freud was treating for hysterical
disturbances. Fliess recommended an operation of the turbinate bone
and one of the sinuses. The advice was accepted. Fliess performed the
operation but had to return to Berlin fairly soon after. On March 4,
Freud wrote Fliess that he was deeply concerned about Emma's
postoperative condition. He mentioned persistent swellings, pain that
required morphine sedation, purulent secretions, a foetid odor and a
massive hemorrhage. Freud called in a prominent Viennese surgeon for
consultation. On March 8, Freud had to write Fliess that the situation
had further deteriorated. Emma had started to bleed profusely from
nose and mouth. The prominent surgeon could not rush to Emma's
bedside forthwith. Freud was forced to call in another specialist, who
removed half a meter of iodoform gauze from the nasal cavity. This had

been used as a packing during the operation but was forgotten by Fliess. A massive hemorrhage followed the cleaning of the cavity. "The foetid odor was very bad" wrote Freud, and he added elsewhere in the same letter:

> It had lasted half a minute, but this was enough to make the poor creature, who by then we had lying quite flat, unrecognizable. In the meantime, or actually afterwards, something else happened. At the moment the foreign body came out, and everything had become obvious to me, immediately after which I was confronted with the sight of the patient, I felt sick. After she had been packed I fled to the next room, drank a bottle of water, and felt rather miserable. The brave Frau Doktor then brought me a small glass of cognac [the liqueur of the Irma dream], and I felt myself again [Schur, 1966, pp. 56–57].

A second passage likewise merits citation.

> I don't think I had been overwhelmed by the blood; affects were welling up in me at that moment. So we had done her an injustice. She had not been abnormal at all, but a piece of iodoform gauze had gotten torn off when you removed the rest, and stayed in for fourteen days, interfering with the healing process, after which it had torn away and provoked the bleeding [p. 57].

Three weeks later Freud could write Fliess that Emma was doing tolerably well (no fever, no more hemorrhages) but, he added: "Of course, she is starting to develop new hysterias from this past period, which then are being dissolved by me" (Schur, 1966, p. 61). During the first half of April 1895 a serious relapse occurred. Several hemorrhages occurred during this second critical period. On April 27, Freud had to write to Fliess: "Eckstein once *again* is in pain; will she be bleeding next?" (Masson, 1984, p. 58). The last letter about the Emma episode that Schur came across (prior to the Irma dream) was written at the end of May. Emma's bleeding had stopped; she was convalescing and had resumed treatment, presumably for hysteria. During the night of July 23–24, Freud (1900) had his famous dream:

Dream of July 23rd–24th, 1895

A large hall—numerous guests, whom we were receiving.— Among them was Irma. I at once took her on one side, as though

to answer her letter and to reproach her for not having accepted
my "solution" yet. I said to her: "If you still get pains, it's really
only your fault." She replied: "If you only knew what pains I've
got now in my throat and stomach and abdomen—it's choking
me"—I was alarmed and looked at her. She looked pale and puffy.
I thought to myself that after all I must be missing some organic
trouble. I took her to the window and looked down her throat, and
she showed signs of recalcitrance, like women with artificial
dentures. I thought to myself that there was really no need for her
to do that.—She then opened her mouth properly and on the right
I found a big white patch; at another place I saw extensive whitish
grey scabs upon some remarkable curly structures which were
evidently modelled on the turbinal bones of the nose.—I at once
called in Dr. M., and he repeated the examination and confirmed
it. . . . Dr. M. looked quite different from usual; he was very pale,
he walked with a limp and his chin was clean-shaven. . . . My
friend Otto was now standing beside her as well, and my friend
Leopold was percussing her through the bodice and saying: "She
has a dull area low down on the left." He also indicated that a
portion of the skin of the left shoulder was infiltrated. (I noticed
this, just as he did, in spite of her dress.) . . . M. said: "There's no
doubt it's an infection, but no matter; dysentery will supervene
and the toxin will be eliminated." . . . We were directly aware,
too, of the origin of the infection. Not long before, when she was
feeling unwell, my friend Otto had given her an injection of a
preparation of propyl, propyls . . . propionic acid . . . trimethylamin (and I saw before me the formula for this printed in heavy
type). . . . Injections of that sort ought not to be made so
thoughtlessly. . . . And probably the syringe had not been clean
[p. 107].

Freud added a brief first account of his feelings before he undertook a
serious analysis of the dream:

The dream has one advantage over many others. It was immediately clear what events of the previous day provided its starting-
point. My preamble makes that plain. The news which Otto had
given me of Irma's condition and the case history which I had
been engaged in writing till far into the night continued to occupy
my mental activity even after I was asleep. Nevertheless, no one
who had only read the preamble and the content of the dream
itself could have the slightest notion of what the dream meant. I

myself had no notion. I was astonished at the symptoms of which Irma complained to me in the dream, since they were not the same as those for which I had treated her. I smiled at the senseless idea of an injection of propionic acid and at Dr. M.'s consoling reflections. Towards its end the dream seemed to me to be more obscure and compressed than it was in the beginning. In order to discover the meaning of all this it was necessary to undertake a detailed analysis [pp. 107–108].

To my mind, there can be no reasonable doubt that the Emma episode and the Irma dream are linked. Greenberg and Pearlman (1978, p. 73) have noted almost twenty points of similarity between Freud's report and analysis of the Irma dream and his report to Fliess about the aftermath of the operation. Schur (1966) presents us with a good summing up:

> Here was a patient treated by Freud for hysteria who *did* have an organic, largely 'iatrogenic' illness; who had narrowly escaped death because a physician really had committed an error; whose pathology was located in the nasal cavity; whose case had confronted Freud with a number of emergencies requiring him urgently to call in several consultants, all of whom had been helpless and confused; Emma's lesion had a foetid odor (propylamil); Freud had had to look repeatedly into her nose and mouth [p. 67].

Schur (1966, p. 70) believes that Freud was not aware of the link between the Emma episode and the Irma dream. Schur accepted Freud's categorical statements that he had no notion what the dream meant and that he never had had occasion to examine Irma's oral cavity. To Schur's thinking, Freud suppressed this knowledge. Others—Greenberg and Pearlman (1978, p. 73), for example—have followed Schur in attributing Freud's forgetting to unconscious censorship. Kuper and Stone (1982) disagree. They assert that Freud deliberately misled his readers: "In the place of what was censored, (Freud) offered what we think are less relevant, even misleading, associations" (p. 1228).

It seems to me that both processes were at work. On one hand, to throw Fliess off the scent, Freud distorted his associations and perhaps even omitted a few elements from the manifest dream. On the other hand, the relationship with Fliess was ambivalent; in many ways Fliess was Freud's surrogate analyst. Some of the more significant issues must have fogged considerably as a result of relations of transference and countertransference.

A STRUCTURALIST CASTLE IN SPAIN

Structuralist Procedures

The manifest content of the Irma dream is divided into five portions: an initial thesis of the dream, an antithesis, a first synthesis, a second antithesis, and a second synthesis (see Figure 1). Each of these stages is constructed around three axes: (i) the nature of Irma's afflictions; (ii) the responsibility of the human actor; and (iii) the nature of catharsis. The empirical basis on which Kuper and Stone (1982) found their exposition is given in the appendix at the end of this paper. Here, by way of example, we will restrict ourselves to relating the initial thesis and its antithesis, and take only the first two axes ("affliction" and "responsibility"). On the first axis—the nature of the affliction—a standard Freudian diagnosis is given: "The illness is sexual-hysterical, the symptoms organic." Kuper and Stone construct this thesis from Freud's preamble and a knowledge of his intellectual development at that time. Thus they assert: "The initial thesis of the dream is that Irma is suffering from hysteria, which has a sexual etiology" (p. 1230). On the second axis (responsibility) the conclusion is that it is caused by the patient. The source probably is the manifest dream: "I said to her: 'If you still get pains, it's really only your fault.' " The antithesis turns the diagnosis to a more orthodox medical standard. The illness is now believed to be organic, with hysterical symptoms. The source here is also the manifest dream: "She looked pale and puffy. I thought to myself that after all I must be missing some organic trouble." Another element that supports this antithesis is: "If only you knew what pains I've got now in my throat and stomach and abdomen—it's choking me." On the second axis, we notice that responsibility is shifted from the patient's shoulders to those of Freud. The source is the same element from the manifest dream: "I thought to myself that after all I must be missing some organic trouble."

The "Central Message"

Kuper and Stone (1982) are convinced that a recapitulation and confirmation of Freud's theoretical ideas is the central message of the Irma dream. The authors mention Freud's efforts to bridge the domains of biology and psychology; the sexual etiology of hysteria; the causes of anxiety neurosis; and the toxic effects of various forms of sexual restraint. This central message, the authors assert, can be revealed only by steering away from idiosyncratic associations and examining the dialectical structure of the dream instead. While I do not wish to contest the authors' claim that some of Freud's theoretical

1. The illness is sexual-hysterical, the symptoms organic.
2. It is caused by the patient.
3. The patient voluntarily resists catharsis (speech).

1. The illness is organic, the symptoms hysterical.
2. It is neglected by the doctor.
3. The patient involuntarily resists catharsis (choking).

1. The illness is organic-sexual.
2. The doctor's negligence made it worse.
3. The doctor induced nasal catharsis, which miscarried.

1. The illness is organic, but a metaphor for hysteria.
2. It passes from the patient to the doctor.
3. The infection causes infiltration (the contrary of catharsis).

1. The illness is organic-sexual hysterical.
2. It is caused by a careless doctor.
3. The infection produces catharsis through the anus (dysentery).

Figure 1. *The Dialectic of Freud's Irma Dream*

From: Kuper & Stone, 1982. Adapted by permission.

notions are reflected in the manifest content of the dream—Kuper and Stone deserve full credit for this finding—too much emphasis on this point can defeat an understanding of other "messages" the dream carries. The other messages seem more important, as I suggest later. These other messages are more than a mere reflection of Freud's intellectual endeavours in the 1890s, more than another form of day-residues; these "communications" deal with the open and the hidden ailments of the psyche. At the end of this study, the contours of these other messages are given, but first I wish to present my objections to the methods and results of the structuralist hermeneutics offered by Kuper and Stone.[5]

5. It is not my purpose to present a critique of structuralism as such. The structuralism of Lacan (1954–1955) or Brodeur (1983), both of whom have attempted a reinterpretation of the Irma dream, is not on the agenda. (I wonder though what Kuper and Stone's reasons might have been for not discussing Lacan's views on the dream of Irma's injection. Lacan was, after all, an influential figure in the structuralist community of Paris.) No other structuralists figure in this paper. However, I have a feeling that Kuper and Stone are right in claiming that they are working within the structuralist tradition. Lévi-Strauss seems to share this view, as is apparent from Kuper and Stone's response to comments on their article. They (1983) are happy to disclose that ". . . perhaps it is sufficient to report that our paper has in fact been read by Lévi-Strauss himself and deemed acceptable by him" (p. 664). This dispels my apprehension that the significance of my critical comments is limited to this one article only.

ARBITRARY CUTS IN THE MANIFEST DREAM

Several portions of the manifest contents are ignored by Kuper and
Stone. Here follow the omitted passages.

A large hall—numerous guests whom we are receiving—Among
them Irma. I at once took her on one side, as though to answer her
letter. I took her to the window and looked down her throat, and
she showed signs of recalcitrance, like women with artificial
dentures. I thought to myself that there was really no need for her
to do that—She then opened her mouth properly. . . .
Dr. M. looked quite different from usual; he walked with a limp
and his chin was clean-shaven. . . . My friend Otto was now
standing beside her as well, and my friend Leopold was percussing her through the bodice [Freud, 1900, p. 107].
(Only the appearance on the scene of Leopold is mentioned by
Kuper and Stone.)

These omissions obviously raise questions about the criteria for inclusion: When is an element of the manifest dream allowed to stay and be
properly placed in the structural-dialectical framework, and when do
we have to throw it out?[6] The authors do not offer justification for their
choice. Some of the passages discarded by the structuralists bring
numerous associations to Freud and are clearly significant to him, the
dreamer. Take, for instance, this example from Kuper and Stone
(1982): "Having noted Irma's pallor and her complaint, which seems to
have little to do with the eventual diagnosis, Freud is delayed by the
false teeth, which Irma does not have" (p. 1229). Why, one wonders,
are we delayed by her false teeth? To Freud these objects are the
takeoff point for a rich series of associations. Kuper and Stone may not
like the method of free association, but they cannot simply dismiss
Freud's thoughts without first explaining why they make these cuts.
Our structuralist critics seem to feel they know better than the dreamer
what should have been in the manifest dream!

OVERDETERMINATION

To the dreamer, one element in the manifest dream may have several
meanings simultaneously. Take, for instance, the dream element "trimethylamin." Freud (1900) has this to say about it:

---

6. According to de Ruijter (1977) a systematic aberration structuralists are prone to
   develop (p. 187).

What was it, then, to which my attention was to be directed in this way by trimethylamin? It was to a conversation with another friend who had for many years been familiar with all my writings during the period of their gestation, just as I had been with his. He had at that time confided some ideas to me on the subject of the chemistry of the sexual processes, and had mentioned among other things that he believed that one of the products of sexual metabolism was trimethylamin. Thus this substance led me to sexuality, the factor to which I attributed the greatest importance in the origins of the nervous disorders which it was my aim to cure [p. 116].

Clearly at least two themes are mentioned simultaneously: the new psychology that Freud was creating, with sexuality as a key variable, and the relationship with his friend Fliess. If we are to judge from what he himself had to say, both were very important to Freud. There may still be other themes involved in the single element "trimethylamin," as has been suggested by Anzieu (1975, pp. 209–210) and Lacan (1954–1955, p. 190), but the two meanings appear to be the minimum "load" in this case. Structural dialectics seems to have no adequate methodology for dealing with "overdetermined" information. Or, to borrow a phrase from Ricoeur (1970, p. 23), the way to a hermeneutics of double-meaning significations is blocked.

HISTORICAL PROPS

When Kuper and Stone construct their first synthesis, they do not limit themselves to materials from the manifest dream. Historical props are employed to ensure the proper development of the dialectical argument. Materials found by Schur (1966) in the Freud archives serve that purpose. Take, for example, these sentences: "We also know that Fliess . . . was implicated in the Irma dream" and "The doctor induced nasal catharsis, which miscarried," and again "That links her illness with Fliess, makes it iatrogenic, and places responsibility on Fliess" (Kuper and Stone, 1982, p. 1230). We have come to know about the crucial role Fliess played only because Schur had been given access to censored portions of the Freud–Fliess correspondence. The whole of the first synthesis depends on one vital "input" from an external domain of knowledge (historical information, censored Freud letters; for other instances, see Appendix). In fact, Kuper and Stone's article could not have been written before 1966, the year Schur's path-breaking paper appeared. This raises the question, what will happen when other investigators get an opportunity to inspect the many letters still under embargo? The implication seems to be that Kuper and Stone would then have to devise a new "logic of the manifest sequence"? Structural dialectics seems to depend on historical knowledge. New disclosures, hence new dialectics.

LATENT MATERIALS TO BOOST DIALECTICS

Here we have an "internal" domain of knowledge: the associations of Freud, condemned as subjective and idiosyncratic by the structuralist critics, but yet utilized to bolster the "logic of the manifest sequence." True, Kuper and Stone only sparingly glean the latent content for clues or elements to shore up structuralist dialectics. Yet on one vital occasion, allowing them to proceed *one* crucial step, they delve deeply into Freud's associations. When the manifest dream gives us: "I noticed this, in spite of her dress" Kuper and Stone surprisingly venture: "It passes from the patient to the doctor" (p. 1232) [second antithesis]. How do they manage to make the jump from "to notice" to "It passes from the patient to the doctor"? The explanation is simple: they had wisely consulted Freud's (1900) interpretation of the dream— that labyrinth of idiosyncratic associations!—where we read that: "*A portion of the skin on the left shoulder was infiltrated.* I saw at once that this was the rheumatism in my own shoulder, which I invariably notice if I sit up late into the night. Moreover, the wording of the dream was most ambiguous: '*I noticed this, just as he did.* . . .' I noticed it in my own body, that is" (p. 113).

In their zeal to avoid unnecessary detours, Kuper and Stone write: "Having noted Irma's pallor and her complaint, which seems to have little to do with the eventual diagnosis, Freud is delayed by the false teeth, which Irma does not have" (p. 1229), meaning that we should not while away with Irma, but get straight to the real business at hand: an analysis in terms of dialectics. But, of course, they knew that Irma in real life had a rosy complexion, and no artificial dentures at all, because they read Freud's dream thoughts. Again, we cannot fail to notice that the structuralists have made good use of Freud's "idiosyncratic associations," which, they assure us, are anathema to them.

This brings us back to a point mentioned before: Procedures such as these put the structuralists in the position of arbiters who may decide the appropriateness of "extra" knowledge for "the logic of the manifest sequence." It leaves us readers in the uncomfortable position of having to accept on faith that this piece of latent content should be incorporated, and that one dismissed—all of this without knowing their criteria for inclusion and while the rhetoric of the "manifest sequence" continues right to the end of the article.

SPURIOUS PROGRESS

By their wording and by particular expressions, Kuper and Stone suggest a development within the dream, a forward movement that carries the dreamer to new insights along the corkscrew path paved with oppositions. This movement is suggested by such words and expressions as "transformations," "themes of sexual causation and catharsis that continue to be developed," "argument," "final resolution," "rules of development," "coherent progression," and "moving in a dialectical fashion from an initial problem to a resolution."[7]

But such progress, if there is any, is the result of streamlining the manifest dream by ignoring parts of it, declaring other portions irrelevant (the delay with the artificial dentures), and claiming that "pale and puffy" had nothing to do with Irma herself. In another instance of generating dynamism in an artificial and arbitrary way, the authors write: "Next Freud and Dr. M. note the lesions in the throat, but these lessen in significance as Leopold finds the dullness and infiltration" (p. 1229). Again, the same question must be asked: who is to decide what is significant and on what grounds? As Erikson (1954, p. 30) knew, long before Schur's (1966, 1972) investigations were to prove him right, two elements stand out most markedly: Irma's throat and trimethylamin, a chemical compound that Erikson, following Freud, strongly associates with Fliess.

When Leopold delivers his diagnosis, are we, as Kuper and Stone suggest, moving to a level of greater significance? What can be the basis for such a conclusion? One can with equal right argue that the middle section of the dream, with its emphasis on Freud's alarm, is the point of gravity in the dream. It is then that Freud sees the lesions in Irma's mouth, which, in Erikson's (1954) words "stare at him like the head of the Medusa" (p. 37).

Kuper and Stone (1982) discern a movement from the surface to underlying phenomena: ". . . this progression from false and superficial manifestations to progressively deeper and more fundamental causes

---

7. Kuper and Stone's article abounds with expressions suggesting movement that is both coherent and unceasing. Among the many examples: "This progression from false and superficial manifestations to progressively deeper and fundamental causes." (p. 1229), and "These two sequences not only move in a coherent direction, down and deeper, they present a typical quasilogical transformation" (p. 1229). Again: "A structural approach, by assuming a coherence in the language and development of the dream, opens the way to a different, simple, and novel explanation" (p. 1230) One wonders again what our structuralist critics of psychoanalysis think about scholars such as Lacan (1954–1955; Kurzweil, 1986), who freely moved from psychoanalysis to structuralism and back again and seem to have been content with both approaches.

parallels Freud's investigations of hysteria. . . ." (p. 1229). But, as we have seen, this theoretical construction (the downward movement) is strongly dependent on unreliable props, viz., their conviction that the artificial dentures do not represent a significant part of the manifest content and that the unnatural pallor belongs to the category of the "false and the superficial." Those who have read Freud's analysis know that for him these clues were just as weighty as everything else, with the exception of the lesions in Irma's mouth and trimethylamin.

The dialectical reinterpretation ends with "dysentery" and the elimination of the damaging toxin. By Kuper and Stone's reasoning, these are the final and decisive chords of a dialectical symphony, the last stage in their journey of discovery. For Freud, however, this was part of an attempt to ridicule Dr. M. (Breuer). The element "dysentery," however, is overdetermined: It serves Freud in his efforts to belittle Breuer, but it also reflects his theoretical ideas about the threat to physical and mental health if toxins remain in the body.

Spurious progress too because Freud, as Kuper and Stone put it with good justification, "Freud consistently treated Irma as though she had a double condition. He treated her for hysteria and yet had Fliess operate on her" (p. 1231). True, the second part of the Irma dream continues to reflect Freud's scientific ideas, but there is no evidence of development, of growth or coherent progress. Freud (1900) sums it up neatly:

> The alternative "either-or" cannot be expressed in dreams in any way whatever. Both of the alternatives are usually inserted in the text of the dream as though they were equally valid. The dream of Irma's injection contains a classic instance of this. Its latent thoughts clearly ran: "I am not responsible for the persistence of Irma's pains; the responsibility lies *either* in her recalcitrance to accepting my solution, *or* in the unfavourable sexual conditions under which she lives and which I cannot alter, *or* in the fact that her pains are not hysterical at all but of an organic nature." The dream, on the other hand, fulfilled *all* of these possibilities (which were almost mutually exclusive), and did not hesitate to add a fourth solution, based on the dream-wish. After interpreting the dream, I proceeded to insert the "either-or" into the content of the dream-thoughts [pp. 316–317].

This insight of Freud seems more acceptable than the authors' assumption that the dream represents an argument that reaches its culmination in the last sentences, when it is discovered that the illness is "organic-sexual-hysterical." As Freud insisted, all these diagnoses were, one by one, options available to a physician with his training and knowledge. Thus coherent progress, resolution, dream-cure, and ordered development are all misleading expressions. Freud simply provides us with a list of possible medical and psychological diagnoses.

THE NEGATION OF MEANING

Central to Freud's thinking is a belief in meaning. Steven Marcus (in Bonaparte et al., 1954) wrote: "In the instance of Freud it was a belief that all human thought and behavior had a meaning and meanings—that they were understandable, purposeful, and a structure and rose to significance" (p. xviii). The method advocated by Kuper and Stone destroys meaning by ignoring parts of the manifest dream, but, worse, by dismissing as irrelevant the dreamer's own effort to make sense out of that hodgepodge of manifest dream elements. I mentioned these points before in connection with the elements "false teeth" and "pale and puffy." There are, of course, more impressive examples to be found in 'the dream of Irma's injection.' To cite Freud (1900):

> *I took her to the window to look down her throat. She showed some recalcitrance, like women with false teeth. I thought to myself that really there was no need for her to do that.* I had never had any occasion to examine Irma's oral cavity. What happened in the dream reminded me of an examination I had carried out some time before of a governess: at a first glance she had seemed a picture of youthful beauty, but when it came to opening her mouth she had taken measures to conceal her plates. . . . The way in which Irma stood by the window suddenly reminded me of another experience. Irma had an intimate woman friend of whom I had a very high opinion [p. 110].

(i) Several association paths lead away from his passage. The first one ("the false teeth") stops momentarily at the theme "recalcitrant women." A second path starts out with "the window" and brings him to an intimate friend of Irma who also suffers from hysterical choking. She happens to be obstreperous as well. A third association is made with "pale and puffy." Freud reopens the first path, moves from false teeth to bad teeth, combines that with pale and puffy, and ends with thoughts about his own wife. Both Irma and his wife share certain drawbacks in comparison with Irma's intimate friend, whom Freud covets as a patient:

Thus I had been comparing my patient Irma with two other people who would also have been recalcitrant to treatment. What could the reason have been for my having exchanged her in the dream for her friend? Perhaps it was that I should have *liked* to exchange her: either I felt more sympathetic towards her friend or had a higher opinion of her intelligence. For Irma seemed to me foolish because she has not accepted my solution. Her friend would have been wiser, that is to say she would have yielded sooner. She would then have *opened her mouth properly*, and have told me more than Irma [Freud, 1900, pp. 110–111].

In combination with the element "standing at the window," the dream elements "pale and puffy" and "false teeth" bring him first to the sexual theme, hardly concealed, and then to the linked theme of wishing to exchange people. The sexual theme is poorly developed, as Freud himself admits ("I had a feeling that the interpretation of this part of the dream is not carried far enough to make it possible to follow the whole of its concealed meaning" (p.111). "Exchanging people" is one of the themes that Freud best developed in this dream. This part of the dream-thoughts is one of the two pertinent bases of material for concluding that dream is the fulfillment of a wish. Thus, far from being trivial elements, "pale and puffy" and "false teeth" are vital links to the dominant theme of "exchanging people" and thus are the building blocks for his theory of wish fulfillment.

(ii) "*I at once called in Dr. M., and he repeated the examination and confirmed it*" (Freud, 1900, p. 111). Only part of this sentence is used by Kuper and Stone, the part dealing with the medical process of repeating and confirming a diagnosis. "At once" plays no role in their thinking, but to Freud it is a crucial element. It reminded him of a woman to whom he had repeatedly prescribed sulphonal. At that time the toxic effects of the drug were insufficiently known, and the patient died from poisoning. If Schur's (1966) data are relevant to an understanding of this dream—and Kuper and Stone leave little doubt on that score—then "at once" is a link between Freud's feeling of despair when it turned out that a patient had died as a result of his medication and the disastrous Fliess operation, recommended if not actually prescribed by Freud. "At once" is a bridge between two states of panic.

(iii) *Dr. M was pale, had a clean-shaven chin and walked with a limp*. The "paleness' is an attribute of Dr. M. (Breuer); the second and third qualities reminded him of his elder brother. Freud reasoned that he fused these two figures in one dream image, because he happened to be ill-humored with the two of them: ". . . they had both rejected a certain suggestion I had recently laid before them" (p. 112). This appears to be the theme of rebellion against an authority figure, be it a father, an elder half-brother, or a mentor (Breuer and, we suspect, Fliess). This theme recurs throughout *The Interpretation of Dreams*. By dismissing these outward appearances, trivial indeed at first glance but yet highly meaningful, Kuper and Stone manage to steer away from those complexes that are of a strong emotional nature and are crucial to an understanding of the dream.

These are three examples of how Kuper and Stone revamp the interpretation of the Irma dream by destroying links to the Freudian themes. The fourth instance of the negation of meaning is of a quite different nature. It concerns the phrase (Freud, 1900, p. 107) "There's no doubt it's an infection, but no matter; dysentery will supervene and the toxin will be eliminated." For Kuper and Stone this means catharsis through the anus—from a voluntary opening of the mouth to an involuntary opening of the anus (one has to admire their inventiveness in discerning oppositions!). The authors' "logic of the manifest sequence" is nearing its end. Toxins produced by sexual restraint are thus eliminated. Freud the thinker had managed to concoct a dream cure for Irma. Unfortunately, his commentary points in a different direction.

Freud's first impulse is to consider this a ludicrous diagnosis. But disciplined by his newly developed routines of systematic free association, he continues pondering the sentence. This brings him to Leopold's diagnosis (diphtheria), which he takes more seriously but finally rejects. A dull area has been located and Freud (1900) adds: "Metastases like this do not in fact occur with diphtheria: it made me think rather of pyaemia" (pp. 113–114). From Schur's (1966) work, we have learned that the threat of pyaemia must have been on Freud's mind when the forgotten gauze was finally removed from Irma's nose two weeks after the operation (March, 1895). It seems unreasonable to shrug off such trains of thought as idiosyncratic associations. These were highly valuable considerations, springing directly from day residues. Kuper and Stone have succeeded in distorting Freud's painful discoveries to the point where they seem little more than absurd pronouncements of a nineteenth-century quack.

Judging from Kuper and Stone's attempt, I conclude that the uncovering of a hidden logic, of an internal dialectic, with structuralists' tools holds out little promise. My objections are directed in particular at the arbitrary and inconsistent nature of the methods advocated. First, the contents of the manifest dream (the authors take from it whatever they fancy) do not appear to suffice for them; they obviously need the help of both external and internal sources—historical information and Freud's own associations. Second, the dialectical progress detected by the authors seems absent. Third, the costs of the deliberate neglect or violation of Freud's system of meanings are considerable. In short, I contend that the structuralists' hermeneutics does not represent a valuable set of techniques for the interpretation of multiple-meaning expressions.

A Dirty World

Kuper and Stone's retreat to their castle in Spain can be understood from a number of angles. An important one is their open revulsion toward the chaotic character and arbitrariness of (some) Freudian dream explanations. Equally plain is their distaste for a theoretical study of unruly passions, "psychosexual fixations," or, more generally, of the forces emanating from the id.[8] To enhance our understanding of their motives let us look again at the Irma dream.

(a) The many interpretations of "the dream of Irma's injection" reminds one of Kurosawa's *Rashomon*: In this Japanese film, the four main characters present their versions of a violent crime: each person projects his or her own emotions or perceived interests in an account of the drama. The Irma dream, the dream to which Freud added the longest commentary of all dreams related in *The Interpretation of Dreams*, has been analyzed repeatedly. The interpretations vary greatly: some stress the ambivalent relationship with Fliess as the important theme; others keep close to Freud's own version. Sexual megalomania is mentioned by three authors (Hartman, 1983; Schatzman, 1982; Swales, 1983a, 6) and disillusionment with the marital relationship (Elms, 1980) also figures. It is a bewildering variety of interpretations.

(b) Examples of arbitrary psychoanalytical "reasoning" are not hard to come by. Erikson (1954), looking at the dream elements "propyl . . . propyls . . . propionic acid," points out that propylon, Freud's association with the first two words, means, in Greek, entrance to the vagina. Propionic, to Erikson at least, suggests *priapic*, or phallic. Erikson adds: "This word play, then, would bring male and female symbols into linguistic vicinity to allude to a genital theme" (p. 26). It seems to

---

8. Spiro (1979) raised this point in his critical discussion of Lévi-Strauss's analysis of a Bororo myth in *The Raw and the Cooked*. Spiro shows how Lévi-Strauss sterilizes sexual and aggressive themes without significant benefits accruing from the operation.

me that little is to be gained by pursuing such an association; we simply do not know whether Freud had this in mind. And if he had, how relevant was it to him? A simple pun or more?

Mahony (1977) feels even freer to speculate. He asserts that the German text of the Irma dream is loaded with double meanings of a sexual nature (p. 84). To uncover these hidden sexual motifs, Mahony advocates that scrupulous attention be paid to "the polysemy of central words . . . overdetermined prepositions . . . the beginnings and endings of words" (p. 85). A few examples of his approach:

A large hall—many guests, whom we receive—
Eine grosse Halle—viele Gäste, die wir empfangen
empfangen: "Conceive," "receive"
"Fang: "claw," "fang"

Mahony offers the following interpretation: "First of all, there is the anticipation in *empfangen* ('conceive,' 'claw') of the vagina dentata of Irma's mouth-vagina and its artificial dentures" (p. 86). Interpreters such as Kuper and Stone have shied away from exactly such wild (undisciplined) speculations. And for good reason. Freud explicitly rejected the association of Irma with "artificial dentures", that was not part of his (Freud's) system of meaning. We have no reason to believe that Freud wished to deceive us here; it seems better to accept his commentary. And how can we be sure that Freud had a vagina dentata in mind when he awoke on Wednesday, July 24, 1895? Support from at least one external source appears necessary before we embrace such speculative ideas. But in this case such confirmation is lacking.[9]

Although Mahony's article contains shrewd insights, its boldness is not always supported by the evidence. Take, for instance, the way Mahony (p. 85) dissects the German original of "it's choking me" *(es schnürt mich zusammen).* "Sperm," is recognized in *Same(n).* In "trimethylamin" he finds "wet-nurses" *(Ammen).* The two words combined bring him to the following statement: "It is obliquely indicated that her mouth is full of sperm *(Samen)* and wet-nurse milk *(Ammen)*, fellatio and breast-feeding are blended" (p. 95). As if this were not enough for any stomach, Mahony asks, "Typographically, are the dashes suggestive of the phallic, a mark of punctuation which

---

9. Mahony (1982) further elaborates this point in a more recent publication: "In the specimen dream analysis in Chapter 2, Freud associates his pregnant wife with Irma and looks into her mouth-vagina. In an act of self-delivery, he emerges from this uterine chapter to the outer world; thus the book as a whole is a maternal object genetically and formally, a metaphor based on the most literal fantasy" (153). One notes that the vagina-dentata of his earlier publication has now disappeared.

Freud defensively removes from the second half of the dream where three other males are protagonists?" (p. 91). Analyses of this type may be partly to blame for the distaste evinced by Kuper and Stone (p. 228) for all those contributions that rely on the unearthing of psychosexual fixations. One more example: Anzieu (1975, p. 204), prodded on by his reading of Erikson (1954), ventures from the dream's first element, "the hall" (vagina and womb), and the verb "receiving" (in German also "conceiving") to the name of this hallowed space, Bellevue. "To a man like Freud," Anzieu suggests, "who knew French well, this [the name] must have been a whole program" (p. 205). One would like to know what sort of program Anzieu had in mind when he wrote this sentence; unfortunately he does not elaborate.[10]

To reduce the number of unwarranted speculations, I suggest two simple methods. First, dream elements, associations, or other pieces of information, should be presented in meaningful clusters or trends. Take, for instance, Anzieu's rumination about the hotel Bellevue. It seems to me there is no apparent connection between "Bellevue" and the elements "hall" and "receive." Anzieu himself makes no effort to establish such a link; he merely suggests it. When Freud (1900) sat down to write his analysis of the Irma dream, he explicitly mentioned the task of combining elements and their associations into larger, meaningful structures (p. 118).

A second and equally useful method would be to look for external confirmation. Freud's letters (Bonaparte et al., 1954) to Fliess are such an external source: they were never meant to be published. As another example, in 1899, when Freud was reading the galley proofs for *The Interpretation of Dreams* (1900), he probably had made up his mind that if *Project for a Scientific Psychology* (1895) was ever to be published, form and content were to be quite different from those of the manuscript he had sent to Fliess in the fall of 1895. This *Project* is therefore considered an external source.

HEADQUARTERS NO LONGER IN CONTROL

Structuralists and depth psychologists part company for reasons more serious than the occasional arbitrariness of the methods employed by followers of both camps. The metaphysical foundations of their work are radically different. Structuralists believe in their "think-

---

10. Around 1900 most European cities and towns had at least one Bellevue and one hotel Terminus to boast. One wonders what the speculations of Anzieu might have looked like had the hotel carried the ominous name Terminus.

ing machine," a central agency dominating the whole of mental life. Depth psychologists hold a very different conception: In their view the psyche is constituted of multiple parts, none of which is strong enough to act as "headquarters" to the psyche (Hillman, 1975, p. 26). How these various entities are called (ego, id, superego, shadow, anima) need not concern us here. The underlying principle is what counts: Our psychological nature is characterized by a plurality of "actors" or "agencies." Mental life can be seen as the result of dialogues among these agencies. In brief, the psyche is an arena; its products (symptoms, dreams, parapraxes, but also "routine behavior") bear its mark. They represent the record of past and current conflict. Mental products are compromises between forces and counterforces.

Complex or conflictual dreams[11] such as "The dream of Irma's injection," as well as most other dreams from *The Interpretation*, reflect those basic divisions within the psyche by being polymorphous: systems of meaning that are multifaceted and multilayered; multifaceted because dreams consist of a number of subsystems, or scripts. Although each script is a production of the dreamer only (Spanjaard, 1969, p. 228), the divisions within the psyche are responsible for their mixed, or compromise, character. Scripts betray the presence of conflicting forces within the psyche. Scripts are often linked. In one dream, these links may be tenuous at best; in another the scripts may overlap or fuse to a considerable extent.

Dreams are multilayered as well: surface and hidden scripts form a hierarchy. This distinction does not coincide with the manifest and latent dichotomy of Freudian dream analysis. Both surface and hidden scripts can influence the manifest and latent contents of a dream. Surface scripts, in my conception, are written by dreamers who succeed in detecting meaningful patterns among disparate elements and who are willing to relate this knowledge to an audience or to themselves. Hidden scripts, however, are never offered overtly. Two main reasons come to mind. A dreamer's abhorrence of the knowledge expected to come to the surface may be so strong that the two crucial processes of dream work—condensation and displacement—stymie his

---

11. I hesitate to attempt a precise delineation of this category of dreams. Such an undertaking, if possible at all, calls for a separate paper. To give only an indication of what I have in mind: Rudi Kaufman's dream (Freud 1900) is not a complex dream, and neither is the type of dream that Freud said he could produce "experimentally": anchovies eaten in the evening invariably produced a dream wherein he gulped cool water (p. 123). Spanjaard's (1969) distinction between the undisguised wishful dreams and the conflictual dreams characterized by hidden intrapsychic conflict appears helpful.

efforts at deciphering. Second, a dreamer may have little wish to inform his audience (or clarify matters for himself!) about the main scripts; he may, for example, practice deception and misinformation. I suggest that the dream of Irma's injection also has its hidden scripts.[12]

THE SCRIPTS OF THE IRMA DREAM

With great clarity Freud presents his first script. It is the "rivalry among colleagues" scenario. This script cogently makes the case for wish fulfillment as *the* causative factor in dreaming. Part of Freud's (1900) argument reads as follows.

> And in the meantime the "meaning" of the dream was borne in upon me. I became aware of an intention which was carried into effect by the dream and which must have been my motive for dreaming it. The dream fulfilled certain wishes which were started in me by the events of the previous evening (the news given me by Otto and my writing out of the case history). The conclusion of the dream, that is to say, was that I was not responsible for the persistence of Irma's pains, but that Otto was. Otto had in fact annoyed me by his remarks about Irma's incomplete cure, and the dream gave me my revenge by throwing the reproach back on to him. The dream acquitted me of the responsibility for Irma's condition by showing that it was due to other factors—it produced a whole series of reasons. The dream represented a particular state of affairs as I should have wished it to be. *Thus its content was the fulfillment of a wish and its motive was a wish* [pp. 118– 119].

Academic reputation and rivalry appear to be the main themes of this first script. The challenge of Otto and the "contradiction" of Dr. M. are both strongly emphasized in the analysis of the dream. Recalcitrant patients also figure as obstacles on Freud's path toward academic success. Key theoretical notions and signs of a struggle to get these accepted appear in both the manifest and latent contents of the dream. This script comes closest to Kuper and Stone's interpretation of the dream.

Right in the middle of Freud's confident exposition of the wish fulfillment theme (and his nocturnal revenge), he allows another

---

12. The next section summarizes parts of my paper on the dream of Irma's injection. (cf. Thoden van Velzen, 1984).

thought to emerge. Unexpectedly (in view of his own "dominant" interpretation) Freud writes: "It seemed as if I had been collecting all the occasions which I could bring up against myself as evidence of lack of medical conscientiousness" (p. 112). This "guilt script" seems as important as the first one, the script to which Freud gave such emphasis. Many reinterpreters of the Irma dream have equally been impressed by the somber mood pervading the dream. Erikson (1954) mentions the fact that the dream starts off in a festive mood (the birthday party at the hotel Bellevue), but that a gloomy atmosphere, full of concern over past mistakes, soon replaces it (p. 32). Mahony (1977) writes that the Irma dream gives him the impression of being "guilt-laden" (p. 94). Cournut (1973) sums it up with the following words: ". . . the dreamer meets only with failure, disappointment, refusal and reproach. On only one account does he have some success: she finally opens her mouth" (p. 84).[13] Schur's (1966) observations are also worth repeating: "The chain of Freud's associations led him far afield. They brought back painful memories of situations in which he could not have failed to feel self-reproach" (p. 51).

Freud's account of the dream of Irma's injection can be read as a litany of self-reproaches. Among the sorrowful reminiscences, that he had recommended cocaine occupies a special place: "The misuse of that drug had hastened the death of a dear friend of mine" (p. 111). The distance between this guilt script and Kuper and Stone's interpretation of the dream is considerable. Here we do not encounter the struggle for mastery of the academic arena and the concomitant endeavours to make a new psychology respectable.

Equally hard to understand from Kuper and Stone's pespective is the "ambivalence script" that Schur (1966) bared. Kuper and Stone make considerable use of the historical information (the bungled nasal operation, the chronology of events between February and July 1895), but they ignore the psychodynamics of the Freud–Fliess relationship. It appears from the letters, particularly from those portions that were first published by Schur, that the relationship between the two men was highly ambivalent, with Fliess functioning as Freud's "surrogate' analyst." Revealing for this script is the mixture of outward praise and covert animosity. This is evident in the passage that is supposed to ridicule Breuer (Dr. M.) (Freud, 1900): "Dr. M. said: 'It's an infection, but no matter. Dysentery will supervene and the toxin will be eliminated (p. 113).

This passage points up the farcical side of the medical profession.

---

13. The translation from the French is mine.

Dr. M. is pictured pontificating as a doctor in a *commedia dell'arte*, strutting through the scene. For Kuper and Stone this element brings us to the final stage of dialectics: catharsis through the anus! However, Freud's chain of associations takes him in a different direction. Whether Freud's associations or Kuper and Stone's interpretation should be accepted depends on the theoretical fruitfulness of these competing hermeneutics. The touchstone could be the extent to which the two thought-sequences fit into models of theoretical significance, baring underlying structures or forces. Kuper and Stone will insist that their treatment of the material does exactly that: as a result of their analysis, the dialectical movement becomes visible. But a careful reading of Freud's text discloses a hidden reality. First, Freud alters the tone of his reflections by shifting the subject: the joke at the expense of Dr. M recedes into the background; the "infection" element comes to the fore. Anxiety is further stressed when he relates how worried he was at the time of his daughter's illness. When associating to dysentery Freud asks the seemingly innocuous question: "Could it be that I was trying to make fun of Dr. M's fertility in producing far-fetched explanations and making unexpected pathological connections?" (p. 114).

Before providing us with an answer, he lets his thoughts wander to instances of medical failure on his part. Then he comes up with a conclusion: "Yes, I thought to myself, I must have been making fun of Dr. M. with the consoling prognosis . . ." (p. 114). But the question should have been answered in the negative. The last thing Freud would blame Breuer for was "[a] fertility in producing far-fetched explanations and making unexpected pathological connections." The cause of their eventual separation is given by Jones (1953) as "Breuer's unwillingness to follow Freud . . . in the far-reaching conclusions Freud was drawing from [the patient's sexual life]" (p. 253). Breuer is described by Jones as dampening Freud's ardor, as displaying a "timid ambivalence" toward Freud, and a "pettifogging kind of censoriousness" (p. 255). It is Fliess, of course, who is the object of his hostile feelings, Breuer serving merely as a displacement-figure, a mask. Of Fliess it could be said that he produced "far-fetched explanations"; only of Fliess would Freud remark that he excelled in making "unexpected pathological connections."

Freud's question—(Could it be . . .) is a bridge between Breuer and Fliess; the passage shows the mechanism of displacement at work. This points to the presence of concealed themes, of hidden scripts. Focusing the discussion on this dream element has an advantage as well as a drawback. We cannot directly compare an argument presented by Freud with one presented by the structuralists; this is always a disadvantage when interpreting hidden scripts. The comparison will have to be between Schur on the one hand, and Kuper and Stone on the other, the positive side being that the dysentery diagnosis figures prominently in both the structuralist and the Freudian interpretative schemes.

The chief difference between the two approaches is the presence of corroborating evidence for the Freudian interpretation, mainly through the letters of Freud to Fliess that were published by Schur (1966). From this correspondence, one gains the impression that Breuer and Freud were then (spring and summer of 1895) on better terms than they had been in the preceding years. From the same source, it is also plain that Freud entertained grave doubts about his confidant (Fliess) during the months following the nasal operation. The correspondence can here serve as an external source of confirmation. But whatever the positive feelings Freud expressed about Breuer, he still held one grievance against the latter. Freud (1900) writes: "But what could be my motive for treating this friend of mine so badly? That was a very simple matter. Dr. M. was just as little in agreement with my 'solution' as Irma herself" (p. 115). This is what makes Breuer fit as the person who could stand at the beginning of a displacement sequence: as with Otto, Breuer had irritated Freud and could therefore be the starting point of a series of associations that ultimately would lead to the man he had such strong but covert hostile feelings about: Fliess.

The structuralist thesis—catharsis through the anus, the final station of a dialectical journey—remains pure guesswork. There is no external corroborating evidence. This is only one of the many examples where the "idiosyncratic" Freudian associations—even in their camouflaged form—offer us a better understanding of what the dream was about than the structuralist can deliver.[14]

The superiority of Freudian hermeneutics is also demonstrated by the interpretation of structuralists' leftovers. Kuper and Stone ignore this element from the manifest dream: "My friend Otto was now standing beside her as well, and my friend Leopold was percussing her through the bodice" (p. 107). Perhaps the evident sexual symbolism of the sentence made Kuper and Stone recoil. However, Emma's case

---

14. At several places in the chapter dealing with the dream of Irma's injection Freud warned his readers that his account was less than the whole story. Schur's (1966) account, written within a Freudian theoretical framework, endeavors to add to the analysis of the Irma dream. Comparing Kuper and Stone with Schur seems a legitimate undertaking when the relative productiveness of the two approaches is in question.

history, which forms part of the *Project* (Freud, 1895), offers a basis for interpreting these elements. Emma fantasized, or had actually experienced, a sexual assault at the age of eight. A shopkeeper had grabbed at her genitals through her clothes. The affect associated with this occurrence or fantasy seems to explain a significant part of her pathology during the time she consulted Freud (1895), later, at puberty, Emma, when entering a shop, had panicked when she found herself alone with two laughing (male) shop assistants. Freud suggested to Emma that her phobia (of entering shops unaccompanied) was linked to both earlier scenes. Emma accepted the link between her fear of being in shops alone and the scene with the two shop assistants, but she rejected a connection with the earlier scene with the shopkeeper. This probably was the solution Freud attempted to get her to espouse.

A combination of elements from the manifest dream and from Freud's associations can be linked to Emma's case history. First, two doctors pursue the examination that was inflicted on a passive patient and was crowned with the injection with a sexual metabolite. The examination is conducted through her bodice. This is not an accidental correspondence to be dismissed as a mere coincidence. Bodily intimacy achieved through the clothes is also suggested by the element from the manifest dream *in spite of her dress*. Freud (1900) gives us the following associations:

> *In spite of her dress*. This was in any case only an interpolation. We naturally used to examine the children in the hospital undressed: and this would be in contrast to the manner in which adult female patients have to be examined. I remembered that it was said of a celebrated clinician that he never made a physical examination of his patients except *through their clothes*. Further than this I could not see. Frankly, I had no desire to penetrate more deeply at this point [p. 113, italics added].

This last sentence is probably Freud's way of saying, "There is more here than first meets the eye, but I do not feel inclined to disclose these matters." After his belittling remark ("only an interpolation"), Freud continues by contrasting adult patients with children in a hospital: the children could be as obstreperous as they wished but had to submit to inspection in the nude. The celebrated clinician's actions Freud was referring to resemble those of the shopkeeper in one vital aspect: a woman's clothes need not restrain a man from achieving bodily contact.

CONCLUSION

Structuralists hanker for a clean world without dirt, where the almighty "thinking machine" holds sway. In this crystal palace greys have been replaced by black and white. Reason is in the driver's seat; the emotional life is kept firmly under the lid. Metaphysical notions underlie all paradigms in the social sciences; all schools have their fairy tales. The reasons for my rejection have nothing to do with this particular fairy tale. As I have tried to argue, Kuper and Stone choose their own guidelines but do not follow them consistently. They use methods that seem arbitrary and inconsistent, and they claim too much success. The fruits of their labor appear limited to a description of a number of scientific ideas Freud held in the early 1890s, ideas that resurface in the dream. Perhaps the results would have been more impressive had Kuper and Stone followed Lévi-Strauss's (1964) key instruction: not to study one myth (or dream) in isolation, but to turn to a large number of cognate myths (dreams) as a basis for structural comparison (p. 12). But doubts linger. The question is whether any realistic analysis can be expected from structuralists, who appear to have turned their back on the psyche's two central activities, the production of emotion and meaning.

The fairy tale of psychoanalysis is different. The polymorphous character of the mind, the tension between repressing agencies and forces striving for expression are responsible for "compromises" in the shape of symptoms, parapraxes, and dreams. The dream of Irma's injection is an example of such a compromise, a fairly complex one, consisting of various scripts. I have suggested that such an approach produces explanations that can stand their ground when confronted with historical material. By comparison, the explanations of the structuralists seem suspended in air.

APPENDIX
MATERIALS FOR KUPER AND STONE'S MODEL (1982)[15]

Thesis 1

1 "The illness is sexual-hysterical, the symptoms organic."
Source: Freud's preamble to the Irma dream, and a general understanding of Freud's intellectual development around 1895. Thus the

---

15. Compiled with the assistance of Peter van Koningsbruggen and Geert Mommersteeg.

authors can write: "The initial thesis of the dream is that Irma is suffering from hysteria, which has a sexual etiology" (p. 1230).

2 "It is caused by the patient."
Source: (manifest dream) "I said to her: 'if you still get pains, it's really only your fault' " (Freud, 1900, p. 107).

3 "The patient voluntarily resists catharsis (speech)."
Source: (manifest dream) ". . . and to reproach her for not having accepted my 'solution' yet" (p. 107)

Antithesis 1

1 "The illness is organic, the symptoms hysterical."
Source: (for the first part of the sentence) "She looked pale and puffy. I thought to myself that after all I must be missing some organic trouble." (second part) "If only you knew what pains I've got now in my throat and stomach and abdomen—it's choking me" (p. 107). Clarification by Kuper and Stone (1982): "Irma's response leads Freud to fear that he missed 'some organic trouble.' This implies that the illness is not hysterical, the cause not sexual." And: "Actually, Irma in the dream describes the classic symptoms of globus hystericus" (p. 1230).

2 "It is neglected by the doctor."
Source: (manifest dream) "I thought to myself that after all I must be missing some organic trouble" (p. 107).

3 "The patient involuntarily resists catharsis (choking)"
Source: (manifest dream) "It's choking me" (p. 107).

Synthesis 1; Thesis 2

1 *"The illness is organic-sexual."*
Source: (manifest dream) "On the right I found a big white patch; at another place I saw extensive whitish grey scabs upon some remarkable curly structures which were evidently modelled on the turbinal bones of the nose" (p. 107). The sexual side of Kuper and Stone's reconstruction of the diagnosis rests on a knowledge of Fliess's theories about a connection between the nose and sexual organs. This link was established by Schur (1966); it is not given in the manifest contents of the dream.

2 "The doctor's negligence made it worse."
Source: The authors have constructed this element from their knowledge of Schur (1966), as is obvious from the following passage: "Freud, of course, omits mention of any negative connections with Fliess, but the dream's next step, the discovery of the scabs on the turbinal bones, points directly to Fliess's involvement. The dream's next thesis mediates the earlier oppositions, Irma's condition is not hysterical, and Freud has not missed an organic illness. Instead Irma has an iatrogenic condition for which neither Freud nor Irma is to blame" (Kuper and Stone, 1982, p. 1230).

3 "The doctor induced nasal catharsis, which miscarried."
Source: Schur's (1966) account of the Fliess' operation. "But the themes of sexual causation and catharsis continue to be developed: the operation Fliess attempted was a drainage of the sinus cavities—a nasal catharsis. Furthermore, given Fliess's theories, which Freud accepted, the nose has a sexual implication" (Kuper and Stone, 1982, p. 1230). "Dr. M. now confirms Freud's finding. By implication he agrees that this is an iatrogenic illness for which Fliess is to blame" (p. 1230). From the manifest dream: "—I at once called in Dr. M., and he repeated the examination and confirmed it."

Antithesis 2

1 "The illness is organic, but a metaphor for hysteria."
Source: (manifest dream) " 'She has a dull area low down on the left.' " That would support the first part of this statement. "A metaphor for hysteria" is defended by Kuper and Stone's insistence that Freud, at every point, continued to view Irma as having a ". . . double condition. He treated her for hysteria and yet had Fliess operate on her" (p. 1231).

2 "It passes from the patient to the doctor."
Source: (manifest dream) "I noticed this, just as he did, in spite of her dress. . . ." (Freud's associations) ". . . the wording in the dream was most ambiguous: '*I noticed this, just as he did . . .*' I noticed it in my own body, that is" (p. 113). Clarification by Kuper and Stone: ". . . in the dream two of the doctors, Leopold and Freud himself, both notice the infiltration in the same way—by feeling it in themselves. This way of noticing in a physical manner in the doctor's own body is also consistent with the code that translates psychological to physical" (p. 1231).

3 "The infection causes infiltration (the contrary of catharsis)."
Source: (manifest dream) "He also indicated that a portion of the skin on the left shoulder was infiltrated."

Synthesis 2

1 "The illness is organic-sexual-hysterical."
Source: (manifest dream) "There is no doubt it's an infection, but no matter; dysentery will supervene and the toxin will be eliminated. We were directly aware, too, of the origin of the infection. Not long before, when she was feeling unwell, my friend Otto had given her an injection of a preparation of propyl, propyls . . . propionic acid . . . trimethylamin (and I saw before me the formula for this printed in heavy type). . . . Injections of that sort ought not to be made so thoughtlessly. . . . And probably the syringe had not been clean" (p. 107).

Comments by Kuper and Stone: "At last the real etiology of Irma's illness is discovered. The disease is caused (1) by an injection of toxic substances 2) with a dirty syringe 3) by a thoughtless doctor, Otto" (p. 1231). And: "Irma's trouble can be traced to her contact with Otto's dirty 'squirter' " (p. 1231).

The last of the toxic substances administered by Otto is trimethylamin. Freud makes it clear that trimethylamin has great significance to him. Kuper and Stone remind us that in Freud's account it was his friend Fliess who pointed out to him that the substance is one of the products of sexual metabolism. "This causes Freud to associate to the importance of sexuality 'in the origin of the nervous disorders' " (p. 1232). "Blame is also given to Otto's sexual inadequacy in the penultimate sentence of the dream: 'Injections of that sort ought not to be made so thoughtlessly.' A thoughtless husband, in Freud's view, could cause anxiety neurosis in a woman" (p. 1232).

2 "It is caused by a careless doctor."
Source: (manifest dream) "Injections of that sort ought not to be made so thoughtlessly . . . And probably the syringe had not been clean" (p. 1232).

3 "The infection produces catharsis through the anus (dysentery)."
Source: (manifest dream) "Dysentery will supervene and the toxin will be eliminated" (p. 107).

BIBLIOGRAPHY

ANZIEU, D. (1959). *L'Auto-Analyse: son Rôle dans la Découverte de la Psychanalyse par Freud; sa Fonction en Psychanalyse.* Paris: Presses Universitaires de France.

—— (1975). *L'Auto-analyse de Freud et la Découverte de la Psychanalyse,* vols 1, 2. Paris: Presses Universitaires de France.

BADCOCK, C. R. (1975). *Lévi-Strauss: Structuralism and Sociological Theory.* London: Hutchinson.

BONAPARTE, M., FREUD, A., & KRIS, E., eds. (1954). *The Origins of Psycho-Analysis: Letters to Wilhelm Fliess,* trans. E. Mosbacher & J. Strachey. New York: Basic Books.

BRODEUR, C. (1983/1984). "L'injection faite à Irma. *Le Coq-Héron,* 89:19–30.

CLARK, R. W. (1980). *Freud: The Man and the Cause.* London: Jonathan Cape & Weidenfeld & Nicolson.

COURNUT, J. (1973). Lettre ouverte à Irma. *Revue Française de Psychanalyse,* 37: 73–93.

ELMS, A. C. (1980). Freud, Irma, Martha: Sex and marriage in the "dream of Irma's injection." *Psychoanal. Rev.,* 67(1):83–109.

ERIKSON, E. (1954). The dream specimen of psychoanalysis. *J. Amer. Psychoanal. Assn.,* 2:2–56.

FREUD, S. (1895) Project for a scientific psychology. *Standard Edition,* 1:281–397. London: Hogarth Press, 1966.

—— (1900). The Interpretation of dreams. *Standard Edition,* 4, London: Hogarth Press, 1953.

GEERTZ, C. (1973). *The Interpretation of Culture.* New York: Basic Books.

GREENBERG, R., & PEARLMAN, C. (1978). If Freud only knew: A reconsideration of psychoanalytic dream theory. *Internat. Rev. Psycho-Anal.* 5:71–75.

HARTMAN, F. R. (1983). A reappraisal of the Emma episode and the specimen dream. *J. Amer. Psychoanal. Assn.,* 31:555–585.

HILLMAN, J. (1975). *Re-visioning Psychology.* New York: Harper & Row.

JONES, E. (1953). *The Life and Work of Sigmund Freud.* Vol. 1. New York: Basic Books.

KUPER, A., & STONE, A. (1982). The dream of Irma's injection: a structural analysis. *Amer. J. Psychiat.* 139:1225–1234.

—— —— (1983). Reply to Comments. *Amer. J. Psychiat.,* 140:664.

KURZWEIL, E. (1980). *The Age of Structuralism.* New York: Columbia University Press.

LACAN, J. (1954–1955). *Le Séminaire de Jacques Lacan (2): Le Moi dans la Théorie de Freud et dans la Technique de la Psychanalyse.* J. A. Miller (ed.) Paris: Editions du Seuil, 1978.

LÉVI-STRAUSS, C. (1955). *Tristes Tropiques.* Paris: Plon.

—— (1964). *The Raw and the Cooked: Introduction to a Science of Mythology.* New York: Harper & Row, 1969.

MAHONY, P. J. (1977). Towards a formalist approach to dreams. *Internat. Rev. Psycho-Anal.,* 4:83–98.

—— (1982). *Freud as a Writer.* New York: International Universities Press.

MASSON, J. M. (1984). *The Assault on Truth: Freud's Suppression of the "Seduction Theory."* New York: Farrar, Straus & Giroux.

NAGERA, H., ed. (1969). *Basic Psychoanalytic Concepts in the Theory of Dreams.* London: George Allen & Unwin.

RICOEUR, P. (1970). *Freud and Philosophy: an essay on interpretation*. New Haven: Yale University Press.

DE RUIJTER, A. (1977). *Claude Lévi-Strauss: een systeemanalyse van zijn antropologisch werk*. Unpublished doctoral dissertation, University of Utrecht.

SCHATZMAN, M. (1982). Freud et Irma. *Spirales: J. Internat. de Culture*, 14: 12–16.

SCHUR, M. (1966). Some additional "day residues" of the specimen dream of psychoanalysis. In *Psychoanalysis: A General Psychology*, ed. R. M. Loewenstein, L. M. Newman, M. Schur, & A. J. Solnit. New York: International Universities Press, pp. 45–85.

—— (1972). *Freud: Living and Dying*. London: Hogarth Press.

SPANJAARD, J. (1969). The manifest dream content and its significance for the interpretation of dreams. *Internat. J. Psycho-Anal.*, 50:221–235.

SPIRO, M. E. (1979). Whatever happened to the id? *Amer. Anthropol.*, 81:5–13.

STRACHEY, J., ed. & trans. (1966). *Standard Edition*, 1. London: Hogarth Press.

SWALES, P. J. (1983). *Freud, Martha Bernays, and the Language of Flowers*. Privately published by the author.

THODEN VAN VELZEN, H.U.E. (1984). Irma at the window: The fourth script of Freud's specimen dream. *Amer. Imago*, 41:245–293.

2
Prophetic Initiation in Israel and Judah

DANIEL MERKUR

Although Jones (1923), Gill and Brenman (1961), Devereux (1966), and Arieti (1976) concurred with the consensus among clinical and experimental hypnotists in equating religious trance with hypnosis, the phenomena of hypnotic dreams have not been discussed in psychoanalytic explanations of ecstatic visions. The present contribution attempts to redress the oversight. Religious uses of hypnotic dreams also provide evidence bearing on the general theory of religion. In the visions, the distinction between stereotyped, cultural religious materials and idiosyncratic religiosity—in a phrase, between "culture and personality"—proceed, as I shall show, in keeping with the distinction between regression in the service of the ego (Kris, 1952) and regression proper. In other words, the distinction is consistent with the intrapsychic, structural division of the conflict-free (preconscious–conscious) portion of the ego and the unconscious, respectively. The unconscious materials were, in some cases, superego manifestations; in others, symptoms of repressed fixations. The theoretic implications of these observations will be developed among my conclusions.

Hypnotic dreams are induced by a hypnotic suggestion to dream immediately following the suggestion, during the hypnotic trance. They vary with the depth of trance from brief and daydreamlike to longer and dreamlike. All seem subjectively to be perceptions of realities rather than imaginations. Products of hypnotic suggestions rather than symptoms of unconscious fixations, hypnotic dreams otherwise closely resemble hysterical dream states. "Every hysterical attack . . . [is] an involuntary irruption of day-dreams" (Freud, 1908, p. 160) with respect its content; but the extent of its symbolization is "completely analogous to the hallucinatory distortions of a dream" (Freud, 1909, p. 229). In theoretic terms, hypnotic dreams may be characterized as daydreams that, occurring during a trance state, undergo reification (Merkur, 1984) and become hallucinations. They also associate with ordinarily unconscious materials and serve as a

conduit for the latter into consciousness. (For a review of the literature, see Merkur, 1985a, p. 166–168.)

THE CULTURAL TRADITION OF INITIATORY VISIONS

The Call of Isaiah (Isa 6:1–13) and Ezekiel's Vision of the Chariot
(Ez 1:1–3:15) belonged, as I shall show, to a tradition of prophetic
initiation that is demonstrable in the northern kingdom of Israel as
early as the ninth century BCE and in Judah from the late seventh
century onward. The tradition was distinguished by a vision of more or
less stereotyped content, in which prophets beheld the proceedings in
the divine council, where Yahweh met with his angels. In myth,
Yahweh functioned as the judge and final authority of the council. The
angels implemented his decisions. The angels were identified with the
"host of heaven"—the sun, moon, and stars—and as the beings that
Yahweh had apportioned to gentiles as their gods. The divine council
met in the house of God, which was at once an earthly Israelite temple
and a mythical location, in heaven or on a paradisal mountain (Mullen,
1980).

An early instance of a vision of the divine council is found in the
legend of Micaiah, a contemporary of Elijah in the northern kingdom
of Israel in the late ninth century BCE.

[19]And Micaiah said, "Therefore hear the word of Yahweh: I saw
Yahweh sitting on his throne, and all the host of heaven standing
beside him on his right hand and on his left; [20]and Yahweh said,
'Who will entice Ahab, that he may go up and fall at Ramoth-
gilead? And one said one thing, and another said another. [21]Then a
spirit came forward and stood before Yahweh, saying, 'I will
entice him.' [22]And Yahweh said to him, 'By what means?' And he
said, 'I will go forth, and will be a lying spirit in the mouth of all
his prophets.' And he said, 'You are to entice him, and you shall
succeed; go forth and do so.' [23]Now therefore behold, Yahweh has
put a lying spirit in the mouth of all these your prophets; Yahweh
has spoken evil concerning you." [24]Then Zedekiah the son of
Chenanah came near and struck Micaiah on the cheek, and said,
"How did the spirit of Yahweh go from me to speak to you?"
[25]And Micaiah said, "Behold, you shall see on that day when you
go into an inner chamber to hide yourself" [I Kgs 22:19–25].

Because the tale of Micaiah had a long life in oral tradition before it
was written down, the primary value of the extant account is its

paradigmatic presentation of religious ideology: the theological explanation of false prophecy. We may note, however, that entering "an inner chamber to hide yourself" (I Kgs 22:25) refers to the means by which the vision was attained. The vision was produced through at least some sensory deprivation in a windowless "inner chamber," or Holy of Holies, in a temple. The precise technique was esoteric; a prophet had to "hide" his activities.

Perhaps 250 years after Micaiah, Jeremiah similarly referred to the vision of the divine council as a precondition of true prophetism. In condemning false prophets, he wrote:

> For who among them has stood in the council of Yahweh
>   to perceive and to hear his word,
>   or who has given heed to his word and listened? (Jer 23:18)

> But if they had stood in my council,
>   then they would have proclaimed my words to my people.
> They would have turned them from their evil way,
>   and from the evil of their doings [Jer 23:22].

A vision of the divine council definitely constituted a prophet's *bona fides*, the vision whose achievement entitled him to status as a prophet. Further references suggest that the vision often had an initiatory significance. The Elohist legend of Jacob's "dream" at Bethel, deriving from the northern kingdom in the ninth century (Jenks, 1977), concerns the very first of Jacob's visions; the biblical term "dream" was a catch-all for hallucinations.

> Behold! a stairway set up on the earth,
>   and the top of it reached to heaven.
> And behold! angels of God
>   were ascending and descending on it.
> He was frightened, and said, "How awesome is this place!
> This is none other than the house of God, and this is the
> gate of heaven" [Gen 28:12, 17].

The "house of God" and "gate of heaven" referred to the divine palace at the top of the stairway, where the angels had council with God. Possibly fathered on legendary Jacob in expression of its authority, the legend of Jacob's dream was the Elohist exemplar of prophetic visions of the divine council. In genre, the narrative was a "belief legend" (Honko, 1964), or paradigmatic account of ecstatic practice. Because a belief legend is believed true and corresponds, however approximately, to living ecstatic practices, it inevitably contributes unconscious—and sometimes also conscious—content to ecstatic experiences; conversely, unconscious associations to the ecstasies influence retellings of the legend.

The legend of Elisha's inheritance of prophetic status from Elijah (II Kgs 2:1–14) includes an account of Elijah's assumption into heaven. In its explicitly initiatory context, the ascension must be understood as the initiatory vision of Elisha.

> As they still went on and talked, behold, a chariot of fire and horses of fire separated the two of them, and Elijah went up by a whirlwind into heaven. Elisha saw it and cried, "My father, my father! The chariots of Israel and its horsemen!" And he saw him no more [II Kgs 2:11–12].

Closely read, the text does not assert that Elijah ascended to heaven. Here as elsewhere, the term "behold" signals the beginning of the description of a visionary experience. The whirlwind, the funnel of a tornado, may be identified with the "pillar of cloud" in which Yahweh accompanied the Israelites in the wilderness. Symbols deriving from the Moses legend were also present in the Call of Isaiah and the Chariot Vision of Ezekiel.

The Priestly account of the Sinai covenant, deriving from late seventh or sixth century Judah (Friedman, 1981), had Yahweh descend onto Mount Sinai amid fire and smoke. The populace at large was forbidden to approach the mountain (Ex 19:9b–13a, 14b–16a, 18; cf. Ex 19:20–25). All heard the ten commandments (Ex 20:1–17). Yahweh then told Moses, Aaron and two of his sons, and seventy Israelite elders to climb the mount. They beheld God and compacted the covenant by sharing food and drink (Ex 24:1–2, 9–11). Moses alone entered the nimbus surrounding God to talk with him (Ex 24:15b–18). The origin legend of the Pentacost feast does not indicate whether it is to be treated as a legend portraying supernatural events or as a belief legend concerning ecstatic practice. Understood in the latter, presumably esoteric sense, Moses initiated the chief priests and tribal elders in his ecstatic techniques. The populace at large was not eligible for initiation. Only priests and elders might behold God. Moreover, only a person who actually participated in the divine council by talking with God qualified for status as a prophet.

Jeremiah's account of his call refers to a rite of initiation, as well as to an ecstasy of initiatory significance.

4Now the word of Yahweh came to me, saying:
    5"Before I formed you in the womb, I knew you.
    Before you were born, I set you apart.
    I appointed you a prophet to the nations."
6And I said, "Ah, Yahweh, God! Look, I don't know how to
speak, for I'm only a boy." 7But Yahweh said to me:
    "Do not say, 'I'm only a boy';
    for to all to whom I send you, you shall go.
    Whatever I command you, you shall speak.
    8Be not afraid of them,
    for I am with you to deliver you, says Yahweh."
9Then Yahweh put forth his hand and touched my mouth. And
Yahweh said to me:
    "Behold, I have put my words in your mouth.
10See, I have set you this day
    over nations and over kingdoms,
    to uproot and to break down,
    to destroy and to raze,
    to build and to plant."
11Then the word of Yahweh came to me, saying, "Jeremiah, what
do you see?" I said, "I see an almond rod." 12Yahweh said to me,
"You have seen well, for I am watching over My word to perform
it" [Jer 1:4–12].

Jeremiah's sight of an almond rod (Jer 1:11) concerned Aaron's rod,
which legendarily put out leaves, blossoms, and almond nuts on one
occasion during the life of Aaron (Num 17:8). It was subsequently
placed before the ark of the testimony (Num 17:10–11), which was kept
in the Holy of Holies in the Jerusalem temple. The Priestly legend of
the rod's origin—which may well have a pre-exilic date (Friedman,
1981)—was meant to account for the cult object that Jeremiah was
shown during his initiation. Using a literary theological formulation
introduced by Amos (Niditch, 1983), Jeremiah carefully recorded that
thinking of the words to name his sight perception was the precondition
of the inspiration of a prophecy. The prophecy depended on a wordplay, which associated šaqed, "almond," with šoqed, "to watch"
(Bright, 1965).
    Reference to his call also occurred in a later prophecy of Jeremiah.

    Your words were found,
        and I ate them.

Your word became for me a joy,
   and the delight of my heart;
and I was called by your name:
   "Yahweh, God of hosts" [Jer 15:16].

Although it is conceivable that the angels surrounding the Divine
throne called Jeremiah "Yahweh of hosts," it is more likely that the
cultic prophet(s) who initiated Jeremiah called him Yahweh as part of
the initiation rite.

The statements that Yahweh touched Jeremiah's mouth with his
hand, placing his words in his mouth (Jer 1:9), and that Jeremiah found
and ate the words of Yahweh, which gave him joy and delight (Jer
15:16), were variants of a stereotyped symbolism. When Ezekiel,
Jeremiah's younger contemporary, gained his prophetic mission, he
was shown a written scroll and told to eat it. He opened his mouth, and
ate, "and it was in my mouth as sweet as honey" (Ez 3:3). In the
Deuteronomic prophecy of a prophet like Moses, Yahweh stated, "I
will raise up for them a prophet like you from among their brothers. I
will put my words in his mouth, and he will speak to them all that I
command him" (Dt 18:18). The oral incorporation of divine words was
already a prominent motif in the Yahwist version of the Moses legend,
which derives from Solomon's era in the 10th century. "Yahweh put a
word in Balaam's mouth, and said, 'Return to Balak, and thus you shall
speak' " (Num 23:5; cf. 23:16).

The symbols of the rod, the edible word of Yahweh, and honey
intersect in various manners in the Old Testament. In the Yahwist
Moses legend, Moses and Israel arrived at the bitter waters of Marah.
"And he cried to Yahweh, and Yahweh showed him a tree. He threw it
into the water, and the water became sweet. There Yahweh made for
them a statute and an ordinance and there he proved them" (Ex 15:25).
Here it was tree, water, and law. In the Elohist version, there was no
water at Massah and Meribah until Moses struck a rock at Horeb with
his rod and water flowed from the rock (Ex 17:5–7). Here the plant had
already become a relic, and the word of Yahweh was mentioned only
through allusion to Mount Horeb, where the law was given. The
Priestly version displays still greater esotericism. At Meribah, where
there was no water, Moses took Aaron's rod from before the ark of the
testimony and twice struck the rock, producing water. Because Yahweh had told him merely to flourish the rod and to speak to the rock,
his action was a sin (Num 20:2–13).

The Song of Moses, which dates to the 11th century, alluded briefly
to the legend of Moses and the rock.

He made him suck honey out of the rock,
and oil out of the flinty rock. (Dt 32:13)

The association of the rock and water here gave way to an association
of rock and honey. Samson found honey in the carcass of a lion on the
first occasion that he prophesied (Judg 14:5–9); while the legend of Saul
relates that during the battle of Aijalon, Jonathan, son of Saul, ate wild
honey in the woods "and his eyes became bright" (I Sam 14:27).
Ezekiel's statement that the written scroll tasted like honey employed
the same symbol in the same initiatory context.

I suggest that the esoteric allusions of the symbolism pertained to the
religious complex surrounding the goddess Asherah, who is best
known as the great mother goddess of Canaanite religion. The consort
of the high god 'El, she was depicted as a nude woman, standing on a
lion, holding one or more serpents in her hands. Her epithets included
"She who treads on the sea," "the Lady of the Lion," and "the Lady
of the Serpent" (Cross, 1973). Olyan (1984) has recently established
that in non-Deuteronomistic circles in the northern kingdom of Israel,
Asherah was an integral part of the religion of Yahweh. In both Israel
and Judah, the Canaanite high god 'El was syncretised with Yahweh,
and Asherah was regarded as Yahweh's consort in at least some
northern circles. The Deuteronomistic reform abolished her cult in the
late seventh century. With the exception of the sacred trees and poles
that were her cult objects (James, 1966), Biblical references to Asherah
were largely suppressed. However, Israelite sculptures depicting
mother goddesses (Albright, 1957), sometimes in conjunction with
serpents (Joines, 1968), are common archaeological finds and attest to
her historical popularity.

Importantly, a further Canaanite epithet of Asherah was "the Living
One," whose Hebrew form *hawwah* is anglicized as Eve (Olyan, 1984,
personal communication). Not a goddess but a legendary woman, Eve
represents a slightly different syncretism of Canaanite Asherah in the
southern kingdom of Judah. Eve remained closely associated with a
snake and with "every tree that is pleasant to see and good for food,
the tree of life in the midst of the garden, and the tree of the knowledge
of good and evil" (Gen 1:9). Moses' tree and the rods of Moses and
Aaron were variant references to the trees of Eden, which integrated
the Canaanite religious materials within the religion of Moses. Since
Asherah was "the Lady of the Lion," the honey that Samson found in
the carcass of a lion (Judg 14:5–9) had the same symbolic meaning as
the water that Moses produced by means of a tree or rod.

It is probable that something was actually eaten as part of the ritual of prophetic initiations. The action may have been purely symbolic, comparable to the ritual consumption of unleavened bread on Passover and in the Christian mass. However, the possibility of a psychoactive substance warrants consideration. In the Eden tale, "every tree that is pleasant to see" (Gen 1:9) can instead be rendered "every tree that is desirable for a vision." The tree that Moses used to sweeten the waters at Marah definitely had active chemical properties.

Whether or not psychoactive substances were used, prophetic initiations definitely involved a ritual that culminated in the initiand's experiencing an ecstasy. The traditional production of ecstasies on demand cautions against assuming psychopathology. Instead, it implies a use of alternate states—which are restricted neither to consciousness nor to the ego. Moreover, the production of detailed visions of traditional, stereotyped content restricts discussion to an alternate state whose contents are capable of being determined in close detail through heterosuggestive, autosuggestive techniques. Hypnotic dreams are the only probable candidate.

The desired form of the ecstasy was a vision of the divine council, mythological imagery shared also with Mesopotamia (Widengren, 1950) and Canaan (Mullen, 1980). In practical terms, the initiand's production of the desired ecstasy established that he had properly mastered the techniques and ideology of prophesying, that he had been taught by an older prophet. In theological terms, a vision of the divine council was necessary because, despite all that his initiator might teach him, the initiand still had to receive his mission and the contents of his prophecies from the divine council. These circumstances are analogous to the esoteric training and stereotyped visions of shamanic initiands (Merkur, 1985a). Interestingly, in the traditional practices of Lapp and Apache shamans, the initiand had to enter within a mountain, where he met gods who gave him a helping spirit and taught him the songs, lore, and rites necessary to control it (Bäckman & Hultkrantz, 1978; Opler, 1941; Boyer, 1979). It is not impossible that prophetic initiations in ancient Israel were adaptations, in an urban, literate culture, of shamanic initiations that had descended from the hunter cultures of East Mediterranean prehistory.

The model of shamanic initiation may, at minimum, be employed as a heuristic parallel. In Inuit shamanic initiations, heterohypnosis, sensory deprivation, and self-hypnosis were deliberately employed in sequence, to cumulative effect (Merkur, 1985a). The analogy is instructive. Israelite prophetic initiations may have used different alternate states in series, as did initiations into the Eleusinian Mysteries of Greece (Wasson, Ruck, & Hofmann, 1978). In result, the evidence suggesting that visions of the divine council were hypnotic dreams is not incompatible with my previous findings that Jeremiah's experience of the words of Yahweh depended on verbal superego inspirations during an intense state of reverie (Merkur, 1985b). Auditions of the words of Yahweh may have followed a ritual use of sensory deprivation or a ritual consumption of psychedelics, whereas visions of the divine council depended on a later use of hypnotic dreams.

Just as the physical setting influences the contents of hypnotic dreams in modern research (Rubenstein, Katz, & Newman, 1957; Newman, Katz, & Rubenstein, 1960), initiatory visions of the divine council replicated the initiation rite in symbolic form. The initiand might journey to the divine palace with the assistance of angels. He might simply find himself in the presence of the divine council. In either event, the heavenly palace was identified theologically with the earthly temple, which the initiand had entered in order to receive his initiation. In his vision, the initiand appeared before God, who occupied an exalted position on a throne and was flanked by lesser beings, the angels. God symbolized the older prophet, who was training the initiand. Angels symbolized people who lacked the status of prophets. Like his earthly prototype, God gave the prophet something to eat. At this point, the vision departed slightly from the rite. For the initiand to succeed, God had to tell him a prophecy that he was to preach as his mission. The initiator could not supply him with a prophecy. He had to acquire one on his own. However, the initiator could call him by the name "Yahweh, God of hosts," heterosuggesting that God now symbolized the initiand. Once the God image that he beheld shifted meaning, the initiand's autosuggestions could supply it with the necessary words of prophecy.

The symbolism generated through suggestion had also deeper, unconscious meanings. Anderson (1927), Niederland (1954), and Zeligs (1974) found Jacob's vision of the ladder and the heavenly palace to symbolize an oedipal triumph over the father. Their results may be extended to the traditional contents of all visions of the divine council. The relation of the initiator and the initiand unconsciously reactivated memories of the father–son relationship. For the initiand to become a prophet meant, unconsciously, that he had to become a father in his own right. He had to be capable of the male role in coitus, which was symbolized by the initial ascension to heaven, an optional feature of the visions. The constant features of the visions provided greater detail. The foodstuff that the initiator gave the initiand to eat condensed two types of symbolism. As a tree, rod, or snake, it symbolized the father's phallus, whose transfer to the son transformed him into a father. As a fluid—water or honey—it symbolized breast milk and, by association, the mother, whose transfer to the son again transformed him into a father. Symbols of both types regularly occurred together: the snake, tree, and Eve; the rod, rock, and water; honey and the lion; honey in the forest of trees, and so on. In the final portion of the vision, the meaning of the God image changed. Because God now represented the initiand, God's commissioning of the initiand as a prophet symbolized the completion of the oedipal triumph. Having acquired both the paternal phallus and the mother, the initiand was in a position to give himself a prophetic mission, that is to be a father in his own right.

THE CALL OF ISAIAH (ISA 6:1–13)

Visions of the divine council contained idiosyncratic materials in addition to their stereotyped contents. Some or all of the idiosyncratic materials may have been produced by suggestions, that is, regressions in the service of the ego. It is equally possible that at least some were spontaneous developments during the alternate states, manifestations of unconscious materials. Unfortunately, legends that had long lives in oral tradition before they were committed to writing do not permit decision on the matter. However, the extant accounts of the visions of Isaiah and Ezekiel do furnish conclusive evidence. The role of folkloristic retelling and literary editing was sufficiently slight that intrapsychic conflicts and other psychic phenomena can still be discerned.

The Call of Isaiah dates to the second half of the seventh century. It is the earliest evidence of a vision of the divine council in the southern kingdom of Judah, as distinct from the northern kingdom of Israel, and its internal evidence indicates the secondary initiation of a Judan prophet into the northern prophetic tradition.

>¹In the year of the death of King Uzziah, I saw my lord sitting on a throne, high and lifted up; and his skirts filled the temple. ²Seraphim stood above him. Each had six wings: with two he covered his face, and with two he covered his legs, and with two he flew. ³One called to another and said,
>   "Holy, holy, holy is Yahweh of hosts;
>   that which fills the whole earth is his Glory."
>⁴The foundations of the threshold shook at the voice of him who called, and the house was filled with smoke. ⁵Then I said: "Woe is me! For I am lost; for I am a man of unclean lips, and I dwell in the midst of a people of unclean lips; for my eyes have seen the king, Yahweh of hosts!" ⁶And one of the seraphim flew to me, having in

his hand a fire-stone in tongs that he had taken from the altar. [7]He touched my mouth, and said: "Behold, when this touched your lips, your guilt was taken away and your sin forgiven." [8]And I heard the voice of my lord saying,

> "Whom shall I send,
> and who will go for us?"

Then I said, "Here am I! Send me." [9]And he said, "Go, and say to this people:

> 'Hear indeed, but do not understand;
> see certainly, but do not know.'
> [10]Make the heart of this people fat,
> and their ears heavy,
> and smear their eyes;
> lest they see with their eyes,
> and hear with their ears,
> and understand with their hearts,
> and be healed again."

Then I said, "Until when, my lord?" And he said:

> "Until cities lie waste
> without inhabitant,
> and houses without man,
> and the soil is utterly desolate,
> [12]and Yahweh removes man far away,
> and the forsaken places are many in the midst of the land.
> [13]And should a tenth remain in it,
> it will be burned again,
> Like a terebinth or an oak,
> whose stump remains standing
> when it is felled:
> the holy seed is its stump.

Because the word *hekal* may mean either "temple" or "palace" (Isa 6:1), the Call of Isaiah may report a vision beheld in the Jerusalem temple (Gray, 1912), or a vision that replicated the temple, or a vision depicting a heavenly palace. If the vision concerns the Jerusalem temple, Isaiah may have stood—or envisioned himself standing—within the inner sanctuary, before the mercy seat on the ark of the covenant, which was conceived as Yahweh's throne. The "throne high and lifted up" (Isa 6:1) was implicitly another throne, suspended in the air. The skirts of Yahweh's robe nonetheless reached the floor. Given that Yahweh was not in heaven but in the Jerusalem temple, his earthly palace, the exceptional extension of his garment would form an image that adapted the notion of Jacob's ladder to the confines of the inner sanctuary. Alternatively, the vision concerns the heavenly palace, and the motif of ascension is explicit.

The *serapim*, literally "fiery ones," were angels that formed Yahweh's council. The conception of fiery, flying angels corresponds to the "fiery chariot and horses of fire" beheld by Elisha (II Kgs 2:11). The earthquake and the smoke attending the sound of the seraph's voice were again variants on traditional images, belonging in this case to the Sinai epiphany in the Moses legend (Ex 19:18–19).

Isaiah's cry of woe in consciousness of his sin (Isa 6:5) followed theologically from the Judan idea that a person cannot see Yahweh and live (Ex 19:21; 33:20). Because Isaiah was being initiated into a different prophetic tradition that prized visions of God, he experienced a conflict of theologies. His cry of woe was attended by a strong affect—the guilt that was alleviated soon afterward (Isa 6:7). Unconscious associations were apparently aroused by the sight of God and facilitated by the emotional motility of the alternate state. Arlow (1951) suggested that the theological prohibition of the sight of Yahweh was unconsciously informed by the fear of beholding the father's phallus. The seraphim's use of their wings to conceal their sex—the term "legs" is a euphemism (Gray, 1912)—may be treated as a displacement of the prohibition.

Isaiah's guilt was alleviated by the events that followed. The conscious expectation that he would be given something to eat unwittingly functioned as an autosuggestion. However, his unconscious wish to be free of guilt caused his vision to deviate from the stereotyped pattern. A seraph went to the trouble of using tongs in order to seize up a fire-stone, on which incense burned in the altar (Engnell, 1949). The contact of the stone with Isaiah's lips enabled him to speak without difficulty. These events removed Isaiah's guilt because reality testing demanded the reverse situation, that the *serap*, "fiery one," could handle the coal with impunity, while Isaiah would be horribly burnt. Implicitly, the absurdity of his experiences led Isaiah to realize that he was hallucinating and that what he beheld on the throne was no more Yahweh than his own lips were burnt.

The conscious expectation—and unwitting autosuggestion—that the figure on the throne would speak to him determined the stereotyped aspects of the next part of his vision. The enthroned being employed the technical theological term "send," and Isaiah replied with the same verb. The exchange constituted Isaiah's commission as a prophet (Engnell, 1949; Widengren, 1950). The further words spoken by the enthroned being manifested the theological concepts that Isaiah had attained in result of his reality testing, which had inadvertently functioned as further autosuggestions. Importantly, Isaiah's unconscious, oedipal associations continued to influence his mood. His guilt was now exteriorized as anger directed against others, which was expressed verbally. "Hear indeed, but do not understand; see certainly, but do not know." An ecstatic vision was not an accurate representation of theological verities.

Isaiah's desire to learn a prophecy (Isa 6:11)—a further stereotyped feature of a vision of the divine council—functioned as a final autosuggestion, guaranteeing that he received one. Since Judah was conventionally described as the tenth part of Israel (Engnell, 1949), Isaiah looked beyond the conquest and deportation of the northern kingdom to the conquest and deportation of Judah. He also anticipated the messianic salvation of Judah. These are classic themes of many of Isaiah's prophecies (Engnell, 1949), whose repetition in the present context is unremarkable. However, the aggression of Isaiah's tone was unusually severe. The aggression was a further displacement of guilt at the idolatry of his vision, once more attesting to unconscious, oedipal associations at the source of his affects.

Further groups of details are almost certainly to be ascribed to the literary process of the reportage. They do not indicate a second literary hand. They merely indicate postexperiential reflections by the prophet on the theological significance of his vision. There was a good deal of literary allusion to the religious complex to which Asherah belonged. The term *serapim* was used in Num 21:6 to refer to venomous serpents. Isa 6:2 instead used the term in its etymological sense, "fiery ones," but the term simultaneously permitted allusion to the snake in Eden. The term *'mt* in Isa 6:4 is generally rendered as "foundations," but only with hesitation. It is traditionally vocalized as *'amot*—the Old Testament contains no vowels—which means "cubits." At minimum, it was an eccentric word choice; the possibility of vocalizing it as *'imot*, "mothers," should be noted, since the "mothers of the threshold" would indeed be its foundations. The wordplay on *'adam*, "Adam; man," and *'adamah*, "soil, earth," which occurs in the tale of Eden (Gen 2:5–7), was used in Isa 6:11–12, where *'adam* must be taken in the generic sense "man, homo." The terebinth and oak in Isa 6:13 refer to the tree of life (Engnell, 1949); while the term *maṣṣebah*, ordinarily a stone pillar sacred to Asherah, was forced to convey the meaning "stump" through a rare use in its etymological sense, "standing." Due to the richness of the allusions to the religious complex involving Asherah, the esoterica of the messianic prophecy are unequivocal. The "holy seed" would not simply be the stump remaining after the tree of

Judah was felled. He would be a *maṣṣebah* sacred to Asherah. In other words, the Judan prophet accepted the religious complex involving Asherah from the northern prophetic tradition.

However, he did not accept the vision of God. With the notable exception of the one instance over which Isaiah felt guilt (Isa 6:5), use of the name "Yahweh" in the Call of Isaiah (Isa 6:3, 5, 12) refers to the God who cannot be seen. By contrast, the term *'adoni*, "my lord" (Isa 6:1, 8, 11) always refers to the being on the throne. The usage was deliberate and consistent with Gen 16:13; Judg 6:22; 13:22. In all cases where the prohibition to behold Yahweh is mentioned and a vision nonetheless occurs, what is beheld is described as an angel, as distinct from Yahweh. Similarly, in the Call of Isaiah, the unseen Yahweh differed from the visible lord. The latter was possibly intended in Isa 6:3c, "that fills the whole earth is his Glory." The term *kabod*, "glory," was a technical theological term in Ezekiel and the Priestly source (Mettinger, 1982). In Ezekiel, it denoted the archangel on the heavenly throne, the immanence of Yahweh in the world.

In all, the Call of Isaiah reports a man suffering hallucinations in whose contents he did not believe, busily scrambling to reassert his customary worldview even as his hallucinations continued. Isaiah could tolerate beholding an angel—the vehicle of revelation—but he was emotionally and theologically opposed to the vision of God. The personal religiosity of his superego had been shaped by his culture during his development; what he encountered later in life, he experienced—in the present case—as cultural alone. In result, he was able to know conflict between his superego religiosity and the religiosity of his regressions in the service of the ego. Due to the strength of his superego and his creative abilities, he resolved his conflict through a theological reinterpretation of the vision of the divine council.

EZEKIEL'S VISION OF THE CHARIOT (Ez 1:1–3:15)

Broome (1946) regarded Ezekiel's Vision of the Chariot as a symptom of paranoid schizophrenia. More sensitive to the traditional aspects of the vision, Arlow (1951) treated it together with the calls of Moses, Samuel, and Isaiah as "a temporary schizophrenoid abandonment of reality and withdrawal of object libido," whose "fusion of ego and superego cathexes . . . corresponds to . . . the hypomanic state." However, as does not occur in psychosis, the prophet subsequently "succeeds in re-establishing the emotional bonds with the world of reality because his message truly corresponds to . . . the collective ego

ideal [which] gives unity and cohesion to the group" (p. 396). Van *So, a typical shamanic vision*
Nuys (1953) thought Ezekiel a catatonic schizophrenic who eventually
recovered sufficiently to put his psychotic ideas to creative, theological
use.

Diagnoses of psychosis, of greater or lesser duration, commonly
seek to account for the very fact of Ezekiel's ecstasies. Because
psychosis is, by definition, socially dysfunctional, the diagnoses are
paradoxical. In order to account for the religious data, a diagnostic
category is innovated—socially functional psychosis—whose existence is otherwise undemonstrated. Reference to a religious use of
hypnotic trance will provide a better account of the data.

Although hypnotic trances of stereotyped religious content do not
furnish evidence of personality, once regressions are commenced in
the service of the ego, they may readily develop into something more.
Adverse reactions to hypnosis may occur (Brickner & Kubie, 1936;
Schneck, 1974). "With the establishment of certain sublimations, a
regressive reactivation of instinctual wishes and indulgence may be
permitted" (Arlow, 1961, p. 384). Just as Isaiah's vision unconsciously
associated with his Oedipus complex, resulting in affects of guilt and
anger, Ezekiel's vision associated with and permitted the manifestation
of unconscious materials of highly personal content. Discussion of
Ezekiel's personality may fairly proceed on the evidence of his deviations from stereotyped, cultural uses of trance states.

The morbidity of Ezekiel's personality cannot be doubted but should
not be overestimated. All of Ezekiel's ecstasies, both audetic and
eidetic, display intimacy with the religious literature then available
together with exceptional creativity in their uses of imagery and
language. Ezekiel may have obtained many of his doctrines at second
hand from Jeremiah, whose preachings were well known to him
(Zimmerli, 1979). As a deportee living in Babylonian captivity, Ezekiel
had reason for grievance. Like Jeremiah, he regarded the Babylonians
as the vehicle of Yahweh's punishment and displaced his anger onto
the sins of Jerusalem and Judah. However, where Jeremiah exhibited
depressive trends (Merkur, 1985b), Ezekiel infused their common
theology with a wrath that involved contempt and, at times, perhaps
hatred.

The three visions in the Book of Ezekiel, additional to the Chariot
Vision, are patent instances of conflict-free, daydreamlike wish-fulfill-
ments. Ezekiel beheld himself transported to the Jerusalem temple,
where he was incensed by the idolatries that he saw practised (Ez 8:1–
11:25). Some years after the death of his wife (Ez 24:18), he envisioned

the resurrection of the dead on the basis of their bones (Ez 37:1-10). Decades after the fall of the Jerusalem temple, he envisioned, in minute detail, the design of the future temple to be built in its stead (Ez 40-48).

The most compelling evidence of pathology consists of an ecstasy soon after the Chariot Vision, in which Yahweh commanded Ezekiel to lie on each side of his body for a specific number of days (390 plus 40), facing a clay model of Jerusalem, while eating food mixed with dung and speaking nothing other than prophecies. He was also to raze his head hair and beard and dispose of the hair in three portions (Ez 4:1-5:4). These actions, on whose basis catatonia has sometimes been diagnosed, were in fact variants of a traditional, ritual practice of war magic (I Kgs 22:11; II Kgs 13:17) in which the brandishing of weapons was believed to destine military victory (Johnson, 1962). Ezekiel humorlessly inverted the practice by enacting the siege of Jerusalem.

The morbid character of some of the trance symbolism cannot be doubted. Eating food mixed with dung was clearly anal in content and compulsive in character. Anal symbolism displaced to the oral sphere may also be seen in the period when Ezekiel lay unmoving on his side and remained silent except when speaking a prophecy. Here retention of language was interrupted by periodic expulsions. Again, Ezekiel's vision of the future temple was no less than obsessive in its concern with extremely minute details. The moral character assumed by Ezekiel's intense anger—his displacement of personal injury by Babylon, through identification with the aggressor, into outrage at his fellow Judans—indicates an overactive and harsh superego, a constellation associated with conflicted anality. Because Ezekiel was a priest, raised from childhood to exercise extreme caution over ritual purity, the anal character of his unconscious conflicts is not surprising.

In discussing Ezekiel's Chariot Vision, the extant text must not be pressed unduly. A few scribal errors and editorial insertions can be identified; several more may be suspected. On the other hand, the severe reductions of the text favored by most Bible critics ought not be followed. Most modern scholars impeach whatever does not conform to their expectations that God, and therefore the "original" content of Ezekiel's vision, must be logical and coherent. The result is a consensus effort to rewrite the extant text—a practice already commenced in the Septuagint translation of the Bible—by omitting the very features that are of keenest interest to psychoanalytic research.

Much of the difficulty of Ezekiel's text stems from the author, who both recorded his vision and burdened his report with a verbosity that sacrifices literary elegance to clarity of comprehension. That the repetitiveness traces to Ezekiel, rather than to a hypothetical "school of Ezekiel" that inserted glosses within the prophet's "original" text, may be proved by a number of features. By emphasizing repeatedly that he had "visions" in which he saw "shapes" and "appearances" that were "like" things in the perceptible world, Ezekiel carefully avoided asserting that the ecstatic phenomena were what they appeared to be. His language was deliberately phenomenological. Ezekiel definitely knew that the symbolic phenomena of his ecstasies were intrapsychic and imaginary. Yahweh twice interpreted the symbolic contents of Ezekiel's ecstasies (Ez 5:5–17; 37:11–14) in a manner consistent with the method of dream interpretation outlined in the Joseph saga (Gen 37:5–11; 40; 41) and the legend of Gideon (Judg 7:13–15). Ecstatic symbolism allegorized what was, to Ezekiel's thought, Divine revelation.

The symbolism of the Chariot Vision was not explained to Ezekiel in the course of his ecstasy. In result, Ezekiel offered his own interpretation, but modestly through the method of intimation. In reporting his vision, Ezekiel consistently and often extravagantly chose words that have double meanings. Some of the wordplays no less than interfere with the manifest reading of the text. The wordplays are internally consistent, however, in developing a second and latent level to the reading of the text that records Ezekiel's associations to his vision.

In my translation, I have attempted, as far as possible, to preserve Ezekiel's word order and syntax. Although a continuous, hypnotic dream is described, I have divided it at natural breaks in the continuity in order to provide running commentary.

¹In the thirtieth year in the fourth month on the fifth of the month, as I was among the exiles by the Kebar canal, the sky was opened and I saw divine visions. . . . ⁴And I saw, behold! a storm wind came from the north, and a great cloud, with a mass of fire and brilliance surrounding it. Out of it—out of the fire—like a radiance of electrum. ⁵And out of it, the form of four living beings. This was their appearance: they had the form of a man on this side, ⁶four faces for each, and four wings for each of them. ⁷Their legs were a straight leg, and the soles of their feet were like the soles of a calf's foot. They sparkled like the radiance of burnished bronze. ⁸A man's hand under their wings on their four quarters, and faces and wings for the four. ⁹Their wings embraced one another. They did not turn as they went. They went each face forward. ¹⁰The form of their faces: the face of a man; the face of a lion on the right for the four; the face of an ox on the left for the four; and the face of an eagle for the four. ¹¹. . . Their wings were separated above

each. Each had two embracing, while two covered their bodies.
[12]They went each face forward. Wherever there was wind to go,
they went. They did not turn as they went. [13]Between the form of
the living beings, the appearance was like burning coals of fire,
like a vision of torches. It moved between the living beings. The
fire was brilliant. Out of the fire went lightning. [14]And the living
beings went and returned, like the appearance of the lightning [Ez
1:1–14].

The thirtieth year (Ez 1:1) may refer to the prophet's age. Priests had
to be thirty years old in order to be ordained (Num 4:30); and, in a
Priestly belief legend (Num 9:4–6), their ordinations were attended by
manifestations of the Glory of Yahweh (Blenkinsopp, 1983).

The vision may have commenced with the sense perception of a
summer storm. Ezekiel experienced it as a traditional storm theoph-
any, originating in Yahweh's mythic abode in the distant north. The
wind providing the basis of the motion of the beings in Ez 1:12 was the
wind generated by the storm. The final images, which moved in the zig-
zag manner of lightning (Ez 1:14), again suggest hallucinatory misper-
ceptions while gazing at real thunderclouds.

Within this framework of sense perceptions—else of a fantasy repli-
cating sense perceptions—Ezekiel beheld an apparition. The "mass of
fire"—an image otherwise unique to the Egyptian plague of hail (Ex
9:24)—appeared out of the cloud. The fire contained an ᶜayin, "radiance; fountain, well; eye." The range of the Hebrew word reflects the
ancient conception of celestial bodies as divine eyes, emitting light as
they observe mankind on earth. Radiating out of the mass of fire were
four ḥayyot, "beasts," here forced to carry its etymological sense,
"living beings." The term is cognate with ḥawwah, "Eve."

The beings had human faces forward but four faces in all. The four
wings were two forward and two behind, given that the human face is
counted as forward. Multipartite beings were a commonplace of ancient Near Eastern religions. In Israel, they were the cherubim whose
spread wings formed the mercy seat, where Yahweh sat, on top of the
ark of the covenant. However, Ezekiel's sight of four faces was a novel
detail.

Ezekiel described the beings as masculine. They had the forms,
hands, and legs of men. Of 45 pronouns referring to the beings, 33 are
masculine plurals; the remainder are the grammatically proper feminine plurals (Greenberg, 1983). The legs of the beings were straight, not
bent at the knees. Their feet terminated in round soles, like those of
calves, and received masculine pronouns (Ez 1:8) rather than the
grammatically proper feminine. Their four faces—man, ox, lion, and

eagle—were all masculine. Hebrew words for the females of the species were not used. Again, the beings' motion was rigid, moving inexorably forward in a straight line.

The masculine language and imagery abruptly yielded to the statement that the wings "embraced one another." Ezekiel's use literally of "a woman to her sister" in order euphemistically to convey "one another" was a bizarre choice of words. Hebrew would ordinarily state "one the second" to convey "one another." Ezekiel similarly forced the word "man" to convey the sense "each." The extravagant choices of language emphasized the presence of an allusion by gender. The beings were male, but their wings were feminine.

Immediately that the wings embraced, Ezekiel insisted that "they did not turn." The verb has also a second sense, "they did not deviate." The "four quarters" of the beings (Ez 1:8) referred to their aerial formation. Between them, as they flew, was a fiery object that moved about and emitted lightning. The living beings moved back and forth in conformance with the lightning, containing it at all times within the space enclosed by their embracing wings. Hence, the beings did indeed "turn." However, they did not "deviate," that is, they did not sin. Ezekiel was implicitly responding to allegations that the matter symbolized by the feminine wings was sinful.

I suggest that the feminine symbolism alluded to Asherah. In a later prophecy, Ezekiel developed the metaphor of Israel as a woman, beloved by Yahweh but who later became a harlot (Ez 16). The prophecy is notable for its extensive and enchanting portrait of the early period of fidelity and for its tone of sorrow at the later harlotry. Ezekiel reverted to the more traditional, angry, and unqualified condemnation of Israel's harlotry only some years later (Ez 23). I suggest that the issue of the orthodoxy or heresy of Asherah came alive for Ezekiel during his initiatory vision, some thirty years after the Deuteronomistic reform sought to abolish her cult.

The attainment of the vision of the quadripartite beings likely exhausted Ezekiel's initial autosuggestion. He had beheld the cherubim, the angels that would escort him to heaven, as Jacob and Elijah had been escorted. The manifestation of feminine symbolism—the womblike image of the embracing wings enclosing fiery ejaculations of lighting—was apparently spontaneous. However, Ezekiel's conscious recognition that feminine symbolism had manifested served unwittingly as an autosuggestion, contributing to his further visions.

[15]As I saw the living beings, behold! One wheel on the earth beside the living beings for each of their four faces. [16]The appearance of the wheels . . . was like the radiance of chrysolite. The

four had the one form. . . . Their construction was like a wheel within a wheel. [17]They went on their four quarters when they went. They did not turn as they went. [18]As for their rims, they had rims and they had dread. Their rims were full of radiance around the four of them. [19]When the living beings went, the wheels went beside them. When the living beings rose from the earth, the wheels rose. [20]Where there was wind to go, they went. . . . The wheels rose with them, for the spirit of a living being was in the wheels. [21]When those went, these went. When those stood, these stood. When those rose from the earth, the wheels rose with them, for the spirit of the living being was in the wheels [Ez 1:15–21].

Although the beings were flying in the air in Ez 1:14, the wheels and beings were abruptly located on the ground in the next verse. Like nocturnal dreams, hypnotic dreams may suddenly shift from scene to scene (Welch, 1936). The new imagery associated wheels with the beings. The relation of the two inverted in the middle of the episode. At first, the beings went and the wheels accompanied (1:19), but the wheels were next discovered to be the motive agency on which the beings depended for their movement (1:20). Again the logic was that of a dream, rather than a thematic composition. Importantly, the wheels, taken from contact with the feminine earth, alluded to the feminine. Far from being an awkward intrusion in a series of masculine symbols, feminine symbols had become the very support of the masculine beings.

The importance of the inversion of status was indicated by the wordplay on *ruah*, which can mean either "wind" or "spirit." At first, Ezekiel intended the former sense. The living beings went wherever there was wind, that is, wherever their wings could carry them. Now, however, the living beings went wherever the wheels went, because the spirit of the beings was in the wheels.

The construction of the wheels, with concentric wheels inside each of them, may refer to an archaic design antedating the spoked wheel of Ezekiel's era (Zimmerli, 1979; Greenberg 1983). More likely, it was an innovation. Because the term for "rims" may instead be rendered "(eye)brows," verse 18b can be read "their brows were full of eyes." The pairing of wordplays draws attention to the subtext. I suggest that the "eyes" on the "rims" symbolized celestial orbs on the revolving sphere of the pre-Ptolemaic celestium; the symbolism would be equivalent to such folkloristic motifs as revolving millstones, the spindle of the fates, rotating thrones and castles, and the like. In depicting celestial orbits as wheels within wheels, Ezekiel's vision innovated imagery to symbolize the prophet's itinerary upward from earth, through the celestial spheres, toward the heavenly throne. Interestingly, the preconscious content of the imagery—a celestial orb within a celestial sphere—resembles the previous image of a fiery object contained within the area bounded by the wings of the living beings. The celestial spheres and the wheels were unconsciously equivalent to the beings' wings.

> 22And the form above the heads of the living beings was a firmament like the radiance of dreadful ice, extended over their heads from above. 23Under the firmament their wings were straight, one toward another. Each had two wings covering . . . his body. 24When they went, I heard the sound of their wings like the sound of many waters . . . a sound of tumult like the sound of a (military) camp. When they stood still, their wings slackened, 25and a sound came from above the firmament over their heads . . . [Ez 1:22–25].

With the recognition that the feminine wheels supported the masculine beings, Ezekiel's resistance to feminine symbolism had been broken, and unconscious materials began to manifest with greater freedom. The beings' wings—again extravagantly described as "a woman to her sister"—supported the firmament, much as the feminine wheels supported the beings. Likening the firmament's composition to *qerah*, "ice" or possibly "crystal," was presumably influenced by its mythic location in the distant north. However, the association of the sound of the wings with the sound of many waters, that is, the depths of the sea, also suggests an unconscious equivalence of ice and water. Both images contrast with the masculinity of fire symbolism throughout Ezekiel's vision.

Ezekiel had now completed his ascension to heaven. In the process, the traditional stereotyped meaning of ascension—the male role in coitus—was resisted. Ezekiel's regressions to supportive, preoedipal, maternal symbolism implies that he experienced unconscious conflict over the traditional oedipal triumph of a vision of the divine council. Of course, Ezekiel interpreted his experience as a favorable reference to religious conceptions that were commonly regarded as heretical. However, the selection of religious imagery was determined unconsciously.

With the next phase of his vision, Ezekiel was obliged once more to autosuggest traditional religious imagery. The wings were let down and ceased to generate their sound, permitting a sound or perhaps a voice (the term *qol* may mean either) to be heard from above the firmament. The visual display moved upward in parallel.

[26]Above the firmament that was over their heads was the form of a throne, like the appearance of sapphire stone. On the form of a throne—on it, from above—was a form like the appearance of a man. [27]And I saw an enclosure for him, like a radiance of electrum, like the appearance of fire, surrounding the appearance of his loins and upward. Downward from the appearance of his loins I saw like the appearance of fire. There was brilliance surrounding about him. [28a]Like the appearance of the bow in the cloud on a rainy day, so was the appearance of the surrounding brilliance. Such was the appearance of the form of the Glory of Yahweh. When I saw, I fell on my face [Ez 1:26–28a].

The reemergence of a masculine motif in the form of the Glory of Yahweh furthers the stereotyped itinerary. On taking in the sight, Ezekiel bowed, rendering homage to the Glory of Yahweh. The sapphire throne was a stereotyped motif; there was sapphire stone at the foot of Yahweh's throne in Ex 24:10. The image otherwise resembled portraits of various ancient Near Eastern gods. The Assyrian Asshur was depicted as emerging waist upwards from a sun disc, whose rays formed a surrounding aura (Zimmerli, 1979). Discussing Ezekiel's vision, Arlow (1951) adduced Greenacre's (1947) observation that the awe of a child in beholding the father's penis may be represented as a halo or aura surrounding a phallic symbol. The image was thus consistent with the oedipal themes of the vision's traditional content.

The visual image of an enclosure of light encasing the upright male torso symbolized coitus. In context, however, the imagery was inconsistent with the traditional latent content of an oedipal triumph. Ezekiel unconsciously yielded the mother to the father and refrained from pursuit of his own oedipal triumph. Interestingly, the word *bayit*, "house," was used in its less frequent, secondary sense, "enclosure," and placed very awkwardly in the sentence. A verb would have been more natural. The word may allude to the Jerusalem temple, conceived as female in coitus with the indwelling Glory.

[1:28b]Then I heard a voice speak. [2:1]He said to me, "Son of man, stand on your legs, and I will speak to you." [2]When he spoke to me, spirit entered into me and stood me on my legs, and I heard what he spoke to me. [3]He said to me, "Son of man, I send you to the sons of Israel, to a nation of rebels who have rebelled against

me. They and their fathers have transgressed against me to this very day. ⁴The sons are hard of face and strong of heart. I send you to them. You shall say to them, 'Thus says my lord Yahweh.' ⁵Whether they obey or whether they decline—for they are a rebellious house—they will know that a prophet was among them. ⁶And you, son of man, do not fear them,
>and do not fear their words,
>although thorns surround you
>and you sit on scorpions.
>Do not fear their words,
>and do not be dismayed at their looks,
>for they are a rebellious house.
⁷You shall speak my words to them, whether they obey or decline; for they are a rebellious house" [Ez 1:28b–2:7].

Since all Ezekiel's expectations culminated in these events, he was told no more than to say, "Thus says my lord Yahweh." There were no specific prophecies for him to foretell. His ambitions—and autosuggestions—were satisfied by the simple fact of his admission to the divine council.

A prophecy of rejection by the intended audience was a stereotypical feature of prophets' calls (Ex 3:19; Isa 6:9; Jer 1:19). It also supported condensations of personal significance. The references, "son of man," "sons of Israel," "they and their fathers," and "the sons" form an elegant literary motif that simultaneously displaced the oedipal conflict with the Glory from Ezekiel to the "nation of rebels." Ezekiel's audience would be "hard of face and strong of heart," expressionless and resolute in their indifference to Yahweh's words. The metaphors also displaced phallic symbolism upwards.

Ezekiel's denial of his own impiety led to a narcissistic identification. Like the Glory, Ezekiel was to suffer Israel's rebellion. He was to display himself, making himself available to be pricked by thorns and scorpions. The homosexual implications of the identification with the Glory were thus displaced in a fashion subserving the stereotypical motifs.

²:⁸"But you, son of man, obey what I say to you. You shall not be rebellious like the rebellious house. Open your mouth, and eat what I give you." ⁹And I saw, behold! a hand was sent toward me. And behold! in it was the scroll of a book. ¹⁰He spread it before me. It was written on the front and on the back. There was written on it lamentation, and mourning, and woe. ³:¹He said to me, "Son

of man, what you have found, eat. Eat this scroll. And go, speak
to the house of Israel." ²So I opened my mouth and he fed me this
scroll. ³Then he said to me, "Son of man, your stomach will eat
and your guts will fill with this scroll that I give you." So I ate it.
In my mouth it was as sweet as honey [Ez 2:8–3:3].

In a very tidy wordplay, Ezekiel stated that the Glory *yiprosh—
either "spread," or "gave an exegesis of"—the scroll. The scroll was
written on two sides in allusion to the tablets of the covenant, which
were similarly written on two sides (Ex 32:15). The imagery simultaneously permitted condensed reference to Ezekiel's literary practice of
wordplay, with double levels of meaning intended in his writings.
Importantly, parchment scrolls were not written on both sides before
the beginning of the common era, when the technology of tanning
improved markedly (Greenberg, 1983).*
    *Greenberg (1983) has noticed the subtle progress of the scene.
Ezekiel was told to eat what he would be given. What he saw was a
parchment scroll, inedible, indigestible, and revolting. He had to be
told again to eat what he had found. He opened his mouth and
received the scroll. Next he had to be told to swallow it. Only with the
assurance that he would digest it did he finally becoming willing to eat,
and only thereafter did he taste honey. The conflict establishes that the
imperative to eat had unconscious origin, despite autosuggestions to
the contrary.*
    *Ezekiel's alternatives, either to defy the father or to submit homo-
sexually to him, symbolized the conflict. The commandment, "You
shall not be rebellious like that rebellious house," removed the self-
deception that Ezekiel had accomplished through displacement of his
own impiety onto Israel. He became conscious of his own guilt. His
atonement consisted of proceeding with the traditional scenario of an
initiatory vision, despite its distaste. Broome (1946) and Arlow (1951)
interpreted the eating of the scroll as an oral incorporation of the
father's phallus. In Arlow's view, Ezekiel accomplished the castration
of the father and claimed the phallus as his own. For Broome, the
fantasy constituted "feminist masochism," a homosexual act of fellatio. The views are not mutually exclusive. An oedipal triumph is
inherently bisexual. Any sharing of a woman by two males is both
heterosexual and homosexual.*
    *On the other hand, I suggest that Broome and Arlow mistook the
preconscious for the unconscious content. The homosexual significance of fellatio masked Ezekiel's conflicts in a manner accommodat-
ing both his ego's censors and the traditional scenario of an oedipal*

triumph. Ezekiel's actual conflicts remained repressed. Conflict over homosexuality was a consciously tolerable substitute. Because Ezekiel's later ecstasies manifested conflicts of anal content, the unconscious equivalence of penis and feces (Isaacs, 1927) in the anal complex may indicate that the roll of leather unconsciously signified feces.

Ezekiel's vision reverted to more traditional content toward the end of the episode, when the scroll proved to taste of honey. At this point, its oral incorporation had latent associations with nursing at the breast, imbuing the scroll with a feminine significance. Because milk and words are first obtained from the mother, they have unconscious equivalence (Wormhoudt, 1949) in any event. Moreover, the rolled edge of the scroll, as it neared Ezekiel's mouth, may have resembled the wheels within wheels of the second episode of Ezekiel's vision.

[4]He said to me, "Son of man, walk and come to the house of Israel. You shall speak my words to them. [5]For you are not sent to a people of deep lips and a heavy tongue, but to the house of Israel. [6]Not to the many peoples of deep lips and heavy tongue that you cannot understand their speech. Had I sent you to them, they would have obeyed you. [7]But the house of Israel will not desire to obey you, for they do not desire to obey me, for all the house of Israel is strong of forehead and hard of heart. [8]Behold! I have made your face harder than the measure of their faces, and your forehead stronger than the measure of their forehead. [9]As adamant is harder than flint I have made your forehead. Do not fear them, and do not be dismayed because of them, for they are a house of rebellion [Ez 3:4–9].

Once Ezekiel had mastered his conflicts and allowed himself to be guided by the traditional initiatory scenario, he arrived at traditional feminine symbolism that happened to dovetail with his own unconscious regressions. Consequently, he was able to complete the scenario in the expected, traditional fashion. His identification with the Glory (Ez 3:7) lost its homosexual aspects. Rather than an identification with an internal object, it had become a displaced symbol for himself. Further, his face and forehead would be harder and stronger than those of the house of rebellion. His oedipal triumph was thus complete. He adopted the role of a father, adamant in chastizing rebellious Israel.

The wordplays in the passage are glaring. The verb *semoᶜa*, literally "hear," idiomatically means "obey" in Ez 3:6b, 7. However, in 3:6a, it was strained beyond its usual range of meanings to convey "under-

stood." Again, the literal phrases "deep lips" and "heavy tongue"
must be treated generously if they are to mean "obscure speech" and
"difficult language," as the manifest reading demands. Ezekiel did
deliberate violence to the Hebrew language in order to develop wordplays equating orality with the hearing and obedience of divine words.
The legend of Moses' speech difficulties (Ex 4:10) may have contributed to the symbolic equation.

> [10]And he said to me, "Son of man, all my words that I speak to
> you, take in your heart and hear in your ears. [11]Walk, come to the
> exilés, to the sons of your people. Speak to them. Say to them,
> 'So says my lord Yahweh, whether you obey or whether you
> decline.' " [12]Then the wind lifted me and I heard behind me a
> voice of great volume when the Glory of Yahweh arose from its
> place. [13]And the sound of the wings of the living beings as they
> kissed one another, and the sound of the wheels along with them,
> and the voice of great volume. [14]The wind carried me and took me.
> I went bitter in the heat of my spirit, but the hand of Yahweh was
> strong upon me. [15]I came to the exiles of Tel-Aviv, who dwelled on
> the Kebar canal, where they dwelled there. I dwelled there seven
> days, overwhelmed among them [Ez 3:10–15].

The itinerary of Ezekiel's return from heaven to earth furnished
stereotypical contents to the concluding imagery. Otherwise the materials summarized his vision by drawing on the contents of earlier
episodes. Two wordplays force themselves on the reader. *Qol*, which
may mean either "voice" or "sound," was used in the former sense in
Ez 3:12, 13, and in the latter in 3:13. Similarly, *ruah*, which may mean
either "wind" or "spirit," was used in the former sense in 3:12, 14, and
in the latter in 3:14. Here is a notable detail. The fourth episode had
used *qol* in reference to the "sound" of the wings and a "sound" or
"voice" coming from above the firmament. The seventh episode used
wordplays to equate orality with the hearing and obedience of divine
words. In the concluding episode, the term *qol* was applied to both the
sound of the wings and the voice of great volume. The consistency of
the associations indicates a subtext. Ezekiel apparently regarded divine words as feminine, so that the very words spoken by the masculine Glory had a feminine significance for him. A tantalizing detail is
Ezekiel's reference to his own bitterness and heat of spirit (3:14),
which contrasts with the icy firmament and its honey. Ezekiel continued to regard himself on the far side of the feminine—the Asherah
complex—but he accepted its esoteric theological validity.

The force of Ezekiel's ecstasy was, in his own word, overwhelming. In undertaking a prophetic initiation, he was obliged to pursue a vision whose unconscious significance as an oedipal triumph aroused intense resistance. Regression to supportive, preoedipal, maternal symbolism, which apparently included the entire experience of audible sounds and language, avoided the repressed conflicts and allowed Ezekiel to complete the visionary scenario. Conflicted materials manifested directly only in Ezekiel's reluctance to eat the scroll. The energy driving the fantasy—the threefold demand that Ezekiel eat despite his autosuggestions to refuse—indicates that the traditional initiatory scenario associated with repressed, fixated materials. In interpreting the symbolism, I have suggested that its homosexual significance as fellatio was a preconsciously tolerable substitution for unconscious ideas of coprophagia. Whatever interpretation is placed on the conflicted imagery, we may conclude that Ezekiel definitely had an adverse reaction to his initiatory vision. It aggravated unconscious conflicts and precipitated a period of acting-out behavior (Ez 4:1–5:4) in which his conflicts manifested more fully.

Conclusions

In Freud's (1930) view, the functions of religious phenomena are simultaneously wholesome and pathological. The stereotyped initiatory scenario, with its unconscious significance of an oedipal triumph, will illustrate. Confronted by the circumstance of becoming a prophet under the tutelage of an older prophet, the initiand experienced a social situation whose unconscious significance was an oedipal triumph. The maturation that was socially appropriate for him was not left to chance but was deliberately encouraged through the fantasy of a hypnotic dream. The stereotyped initiatory scenario, whose unconscious significance was similarly an oedipal triumph, guided him through his development from layman to prophet. Left to mature on his own, the novice prophet might have felt hesitation, anxiety, or guilt, but these negative possibilities were avoided because the stereotyped fantasy asserted that it was proper and desirable for him to proceed as he did. However, the benefits of the stereotyped initiatory vision—its adaptations to social realities—were achieved at the expense, in Freud's (1930) words, of an "intimidation of the intelligence" by the "state of psychical infantilism" and "mass-delusion" consisting of the religious beliefs themselves (pp. 84–85).

In the prophets' experiences, stereotyped cultural materials were produced through regressions in the service of the ego, which are collaborations of conscious and preconscious ego materials (Kris, 1952). As conflict-free ego materials, they were superficially integrated within the prophets' personalities. They were data committed to memory, as distinct from materials formative of character. By contrast, the personal or idiosyncratic aspects of the prophets' visions stemmed from deeper aspects of their personalities. Once conflict developed, defense proceeded spontaneously through unconsciously determined regression. Each prophet reacted against—better, regressed from—the cultural stereotype in an individual way. Isaiah's conflicts with the stereotype manifested superego materials, but Ezekiel's conflicts manifested fixated repressions. Between them, the idiosyncratic materials in the prophets' visions furnish instances of hypnotic dreams both "from above" and "from below."

These observations have consequences for the general theory of religion. Freud (1927) maintained that the superego functions as the psychic representation of culture and opposes the natural, instinctual drives. Religiosity is among the superego's activities. By contrast, the prophets' visions evidenced two types of religiosity. In each case, cultural religiosity was internalized within the conflict-free ego sphere. This ego religiosity was manifestly distinct, in Isaiah's case, from his superego religiosity. Superego religiosity is directly consequent of the formative development of the superego during the early years of childhood (Freud, 1927). By contrast, ego religiosity may presumably be acquired in later years and may never attain comparable internalization. The two types of religiosity may or may not be in agreement with each other. In cases of conflict, ego religiosity can be experienced as a cultural expectation that is variously subject to denial or compromise, as different parts of Isaiah's vision establish. I suggest that it may also be subject to subscription, despite one's better judgment and misgivings. Again, ego religiosity may conflict with unconscious fixations, as Ezekiel's vision proves.

By introducing the distinction between ego and superego religiosity, I suggest that ego religiosity, experienced as cultural religious expectations, may guide behavior by providing symbolic solutions of unconscious conflicts. In furnishing models for successful adaptation, ego religiosity may have a psychic function analogous to that of play (Merkur, 1981). Superego religiosity, by contrast, always has the quality of real values and ideals.

Ego religiosity can furnish only those models that have been attained historically within a culture. The conflicts most frequently encountered are those whose solutions are most likely to be valued by the culture as a whole. In result, they are the conflicts whose solutions are most likely both to be developed and to be celebrated in religion. However, ego religiosity is simultaneously subject to conflict with both the superego and unconscious fixations. Consequently, religions—considered as wholes—are under constant pressure "from above" as well as "from below" to devise solutions to conflicts that have not yet been addressed. Religious materials may include presentations of the problem, as well as the solutions attained. A belief legend, such as Jacob's vision at Bethel, unconsciously presented a solution. However, Ezekiel's Chariot Vision was imitated for centuries by the Jewish *merkabah* mystics and attracted millennia of commentary in the search for a solution to the problems that it posed. (By contrast, it did not attract similar attention from Christian exegetes, presumably because its problems were trifling when compared with those presented by the Jesus legend.)

The relationship between cultural and personal religiosity is analogous, at the cultural level, to oysters' productions of pearls in response to irritation. Regressions in the service of the ego associate with, and induce the manifestations of, regressions proper. In turn, the regressions become topics for further regression in the service of the ego, through theological creativity that is unconsciously aimed at resolving the unconscious conflicts. At the cultural level, the process is cumulative. In all societies, the cultural heritage grows when it expands to include solutions for increasing numbers of conflicts. A society with a limited cultural heritage is able to resolve only a small number of unconscious conflicts through its cultural expressions. Individual culture members are consequently unable to find comfort in other than highly circumscribed lives. By contrast, a society with a rich cultural heritage, that addresses a great range of unconscious conflicts, produces individuals capable of greater versatility. Sufficient versatility may eventually see to the obsolescence of traditional religious forms themselves. In their task to guide adaptation, religions do the best they can. In resolving one conflict, they can render another acute, as the case of Ezekiel proves. That religions advance only slowly speaks of their points of departure more than of their methods and goals. Like analysands, they must be carefully prepared before they can become willing to accept the validity of insights.

BIBLIOGRAPHY

ALBRIGHT, W. F. (1957). *From the Stone Age to Christianity: Monotheism and the Historical Process,* 2nd ed. Garden City, NY: Doubleday.

ANDERSON, F. A. (1927). Psychopathological glimpses at the behavior of some biblical characters. *Psychoanal. Rev.,* 14:56–70.

ARIETI, S. (1976). *Creativity: The Magic Synthesis*. New York: Basic Books.

ARLOW, J. A. (1951). The consecration of the prophet. *Psychoanal. Quart.*, 20:374–397.

——— (1961). Ego psychology and the study of mythology. *J. Amer. Psychoanal. Assn.*, 9:371–93.

BÄCKMAN, L. & HULTKRANTZ, A. (1978). *Studies in Lapp Shamanism*. Stockholm: Almqvist & Wiksell.

BLENKINSOPP, J. (1983). *A History of Prophecy in Israel*. Philadelphia: Westminster Press.

BOYER, L. B. (1979). *Childhood and Folklore: A Psychoanalytic Study of Apache Personality*. New York: Library of Psychological Anthropology.

BRICKNER, R. M., & KUBIE, L. S. (1936). A miniature psychotic storm produced by a superego conflict over simple posthypnotic suggestion. *Psychoanal. Quart.*, 55:467–487.

BRIGHT, J. (1965). *Jeremiah: A New Translation with Introduction and Commentary*. Garden City, NY: Doubleday.

BROOME, E. C. (1946). Ezekiel's abnormal personality. *J. Bib. Lit.* 65:277–292.

CROSS, F. M. (1973). *Canaanite Myth and Hebrew Epic: Essays in the History of the Religion of Israel*. Cambridge, MA: Harvard University Press.

DEVEREUX, G. (1966). Cultural factors in hypnosis and suggestion: An examination of some primitive data. *Internat. J. Clin. Exp. Hyp.*, 14(4):273–291.

ENGNELL, I. (1949). *The Call of Isaiah: An Exegetical and Comparative Study*. Uppsala Universitets Arrskrift: 4. Uppsala: A.-B. Lundequistska Bokhandeln.

FREUD, S. (1908). Hysterical phantasies and their relation to bisexuality. *Standard Edition*, 9:159–166.

———. (1909). Some general remarks on hysterical attacks. *Standard Edition*, 9: 229–234.

———. (1927). The future of an illusion. *Standard Edition*, 21:5–56. London: Hogarth Press, 1961.

———. (1930). Civilization and its discontents. *Standard Edition*, 21:61–145, 1961.

FRIEDMAN, R. E. (1981). *The Exile and Biblical Narrative: The Formation of the Deuteronomistic and Priestly Works*. Chico, CA: Scholars Press.

GILL, M. M., & BRENMAN, M. (1961). *Hypnosis and Related States: Psychoanalytic Studies in Regression*. New York: International Universities Press.

GRAY, G. B. (1912). *A Critical and Exegetical Commentary on the Book of Isaiah, I – XXVII*. Edinburgh: T. & T. Clark.

GREENACRE, P. (1947). Vision, headache and the halo: Reactions to stress in the course of superego formation. *Psychoanal. Quart.*, 16:177–194.

GREENBERG, M. (1983). *Ezekiel 1–20: A New Translation with Introduction and Commentary*. Garden City, NY: Doubleday.

HONKO, L. (1964). Memorates and the study of folk beliefs. *J. Folklore Inst.* 1:5–19.

ISAACS, S. (1927). Penis-faeces-child. *Internat. J. Psycho-Anal.*, 8:74–76.

JAMES, E. O. (1966). *The Tree of Life: An Archaeological Study*. Leiden: E. J. Brill.

JENKS, A. W. (1977). *The Elohist and North Israelite Traditions*. Missoula: University of Montana/Scholars Press.

JOHNSON, A. R. (1962). *The Cultic Prophet in Ancient Israel*, 2nd ed. Cardiff: University of Wales Press.

JOINES, K. R. (1968). The bronze serpent in the Israelite cult. *J. Bib. Lit.* 87:244–256.

JONES, E. (1923). The nature of auto-suggestion. *Internat. J. Psycho-Anal.*, 4:293–312.

KRIS, E. (1952). *Psychoanalytic Explorations in Art*. New York: International Universities Press.

MERKUR, D. (1981). The psychodynamics of the Navajo Coyoteway ceremonial. *J. Mind & Behavior*, 2(3):243–257.

—— (1984). The nature of the hypnotic state: A psychoanalytic approach. *Internat. Rev. Psychoanal.*, 11(3):345–354.

—— (1985a). *Becoming Half Hidden: Shamanism and Initiation Among the Inuit*. Stockholm: Almqvist & Wiksell.

—— (1985b). The prophecies of Jeremiah. *Amer. Imago*, 42(1):1–37.

METTINGER, T.N.D. (1982). *The Dethronement of Sabaoth: Studies in the Shem and Kabod Theologies*. Lund, Sweden: Gleerup.

MULLEN, E. T. JR. (1980). *The Divine Council in Canaanite and Early Hebrew Literature*. Harvard Semitic Monographs, 24. Chico, CA: Scholars Press.

NEWMAN, R., KATZ, J., & RUBENSTEIN, R. (1960). The experimental situation as a determinant of hypnotic dreams: A contribution to the experimental use of hypnosis. *Psychiat.*, 23:63–73.

NIDITCH, S. (1983). *The Symbolic Vision in Biblical Tradition*. Chico, CA: Scholars Press.

NIEDERLAND, W. G. (1954). Jacob's dream: With some remarks on ladder and river symbolism. *J. Hillside Hosp.*, 3:73–97.

OLYAN, S. (1984). The reform cult of Jeroboam and the Asherah of Samaria. Presented at meeting of the Society of Biblical Literature, Chicago. An expanded version, entitled "Asherah and the Cult of Yahweh in Israel, appeared in *Problems in the History of the Cult and Priesthood in Ancient Israel*, unpublished doctoral dissertation, Harvard University, 1985.

OPLER, M. E. (1941). *An Apache Life-Way: The Economic, Social, and Religious Institutions of the Chiricahua Indians*. Chicago: University of Chicago Press.

RUBENSTEIN, R., KATZ, J., & NEWMAN, R. (1957). On the sources and determinants of hypnotic dreams. *Can. Psychiat. Assn. J.*, 2:154–160.

SCHNECK. J. M. (1974). Observations on the hypnotic nightmare. *Amer. J. Clin. Hypnosis*, 16(4):240–245.

VAN NUYS, K. (1953). Evaluating the pathological in prophetic experience (particularly in Ezekiel). *J. Bible & Religion*, 21:244–251.

WASSON, R. G., RUCK, C.A.P., & HOFMANN, A. (1978). *The Road to Eleusis: Unveiling the Secret of the Mysteries*. New York: Harcourt Brace Jovanovich.

WELCH, L. (1936). The space and time of induced hypnotic dreams. *J. Psychol.*, 1:171–178.

WIDENGREN, G. (1950). *The Ascension of the Prophet and the Heavenly Book*. Uppsala Universitets Arsskrift:7. Uppsala, Sweden: A.-B. Lundequistska Bokhandeln.

WORMHOUDT, A. (1949). The unconscious identification words-milk. *Amer. Imago*, 6(1):57–68.

ZELIGS, D. F. (1974). *Psychoanalysis and the Bible: A Study in Depth of Seven Leaders*. New York: Bloch.

ZIMMERLI, W. (1979). *Ezekiel 1: A Commentary on the Book of the Prophet Ezekiel Chapters 1–24*. Philadelphia: Fortress Press.

3

The Cult Phenomenon and the Paranoid Process

W. W. MEISSNER

Everyone who reads the newspapers or listens to radio or watches television or reads the morning paper in our society cannot avoid the phenomenon of cults. The rapid effulgence of a large number and bewildering variety of new and fragmentary religious movements and religious groups espousing a wide and often wild spectrum of religious beliefs and convictions cannot have failed to impress itself on even the casual observer. The outburst of cult expressions that was characteristic of the sixties and seventies seems to have extended itself in somewhat modified fashion into the present decade.

The phenomenon of the cults has not impressed itself on public consciousness by virtue of anything particularly inherent in the cults themselves, but rather by reason of their secondary effects in the public domain. These public reverberations may take many forms: proselytizing; religious demonstrations by large numbers of people, often making a more vivid impression by reason of the unusual character of the religious group's public behavior; legal processes attendant to the acquisition of properties by more affluent cults; legal struggles between cult groups and embittered and embattled parents who are struggling to recapture their offspring from involvement in cult activities and submission to cult influence.

Within the swirling turmoil and often bitter conflicts of these public events, there is another, more private, less observable level of the interplay of inner, subjective events and powerful forces of influence generating and sustaining the phenomenon of the cults. This complex interweaving of inner forces and external influences has been the focus of considerable sociological and psychological interest in recent years. I shall refer to it here as the "cult phenomenon" (CP). My interest in the present study is in the interplay between structural aspects of the organization of religious movements and the internal, dynamic processes generated intrapsychically by the mechanisms of the paranoid process (Meissner, 1978).

The attempt to gain some initial focus on the CP must lead beyond preliminary attempts at definition to a discussion of the functional role of CP in the various contexts within which it finds expression. Religious groups comprise a heterogeneous spectrum of widely varying forms of organization and integration, and in each of these the CP finds its variant expression conditioned by the context within which it operates. This leads inevitably to a consideration of a typology of religious groups and religious movements as a means of gaining a better understanding of the contexts in which the determinants affecting the CP come into play. In addition to these typological variants, there are also extrinsic factors that shape and influence the patterning of intrinsic factors within any given religious group.

I will develop the argument in the following steps: first, a discussion of the nature of the CP; second, a focusing of the relevant aspects of the paranoid process; third, a reconstruction of available religious typologies; fourth, a consideration of patterns of change in the organization of religious movements; fifth, a discussion of the patterns of change and structure within religious groups that reflect the influence of the paranoid process; and finally, some conclusions regarding the nature of the CP based on these considerations. My intention here is not to explore the specific dynamics of particular religious systems— that effort is left to future endeavors—but to provide a framework for a reflection on the nature of religious structures and movements that allows these phenomena to be understood in the context of underlying psychological motives and forces. The focus of the mediating variables in this approach is on the paranoid process.

THE NATURE OF THE CULT PHENOMENON (CP)

A preliminary description of the CP can serve as a starting point for our further investigation. The cult phenomenon expresses a general tendency to factionalization in human religious experience and in the organization of religious groups. The CP is active and finds expression in all forms of religious experience, thriving on the tendency to form factions or subgroupings, to set up divergent or deviant elements of belief at variance with, or even in opposition to, more generally accepted belief systems of a given religious organization or organizations.

The definition raises the question of whether the CP operates only within previously existing religious groupings and organizations, or whether it includes in its field of expression the initiation of separate and divergent religious groups. The immediate answer is that our understanding of CP is intended to embrace the full range of such contingencies. But a more adequate answer will involve a more careful look at the typology of religious organizations and movements within which the CP may come into play.

At the same time, as we shall see, religious beliefs and practices always are contaminated by a highly individual, personal, and idiosyncratic dimension. Not only is the inherent variation of individual patterns of belief within a shared belief system part of the problem, but there are also almost completely idiosyncratic, even delusional, belief systems that by reason of their religious quality and emphasis can reasonably be regarded as religious phenomena. Consequently, while the consideration of religious phenomena as expressions of group processes has a certain utility, other forms of nongroup-related or nongroup-involved religious expression continue to play a vital role.

The CP, then, takes place within a specifically religious context. As an aspect of religious experience, the CP shares in the diversity, complexity, and uniqueness of religious phenomena. Although the CP can be regarded as a specifically religious expression and process, it does not take place without a complex array of influences that can be described in both psychological and sociological terms. The psychological factors—the mechanisms, motives, and processes in the inner world of the believer—are continually and inexorably influenced by aspects of the surrounding environment. These factors can be variously described in terms of social, cultural, economic, and political factors.

THE PARANOID PROCESS

My objective here is to link these aspects of religious organizations and movements to aspects of the paranoid process as a means of articulating some of the basic psychological mechanisms inherent in the CP. The paranoid process was defined originally in clinical terms (Meissner, 1978), but finds its natural extension in the dynamics of the CP (Meissner, 1984). The clinical understanding of the paranoid process is rooted in the introjects, the drive-dependent and defensively motivated internalizations drawn from significant object relationships during the course of development and life experience. To the extent that these introjects are pathologically derived, they provide a core formation of pathogenic structures around which one organizes one's inner world and pathological sense of self. These formations, to the extent that they have been analyzed, are organized in terms of aggressive and narcissistic polarities: The aggressive themes tend to be cast in terms of aggressive (victimizing) and victim (victimized) configurations, and the narcissistic dimensions take the form of superior and inferior configurations. To the extent that one or another of these configurations comes to dominate the subject's internal world, the self is experienced as aggressive, hostile, and destructive; vulnerable, weak, impotent, and helpless; special, entitled, omnipotent, even grandiose, or, alternatively, inadequate, inferior, worthless, and shameful (Meissner, 1978, 1986). The combinations and interactions of these components of the self system are the basis for the pathology of the self and for its variant characterological and symptomatic expressions.

The significance of the introjective configurations for our present consideration is that they provide the foundation for defensive patterns of projection that can color and otherwise shape the subject's experience of significant objects in his environment. The interaction of projection and introjection influences the experience of the relationship between the self and outside objects from very early on in the infant's career, and they continue to play a role in all subsequent phases of development and life experience. Any aspect of the introjective configuration can serve as the basis for projection; but usually when one polarity becomes the dominant focus of self organization, the opposite polarity is projected. Thus, if the patient experiences himself predominantly as weak, vulnerable, and victimized, his tendency is to project the opposite configuration so that he experiences certain key figures in his environment as powerful, threatening, or even persecuting. These vicissitudes play a powerful and central role in the development of transferences, not only in the psychoanalytic setting, but in a wide variety of life circumstances.

Such projective propensities—common as they are to the human condition—are inherently unstable and precarious, particularly where they may come into contradiction with or fail to find adequate sustaining confirmation in the external world. They require a framework, a sustaining organization of conceptual integration, to allow them to take on further meaning and relevance. This construction is provided by the paranoid construction, that is, a cognitive elaboration that justifies and sustains the patterns of projection and lends them a context of purposeful intention and meaningful connection. Such paranoid constructions, while they may take the form of conspiratorial hypotheses in their pathological renditions, more usually in the common run of human experience find expression in various forms of ideology or belief systems. Religious belief systems are obviously primary expressions of this process, but similar constructions, often serving similar functions, can be found articulated in political, social, and even cultural terms. The paranoid construction not only provides a sense of cognitive integration and purposeful organization intrapsychically, but it also serves to connect the ideology to a given group structure and reinforces the sense of belonging, of common commitment and participation that goes along with adherence to a group context and its related group culture. This dynamic is seen with dramatic clarity in the adherence to religious groups and their doctrinal ideologies.

RELIGIOUS TYPOLOGIES

The nature and function of the CP varies with the religious context within which it operates; the CP will enjoy a variety of forms of expression depending on the organization and structure of the religious context within which it takes place.[1] The effort to categorize and identify forms of religious structure is a long-standing enterprise in the sociology of religion. However valid and meaningful the enterprise, the achievement of a valid and consensually acceptable typology has remained somewhat elusive, largely because of the complexity of religious forms and the difficulty of categorizing forms of religious organization and expression that have a mixed and heterogeneous character.

The primary distinction goes back to the work of Max Weber and Ernst Troeltsch. For Weber, a "church" was "a community organized by officials into an institution which bestows gifts of grace" (Gerth and Mills, 1946, p. 288). In Weber's terms, church organization was hierocratic, bureaucratic, and hierarchical in its structure. As Weber comments: "For the church, being the holder of institutionalized grace, seeks to organize the religiosity of the masses and to put its own officially monopolized and mediated sacred values in the place of the autonomous and religious status qualifications of the religious virtuosos" (p. 288).

On these terms, then, Roman Catholicism would certainly qualify as

---

1. The enterprise faces the quandaries of the one-and-the-many that arise in any form of categorization. My view is that we are seeking to illuminate general mechanisms that find different forms of expression in different contexts. They are generalizable to the extent that they share certain similarities, but they cannot be reduced to a univocal category because of inherent differences. The conceptualization and reasoning thus becomes analogical rather than univocal. The problem is common to all theorizing in the human sciences.

a church, but curiously enough the Baptist church would not. The essential note here is that a church is a natural social grouping, similar to the family or the nation, whereas a sect is regarded as a form of voluntary association of religious believers, similar in nature to such secular versions as fraternal organizations or clubs of various kinds. Members are born into the church, but they must join a sect. The church is an organized institution, frequently national in extent and emphasizing the universalism of the gospel message. This churchly inclusivism is opposed by the exclusivism of the sect, which tends to appeal to individualism rather than having a group emphasis and stresses its unique ethical demands. While the sect usually demands some form of religious experience as a requirement for membership, church membership tends to be more socially obligatory, a consequence of birth, requiring no special individual conditions for its accomplishment. As Niebuhr (1929) observes, these differences in structure also tend to be associated with differences in ethical emphasis and doctrine. The institutional church attaches a high degree of importance to the sacramental means of grace that it oversees. It emphasizes doctrinal orthodoxy, the observance of proper ritual in the administration of sacraments and orthodoxy in doctrinal teaching by an official clergy. It seeks to train youthful members to a certain degree of conformity in thought and practice in order that they fulfill their roles as proper church members. In this dichotomy, then, the church stands on the side of established and institutionalized structure, with formalized and organized systems of worship, practice and belief and with a hierarchically organized and authoritative leadership.

In contrast, the sect attaches its primary emphasis to the religious experience of the members prior to their joining the group. It espouses the priesthood of all believers, thus denying any significant or meaningful disparity between an official clergy and the laity, and tends to regard the sacramental aspects of religious practice as mere symbols of fellowship or pledges of allegiance. Lay inspiration is preferred to any form of theological or liturgical expertness as might be found in an officially designated and trained clergy. The sect, then, occupies the opposite pole of structural integration, de-emphasizing formal structure and leadership and emphasizing the openness to individual inspiration and impulse rather than formal doctrinal requirements.

As an inclusive social group, the church tends to be closely allied with national, economic, and cultural interests. The nature of its organization links it to a certain accommodation of its ethical norms to the ethics of the civilization in which it endures. It thus tends to represent the morality of the respectable majority rather than that of a heroic minority. In contrast, the sect is always a minority group that maintains a relatively separatist and semiascetic attitude toward the world. Such isolating attitudes are reinforced by persecution. The members of the sect hold to their unique interpretation of ethics with great tenacity, preferring isolation to compromise. As Niebuhr (1929) observes,

> At times it refuses participation in the government, at times rejects war, at times seeks to sever as much as possible the bonds which tie it to the common life of industry and culture. So the sociological structure, while resting in part on a conception of Christianity, reacts on that conception and re-inforces or modifies it [p. 19].

There have always been difficulties in trying to integrate empirical observations with Weber's ideal types (Stark and Bainbridge, 1979). A somewhat different approach to the relationship between church and sect was provided by Niebuhr (1929). Niebuhr saw that the existing typology was unwieldy and poorly suited to the analysis of American Protestant sects. Giving the typology a somewhat different emphasis and focusing the implications of the typology on the process of reconciliation with the world, Niebuhr argued that a sect was essentially a relatively unstable form of religious organization that over time became gradually transformed into a church. The church represented a more stable and enduring form of religious organization. By the same token, however, the failure of the new church structure to meet the needs of many of its members continued a process of cyclic evolution, sowing the seeds of discontent, which led to further schism and the splitting off of new sect formations. Niebuhr envisioned an endless cycle of birth, transformation, splitting, and rebirth of religious movements in a constant process of division and cyclic reorganization.

Another facet of this complex problem was brought into focus when Johnson (1963) argued that religious groups could be more effectively classified by appealing to a single attribute, namely, the form of the relationship between the religious group and its social environment. He concluded on this basis that a church could be regarded as a religious group that accepted the social environment in which it existed, whereas a sect was a religious group that essentially rejected the social environment. This way of viewing religious group organization reflects the degree to which a given religious group may be in a state of tension with its surrounding social environment. Consequently, not only established churches but also a variety of religious institutions occupy a more stable sector of the social structure and provide a cluster of roles, norms, values, activities, and beliefs that contribute to and maintain the stability of social structure. On Johnsons's axis, extending from contexts of low tension to those of high tension, religious institutions would occupy the low tension end of the axis, whereas religious movements would occupy the opposite high tension area.

While religious institutions can adapt to social change, religious movements may have as their goal either the advancement or the prevention of social change. Religious movements, then, are forms of social movement that aim at causing or preventing change in a system of beliefs, values, symbols, and practices that are religiously based and oriented. Moreover, analogously to the analysis of sects and churches advanced by Niebuhr, religious movements may be seen as striving in the direction of becoming religious institutions and thus seeking a position as the dominant religious belief system in a given society. The degree of tension often associated with sect movement and sect formation is equivalent to a form of subcultural deviance marked by difference, antagonism and separation (Stark and Bainbridge, 1979).

Following Johnson's (1963) suggestion, when religious movements evolve toward lessened tension with their social and cultural environment, they can be regarded as church movements, regardless of the length of time that it may take a given sect to follow this process. When such groups move toward higher tension with the social and cultural environment, they may be regarded as sect movements. Thus, toward the polarity of higher degrees of tension, the emergence of religious groups is cast in terms of social and subcultural deviance; at the level of lower tension, the movement may be cast in terms of increased social integration.

In reviewing the church–sect typology, Yinger (1957) has emphasized the stabilizing social function of the church insofar as it becomes an integral part of the existing social order and thus functions in such a way as to preserve, determine, and stabilize that existing social structure. The inevitable tendency in such situations is for the church to be drawn into the service of preserving the existing power structure and the influential position of the dominant or established classes of the society. In this sense, the church becomes the facilitator and enforcer of social order. In Yinger's view, however, the sect takes a diametrically opposed posture vis-à-vis the surrounding society. Rather than emphasizing the importance of communal goals and social organization, the sect directs its emphasis to the level of individual needs. Yinger comments:

But if some of these needs are—or are thought to be—a product of the very society which the religious system also supports, they are unlikely to be successful with those who feel those needs most strongly. When, due to compromises with the secular powers, rigidity of ecclesiastical structure, the failure of doctrine and ritual to change as pervailing personality inclinations change (what are appealing symbols to one generation may lack meaning to another), when, that is, the system loses some of its ability to satisfy various individual and group needs, it promotes sectarian development [p. 145].

Broadening the implications of the term "sect" so that it refers to any religious protests in which individual religious needs have become obscured or overriden by an emphasis on social and ecclesiastical order draws the analysis of church and sect more strongly into the psychological sector and away from its strictly sociological implications. The religious sect becomes a religious movement in which the primary emphasis falls on the satisfaction by religious means of a variety of basic human and individual needs. It is thus a revolt against a previously existing religious system in which these needs were inadequately responded to (Yinger, 1957).

In these terms the sect organization carries within it the seeds of divisiveness and ultimate anarchy, just as the organization of church structures might tend toward authoritarianism and rigidity. Yinger (1957) observes:

In the logical extreme, the sect emphasis on religious beliefs and practices that are efforts to deal with individual needs—with a minimum attention to the function of social integration—leads to anarchy. The sectarian associates order with the disliked order of the church and society in which he feels his needs are smothered. This may lead to the avoidance of any political claims over him, the rejection of some of the moral standards of society (note the various experiments of extreme sectarians, with new patterns of sexual morals or forms of marriage), and the repudiation of other aspects of the supposed wicked society—learning and art, for example. Seldom is this potentiality for anarchy carried to the extreme, but the tendencies are there, just as the tendencies for authoritarian rigidity are present in the church [p. 147].

Stark and Bainbridge (1979) have noted that Niebuhr's analysis of the formation of sects applies almost exclusively to schismatic religious movements that originated as an internal action of another previously existing religious body. But obviously this is not the only form of religious movement that exists in high state of tension with the surrounding sociocultural environment. Such religious movements may have no prior history of organizational affiliation to another religious group and may, in fact, lack any close cultural continuity with or similarity to such groups. These nonschismatic deviant religious groups may represent either a form of cultural innovation, to the extent that they add some distinctive feature to the more familiar characteristics of religious groups in the culture, or a type of cultural importation in that they represent or form an extension of a religious body already established in some other cultural setting.

Consequently, both cults and sects may be regarded as deviant religious bodies that exist in a relatively high state of tension with the surrounding sociocultural environment. From this point of view, the sect is specifically a schismatic movement that breaks off from a previously existing religious organization. Cults in this perspective do not have a prior tie with the previously existing religious body. The cult may be imported from an alien religious context, or it may have originated in the host society by way of innovation rather than schism. In any case, the cult comes to represent something new in relationship to the existing religious movements in a given society. If it arises by innovation within the society, it brings to that culture a new revelation or insight, justifying its claim that it is somehow different or unique. Usually, imported cults have little in common culturally with the already existing faiths. Consequently, although they may be ancient in their society of origin, they present themselves to the new social context as something new and different.

The difficulties in application of the classic typologies and the classificatory confusion to which such attempts gave rise have led to attempts to offer more refined typologies that may better suit the variety of religious groups and the needs of more scientific analysis. I will discuss two such refinements here, one based on primarily ideological grounds, and the other more specifically organizational.

In his analysis of sect development in Protestant Christianity, Wilson (1959) describes four types of sects, each characterized in ideological terms by the inherent values and patterns of social relationships found in it. The first type he calls *conversionist*, by reason of its function of altering the world through the conversion of mankind. *Adventist* sects tend to predict such a drastic alteration of the world; but rather than promoting this final dispensation, they seek to prepare themselves for the inevitable change. *Introversionist* sects tend to reject the world's values and try to replace them with higher ethical values of their own.

And, finally, *gnostic* sects tend largely to accept the goals of the world, but seek to find new and esoteric means to their achievement.

The implications and correlates of each of these ideological approaches are spelled out in the following terms.[2] The conversionist sect centers its teaching and activity on evangelism, typically in a more orthodoxly fundamentalist or pentecostal fashion. The bible is taken as the sole guide to the good life and is accepted in more or less strictly literal terms. The test of fellowship to the communion is a conversion experience and the acceptance of Jesus Christ as one's personal savior. Individual guilt for personal sin and the need for redemption through Christ hold a central place in the doctrine of such sects. No one is excluded from potential salvation, and the techniques for obtaining conversion and commitment are generally revivalist. Conversionist sects are generally distrustful of or indifferent toward other denominations and churches, which they see as having diluted or betrayed the Christian message. They are hostile to clericalism, to any forms of special clerical learning, and particularly any modernist tendencies. Modern science, especially geological or evolutionary theories, are anathema. Examples may be found in the Salvation Army and in various pentecostal sects.

The adventist sects may also be regarded as revolutionists, emphasizing a future revolution against the present world order and the institution of a new, pure, and more sanctified Christian dispensation. Emphasis is on the role of the bible, particularly on those passages in which the time and circumstance of the second coming of Christ is predicted. Christ is not only savior but divine leader, who exacts a high moral standard from his followers. A share in the new dispensation and in Christ's new kingdom will be limited to those who have maintained doctrinal and moral purity. Acceptance into the fellowship tends to be predicated on a thorough understanding of doctrinal teachings rather than on any conversion experience. Quick conversions are not sought, and revivalism is regarded as trivial and emotionally misguided. Established churches represent the anti-Christ, and clerical learning is devalued. Such sects are hostile toward the wider society; they emphasize separation from the world and anticipate the overthrow of the present society. Examples may be found in the Jehovah's Witnesses and the Christadelphians.

Introversionist sects are pietistic. They direct their followers away

---

2. This analysis is based on the characteristics of American Protestant sects, but may have analogous application to other sectarian contexts.

from the world, focusing more intently on the life within the community and particularly to possession of the spirit. Reliance is placed on the inner illumination, regarded as the voice either of conscience or of the Holy Spirit. The bible is a source of inner inspiration and ethical insight. The letter has submitted to the domination of the spirit, so that doctrine is de-emphasized and the deepening of the experience of the spirit assumes a central position. The members of the sect regard themselves as an enlightened elect, and a strong ingroup morality is evolved. Evangelism has little or no place, and the inclination of the sect is to withdraw from the world or to allow its members only the degree of activity in the world that is consistent with human betterment. There are no spiritual guides or official clergy. Examples include some holiness sects, the Quakers or the Amana Community.

The gnostic sects hold to a special body of esoteric teaching, usually involving a revived interpretation of some essential Christian teaching. The position of the bible is more or less secondary or subsidiary to the sect's own religious gnosis. Christ is viewed more as a guide or exemplar of the truth rather than a savior. Mystical teachings are often replaced by exclusive and esoteric forms of mysticism, which can only gradually be understood. Secular scientific teachings are replaced by forms of cosmology, anthropology, or psychology that reflect elements of the religious system. Although conversion does not play a significant role in such sects, instruction and guidance are offered to the outsider, in the hope of leading him along various stages to deepening understanding and enlightenment. Often there is a charismatic leader or succession of such leaders who articulate the enlightened teaching of the sect. Other religious groups are regarded with indifference or as ignorant or backward. Secular knowledge or scientific learning is generally acknowledged as valid and useful, except where it comes into opposition with sect doctrine. The gnostic sectarian tends less to withdraw from the world than to try to exploit his special gnosis for either changing the world or improving his own position in it. Examples of such sects are the Christian Science Church, the New Thought sects, and the Order of the Cross.

Another attempt at typological refinement, cast in more strictly organizational terms, was that offered by Yinger (1957). Yinger based his typology on two primary characteristics, namely, the degree of inclusiveness of the members of a religious group and the degree of emphasis given to the function of social integration as contrasted with the emphasis on the function of personal need in the religious group. On this basis, he developed a sixfold classification of religious groups.

The first form of religious group is the *universal church*. The universal church is a religious structure that functions well in support of social integration while at the same time satisfying many of the personal needs of its members on all social levels. It is universal in the twofold sense that it excludes none of the members of the society from its fold and strives to satisfy the two major functions of religious systems. In such groups, there is an inherent commitment to maintaining the social order that is favorable to the existence of the religious group and the minimizing of individualizing tendencies that would lead to schism. The problem for the universal church is one of continual adaptation to the balance of social and individual needs and the need for maintaining the allegiance of most of the members of the social fabric.

The second form of religious group is the *ecclesia*, which extends at least potentially to the boundaries of the social order and embraces all levels of society. But the ecclesia does not encompass sectarian tendencies as successfully as does the universal church. In the ecclesia, adjustment to the dominant elements of the social order is so strong that it may exclude or frustrate the needs of the lower classes. It is better adapted to reinforcing the existing patterns of social integration than to meeting the personal functions of religion. The ecclesia, therefore, is vulnerable to indifference, sectarian protests, and secular opposition. Consequently, Yinger views the ecclesia as in a sense the universal church in the process of rigidification. Thus, while the ecclesia is professedly universal in its intention and tends not to be in a position of open conflict with the social order, it is nonetheless conservative in its orientation and particularly in its identification with national groupings. Thus, established national churches lean toward the ecclesial type. Both the universal church and the ecclesia fit the classic definition of the church in the Weber-Troelsch typology.

The *class church*, or *denomination*, enjoys less universality even than the ecclesia. It is limited not only by class, racial, and even regional boundaries, but also insofar as it minimizes the sectarian tendency to withdraw or criticize. It has some of the characteristics of a church in that its agreement with the secular order is substantial if not complete. Sectarian elements are not foreign to such class churches; often these denominations begin as sects and do not completely escape the sectarian influence. Generally, denominations tend to be conventional and seem to have moved to a position of greater compromise with the existing social order. In a pluralistic society, Yinger observes, sectarian tendencies would be more likely to express themselves in some form of schism rather than maintaining a relationship with the general religious grouping, as would be the case in a universal church.

The range of sectarian tendencies is quite broad, however, and includes, for example, Congregationalism, with its rather developed sectarian tendencies, and Lutheranism, which tends to enjoy a greater degree of secular accommodation.

Continuing along the scale of the degree of universality and of emphasis on social integration, the next type of religious group is the *established sect*. The structure of religious sects is inherently unstable, so that the group either disintegrates when the original members die or it develops a more formal structure along with techniques for gaining new members and prolonging the life of the sect. As the primarily lay character of the first generation wanes, professional leaders tend to emerge to fulfill similar functions. The economic or social status of the sect may also improve. Direct challenge or opposition to the social order usually subsides. In Yinger's opinion, those sects will develop into denominations that originally emphasized problems of individual anxiety and sin and whose primary efforts were directed to reducing the burdens of guilt and confusion. Middle-class sectarian developments usually follow this pattern; Methodism might be an example. In contrast, those sects whose original focus and concern was predominantly with the evils of society develop in the direction of established sects. Such groups, for example, the Anabaptists and Quakers, might make demands for social justice and reform, or they might withdraw from society by establishing isolated communities and refusing to fulfill social obligations.

The *sect*, occupying the next position in this progressive typology, does not differ significantly from the classic description of the sect provided by Troeltsch (1931). Sects can be distinguished by the need underlying their origin and the pattern of response to that need. Response to an unfulfilled or unsatisfied need can take the form of acceptance, aggressive opposition, or avoidance. Middle-class sects are likely to accept the existing social order without significant challenge. Such groups are more likely to localize the difficulties in the order of religious failures more than in the social order as such. In contrast, lower-class sects react more strongly to the problems of poverty and powerlessness, thus interpreting the Christian message in more radical and ethically provocative terms. In their view, society is inherently evil and only true religion has the power to reorganize the social order. Such radical and strong opposition leads almost predictably to failure, so that such groups either disintegrate or are transformed into some other more persistent type. Yinger cites the Anabaptists as an example.

Sects may also originate in a pattern of avoidance, which may express itself in the devaluation of the importance of this life and an attempt to salvage one's hopes in the supernatural world or the afterlife. In the meantime, the problem of facing the world can be mitigated by joining together into a fellowship of like-minded sufferers. This form of sectarian protest faces the hard facts of life, particularly as they afflict the lower classes in the form of poverty, injustice, and impotence. Yinger classifies Adventist, Pentecostal and other forms of utopian or millenarian sects as forms of avoidance groups, since their beliefs and practices seem to entertain a common function, namely, the struggle with life's problems and difficulties by a transformation of the meaning of life and the substitution of some form of religious status for the lack of social status.

The last form of religious grouping in Yinger's classification is the *cult*. The connotations of the cult include small size, a yearning for mystical experience, minimal organizational structure, and the presence of a charismatic leader. These groups represent an even sharper break from the dominant religious tradition than the sects. The cults occupy the farthest extreme from the universal church. Cults are usually short lived, local in extent, and centered on the teaching and charismatic influence of a dominant leader—a characteristic that sets the cult in opposition to a sect, in which reliance is placed on a broader distribution of lay participation. Because of its small size and dependence on the leader, the cult is not likely to develop into an established sect or denomination. The emphasis is almost exclusively on individual needs, with little regard or interest in questions of social order and social integration. Cults are religious mutants, extreme variations in the spectrum of processes by which people try to solve the problems of existence by religious means.

We can note with regard to these refined typologies that the CP, as we have been attempting to describe it, has a role at all levels of religious organization and finds its unique expression in various contexts of ideology and value orientation. In all forms of religious grouping, the CP operates in a process of constant tension and interaction. These forces play themselves out in those circumstances in which cultic or sectarian groupings shift progressively toward more consolidated, more socially acceptable, and better socially integrated forms of religious organization, that is, that of the established sect, denomination, or church.

The CP, however, concerns itself with those forces that come into play in the origin of sects, cults, or other forms of schismatic or deviant religious organization. Even within more consolidated church structures, like that of the universal church or the ecclesia, the CP plays a

role in a variety of contexts and with a variety of effects and connotations.

The dynamics of the paranoid process, too, play themselves out at
all levels of religious typologies. The processes of ingroup adherence,
membership, and commitment to the given ideology of the church may
take a different form of expression from that in the sect, but the same
basic processes are involved. Such adherence to the church structure
centers on institutional commitments and formalized ritual practice,
along with acceptance and belief in an established and usually credally
organized doctrine. The sect, however, puts its emphasis on religious
experience, on individual inspiration rather than on formal structure.
But in both cases, adherence to the group norms is primary, and
patterns of rejection and opposition to outgroups is reinforced. The
true religious spirit and conviction is found within the group, not
outside it. Because of its separatist and minority status, the sect, even
more than the church, casts its role in opposition to outgroups, viewing
the outgroup ideology and ethics as antithetical or even threatening.
These processes, so common in religious movements, reflect the
workings of the paranoid process, by which undesirable or conflictual
aspects of internal attitudes or characteristics are attributed to the
outgroup, and the more sustainable aspects of the inrojective configuration are retained and supported by doctrinal and membership commitments. In this sense, religious belief systems and group participation are powerful contributors to the maintenance of narcissistic
equilibrium. By adherence to the religious group and its ideology, one
compensates for one's own sense of inner inadequacy, shame, and
worthlessness, by substituting a sense of purposeful belonging and
participation in the religious organization—thus sharing in the value,
esteem, and meaningfulness of the group.

These processes set the stage for dynamic patterns of interaction
between the religious structure and its environment. The extent to
which the church is able to meet the psychological needs of its
members determines the level of its stability or the disposition toward
schism and sect formation. The religious group likewise exists in more
or less tension with the surrounding society. The mechanisms of the
paranoid process play a decisive role here, determining the extent to
which individual members find support and security in the group
ideology and experience their adherence to the group ideals as congru-
ent with or in conflict with the prevailing norms of the society and
culture. Thus religious institutions will adapt to social change, whereas
religious movements will set themselves against the social matrix and

seek to bring about social change. In this context, projections and their correlative construction can reinforce, and at times even distort, these tensions and differences, so that differences become antitheses and divergences are magnified into hostilities. The schismatic tendencies in both sects and cults can be taken, then, as reflecting the paranoid process at work in promoting, intensifying, and justifying the differences and preferences that arise out of individual needs.

The ideological patterns that find expression in various types of sects can be taken as patterns of expression of the mechanisms of the paranoid process. Conversionist sects endorse a specific belief system and set a high priority on the conversion of nonmembers. Their adherence to the ingroup ideology is matched by the degree of distrust of and hostility to other religious groups, which are seen as contaminating and distorting the true Christian message and practice. The emergence of a projective system, with its devaluing of the outgroup and elevation of the ingroup, is clear. Projective tendencies would see other religious groups as hostile or even persecuting—certainly threatening. Narcissistic needs are met largely by adherence to the group ideology and by an assumption of its higher value and religious superiority.

Adventist sects would see contemporary life as negative and religiously false or corrupt. Paranoid mechanisms undoubtedly play a role in the genesis of such perceptions and lead to a commitment to the idea of the overthrow of the present world and its replacement by a new and more sanctified one. The narcissistic reconstitution in such a belief seems vivid and is matched by the conviction that only those who have been pure and faithful will be allowed into the new world. Not only is there a radical selection between those who belong and those who do not, but the antipathy of such sects toward other religious movements and society at large is marked. Paranoid mechanisms, particularly involving hostile or aggressive projections, serve to justify visions of the destruction of the present order by some form of violent eschatological upheaval and even, in the more radical sects, endorsement of the present means of such revolution.

Antipathy toward the world is found in introversionist sects as well, but the strategy for dealing with it is one of withdrawal. The tactic parallels that often seen in paranoid patients, who are threatened by persecuting forces from the outside: some will respond to the fear and vulnerability by aggressive counterattack; others will respond by fearful retreat and isolation. Introversionists retreat from the world into a cocoon of inner illumination and dependence on the guidance of the Spirit. The members become an enlightened elect, a resolution admirably suited to sustaining narcissistic needs and redressing the balance of narcissistic vulnerability. The world is often seen as threatening and even hostile, to be avoided rather than challenged.

In gnostic sects, the ideology, in the form of the special gnosis of the sect, assumes the dominant position. This special doctrine sets the members apart from others and gives them superior religious status. Special mystical knowledge and experience raises them above non-members and grants them a position of privilege and grandiose enhancement. This dimension is often reinforced by the role of a charismatic leader, who embodies or propounds this special gnosis. Correspondingly, other sects and religious groups are looked down on and regarded as inferior. In such contexts, the projective mechanisms seem to operate on primarily narcissistic grounds, without the degree of aggressive contamination seen in other contexts. The preservation of narcissistic superiority through special gnosis is matched by the projection of narcissistic inferiority to outside groups. The projective system is enhanced and consolidated by the dictates of the special gnosis, which serves as a confirming and justifying ideology.

PATTERNS OF CHANGE

In his elaboration of the church–sect typology, Niebuhr (1929) emphasized the minority status of the sect in contrast to the more established and socially integrated position of the church. As a minority, the sect necessarily isolates itself from, and in a sense is hostile toward, its surrounding social environment. It prefers isolation to compromise, refuses to engage in political or social efforts, turns its back on participation in government, and in general seeks to cut its ties as much as possible with the common life of the society and culture in which it lives. At least in the context of the Protestant history that Niebuhr was addressing, the sect has usually been the offspring of an outcast minority, taking root in the religious revolts of the poor and of those who found no meaningful place in the church or state. Moreover, the pattern of separation and hostile disengagement seems to reflect the influence of paranoid mechanisms magnifying differences and reinforcing patterns of hostile interaction.

But social forces come to play upon this rebellious outcast with seemingly inexorable effect. Sectarianism is almost always altered in the course of time by the processes of birth and death and the shifting configuration of social pressures that draw the outcast sect closer to the mainstream. Niebuhr (1929) wrote:

By its very nature the sectarian type of organization is valid only for one generation. The children born to the voluntary members of the first generation begin to make the sect a church long before they have arrived at the years of discretion. For with their coming the sect must take on the character of an educational and disciplinary institution, with the purpose of bringing the new generation into conformity with ideals and customs which have become traditional [pp. 19–20].

The sect's new generation rarely has the strength of conviction or fervor that characterized its founders. The convictions that were tempered in the white heat of conflict, persecution, and martyrdom give way to gentler sentiments and the need for accommodation. Isolation from the surrounding social order becomes increasingly difficult. Even the frequently observed discipline of hard work and spartan living contributes to the economic well-being of the sect, and with the increase of wealth the opportunities for cultural enrichment and greater involvement in the economic life of the surrounding society become possible and less easily avoided. The process of compromise and accommodation begins to take hold. The spartan and idiosyncratic ethics of the sect begin to shift gradually toward a more churchly form. Even the place of lay leadership in the sect begins to give way to a more theologically educated and ritually sophisticated clergy. Children are born and infant baptism once again takes its place as the means of incorporation and salvation. In short, the sect is transformed into a church.

Along the same line, Yinger (1970) has observed that the sectarian tendencies carry the potential for anarchy and for the negation and avoidance of any social claims or pressures. But in fact the sect cannot exist outside of the social order and consequently cannot avoid the problem of order. Even in the most isolated cultic communities, the problem of establishing and maintaining some form of order to insure the continued existence and functioning of the group begins to assert itself. The original needs that prompted the forming of the sect or cult may change over time, particularly if the socioeconomic context in which the sect members live improves. Leadership is impelled to want to continue itself, to find ways to assure the continuity of power. And with the coming of the second generation, the problem of voluntary membership must be dealt with since it demands the training and integrating of children into an existing social order. Thus, in keeping with Niebuhr's formula, the sect moves inexorably toward a more

churchly organization and standing. As Yinger (1970) notes, particularly in mobile societies, where the problems of maintaining social
order and the pressure of individual human needs constantly impinges
on social structures to generate a process of continuous change, the
dialectic between church and sect has fertile ground in which to
flourish.

The tendencies to follow given patterns of social reorganization and
change may reflect the inherent dynamics of the sect itself, the variations of which we have already have had some suggestion. Wilson
(1959) suggests in his analysis of sect development that sects that are
characterized by a general democratic ethic, that stress intense subjective experience as a criterion of admission, that stand on a more rigidly
fundamentalist tradition, that emphasize evangelism and revivalist
techniques, and that seek to accommodate dislocated groups are more
likely to shift in the direction of a churchly form of organization, a shift
that Wilson refers to as denominationalizing tendencies. These tendencies are all the more intense if the sect is relatively unclear about who
belongs to the potentially saved community and extends its rules of
endogamy to include anyone who is saved.

Moreover, the trends will be accelerated if moral injunctions are not
clearly distinguished from traditional morality and if it accepts simple
remorse for sin for readmission to the fellowship. Denominationaliza-
tion is even more powerfully enforced when the sect inherits or
develops any sort of preaching ministry or pastorship. In his typology,
Wilson would see the conversionist sects as the most likely to shift in a
denominationalizing direction. By the same token, adventist and introversionist sects are least exposed to this trend, since they institute
processes to prevent these denominationalizing influences. I submit
that denominationalizing tendencies coexist side by side with the CP in
any form of religious movement or group. The extent to which one or
another process assumes the ascendency and determines the future
direction of the evolution of the religious group—whether in the
denominationalizing or churchly direction or in terms of maintenance
of the sectarian position or even in the further evolution of new
sectarian subgroupings—is a matter of the confluence of a large number of complex factors that operate both within the religious group and
outside it. Paranoid mechanisms operate in this context to maintain
aspects of separation and ingroup–outgroup isolation. The need to
maintain such isolation, to see outgroups as enemies in some fashion,
to maintain a sense of ingroup superiority, all are abetted by the
paranoid process. Denominationalizing tendencies seem to run counter
to these forces. Paranoid mechanisms, if anything, move in the oppo-

site direction, toward further isolation, exclusivism, and sectarian division.

THE INTERNAL STRUCTURE OF RELIGIOUS GROUPS

The development of some form of centralized organization may be in response to a variety of needs, including pressure from the surrounding society for conformity of various kinds, for example, education, the payment of taxes, or even in times of war for service to one's country. But as Wilson (1959) notes, the tendency to central organization should not be equated with the denominationalizing tendency. Centralizing may reflect a further development of paranoid tendencies moving toward consolidation of the ingroup structures as a buffer against threatening outside pressures. The group structure thus becomes more closed than open. In fact, centralized control may operate quite effectively to oppose any such denominationalizing tendencies, as is the case in the Jehovah's Witnesses. Insofar as the organization may represent a departure from the original sect ideal, it may evolve as a response to some external threat to the sect's values.

An important question here is whether or not those who assume the position of centralized responsibility in fact become professional public functionaries, that is, with specifiable functions that become institutionally differentiated and lead into the specialization of roles. Where the concept of the special training of religious leaders enters the picture, a decisive step toward denominationalism is taken. Where the structure of doctrine and the internalization are more clearly articulated, the tendency toward schism is greater. Schism most often involves questions of doctrinal or ritual purity, and a successful separation usually finds a charismatic leader in the inner elite of the movement.

The Degree of Separateness from the World

The sect is usually committed in some degree to keeping itself isolated from the world and to maintaining its distinctness, to members and nonmembers alike. This is achieved by two principal types of mechanism: isolation and insulation (Wilson, 1959). The isolation may be geographic or local, but the maintenance of this form of isolation usually requires some form of communistic organization. Generally, the sects that aspire to this form of social isolation and avoidance of alien influences are of the introversionist type. The isolation may also be linguistic as it is, for example, with the Mennonites, the Hutterites, and the Doukhobors. The mechanism of insulation involves behavioral rules that are set up to protect sect values by reducing external influences when contact must occur or is permitted. Such insulating devices may include distinctive dress, again as among the Mennonites, Hutterites, and some early Quakers. Group endogamy is also an effective means of isolation, as it is in many adventist and introversionist sects.

The degree of separateness in general reflects the extent to which the world or some part of it is experienced as alien, threatening, corrupt, sinful, or dangerous. The degree of isolation and insulation corresponds to the level of paranoid intensity in which the group and its adherents were experienced as vulnerable, weak, impotent, and potentially if not actually victimized, by outside influences. This expression of the victim-introject may mesh with more realistic considerations having to do with cultural and value diffusion due to outside influences. But the need to adhere strongly and rigidly to sect values itself reflects the operation of the paranoid process.

Coherence of Sect Values

Sects also vary in the degree of coherence of sect values. Clearly, the maintenance of separation from the world is one device for maintaining a particular constellation of values embraced by a given sect. One can anticipate a certain degree of tension resulting from the conflict between the ideals and values of a given sect or cult and the ideals inherent in the wider society and ultimately expressed in the workings of the state.

One of the basic conflicts related to the issue of isolation and separation arises from the frequently heard injunction to go out and preach the gospel and convert the multitudes. Such evangelism necessarily implies exposure to the world and the accompanying risk of alienation. It also means that the sect must open itself to the acceptance of new members, throwing an extra burden on the process of selection and admission to insure the incorporation of members who are completely socialized to the sect's point of view. Introversionist and gnostic sects do not experience tensions of this type, because they do not seek to evangelize, or do so only by highly formalized processes. Adventist sects, however, accept the responsibility of preaching the kingdom and warning the world about portending disaster, but their agents are sent out into the world only after thorough indoctrination and testing of allegiance. The tension between isolation and evangelism is found most exquisitely in the conversionist sects, who are least able to protect themselves on these points of vulnerability.

The desire for separateness and the associated values creates certain distinct tensions for the sect and for its members. Wilson (1959) describes a point of optimal tension at which any greater degree of hostility toward the world would imply direct conflict, and any less degree of hostility would signify potential accommodation to worldly values. He lists the typical issues about which conflicts of this sort arise. They include: convictions as to what constitutes true knowledge in the view of the sect as opposed to that of society, often leading to conflicts concerning the manner of education; the refusal to recognize legitimate social and legal prescriptions and the refusal to accept conventional pseudosacral practices such as oath-swearing; withdrawal from political participation, for example, refusing to vote, to salute the flag, to recite the oath of allegiance, and the like; conscientious objection to military service; refusal to recognize marital and family regulations imposed by civil authority; objection to and resistance against state-required medical procedures; disregard of economic institutions, such as the refusal to register land ownership or to join labor unions. Even in a flexible and pluralistic order, there are limits to which the sect can go in its efforts to depart from accepted moral norms. Beyond a certain limit, a sect inevitably comes into conflict with society. As Wilson (1959) observes:

> But the sect itself, in pursuit of its values, in its search for exemption, may experience change of character. It must, for instance, develop agencies to treat with a state; to preserve its values it must be thrust into new types of social action, new contact with worldly organization—perhaps even fighting its case in the law courts of "the world," although this conflicts with the desire of most sects to be a law unto themselves. Action to reduce external tensions may in this way generate new internal tensions as the sect departs from old practices and values [p. 12].

Group Commitments

A significant level of commitment to the sect is required of the individual member. The commitment may be a general and ideological one, or it may imply the acceptance of and submission to the commands and directives of a charismatic leader. In gnostic sects, as Wilson (1959) points out, commitment may be simply to the leader or to the ideological position of the movement. The member gains no advantage from the special gnosis of the sect unless he accepts the implicit world view that is involved. There may be moral correlates involved, for example, injunctions to abstain from certain forms of food or drugs, tobacco, alcohol, or sex. Introversionist sects, which may or may not have recognized leaders, who may or may not have any distinctive charisma, require a distinctive moral commitment. Certain forms of behavior are prescribed, along with a strong commitment to the fellowship itself. Adventist groups require a strong commitment to specific doctrines and specific moral practices. But conversionist sects are less sharply exclusive in their demands and may even extend the conditions of fellowship elastically to embrace any born-again believer.

The quality of social organization plays an important role. Introversionist and adventist sects are *Gemeinschaften*, in which fellowship itself becomes an important value. Group relationships are primary and face to face, and the individual's role and function as a sect member takes predominance. Membership is patterned along family lines rather than individual lines, and the sect values are often mediated by the kin group. Conversionist sects share these general characteristics only partially; the concept of brotherhood for them extends beyond sect boundaries, and its standards are more inclusive and less rigorous. Acceptance into the sect is easier, socialization is less intense, and the loss of membership is more frequent.

In contrast, gnostic sects are structured more along *Gesellschaft* lines. The pattern of relationships is more or less secondary, and commitment to the sect ideology and to the leadership takes precedence. An impersonality of relationships may even be preferred, since it is the occult gnosis, the ideology that is important. Sect affiliation may often be easily concealed so that the member can withhold his membership from the judgment and potential disapproval of the outside world.

THE NATURE OF THE CULT PHENOMENON

The delineation of these multiple aspects of religious typologies makes it abundantly clear that any discussion or investigation into the CP must take into account multiple dimensions of the phenomenon and must be prepared to find its subject matter displayed in a variety of heterogeneous and divergent contexts. We will not be able to fix on a simple or unequivocal understanding of the CP that would allow us to deductively comprehend the full scope its concrete and vital expression.

At this point, however, we can assume that the CP can meaningfully be identified in all religious settings and that in each of these settings there will exist a degree of tension and interaction between the CP and those forces and influences that lead toward the persistence, continuity, and increasing stability and reinforcement of social integration within the religious system. The paranoid process intends to focus the mechanisms and motivations that contribute to and drive those tendencies of religious movements toward divisiveness in religious organizations and the development of deviant religious belief systems.

The basic characteristics of sectarian and cult movements, then, are: exclusivism, responsiveness to and determination by individual needs, resistance to hierarchical structure, separation and isolation from the dominant social environment, a high degree of tension between such deviant movements and the prevailing social institutions, and divisiveness and anarchy. These characteristics are manifestations of the operation of the paranoid process, based in individual dynamic patterns but reflected in group processes. The CP expresses itself in the development of ingroup processes that delineate the boundaries of the group from the surrounding milieu and foster those attitudes which make the ingroup the repository of truth, virtue and salvation, while the outgroups are rejected as misguided, false, and untrustworthy.

Sect formation represents a pattern of revolt on any of a number of grounds. For lower-cast sects, the revolt is a rebellion of the underprivileged, the powerless, the disenfranchised—with reference to the context of meaningful religious participation and influence. Individual needs are not met by the existing religious structure and revolution follows. The revolution expresses itself in withdrawal and isolation and the integration of a set of values and beliefs that stands in opposition to the prevailing values of the existing society or the system of beliefs of the existing religious traditions. In the formation of cults, these tendencies are often carried to an extreme—with minimal structure, searching for and valuing of mystical experiences (at times drug induced), attachment to a charismatic leader, and a sharp oppositional break with religious traditions.

These developments are a reflection of underlying psychological processes and motivations. I propose that sectarian developments, and thus the operation of the CP, are motivated by basic needs to bolster the individual's faltering sense of identity and thus answer to internal issues of vulnerability and powerlessness. In terms of the paranoid process, these aspects of the individual's self-structure are organized around intrapsychic introjective configurations in respect to which the person feels and experiences himself as weak, powerless, victimized, disadvantaged, inadequate, inferior. In clinical terms, these characteristics are readily recognized as aspects of pathogenic introjects (Meissner, 1978). The paranoid process operates to dissociate and externalize these aspects of the individual's self system by way of projection. This relieves the individual of the feeling of being afflicted by such shortcomings, and provides the means by which these limitations and deficiencies can be attributed to the outside world. The projective system is then bolstered and consolidated by means of a paranoid construction that rationalizes, defends, and justifies the projections. The paranoid construction gives rise to the deviant belief system, which supports and gives meaningful coherence to the projective elements.

By adherence to the belief system, whether cast in terms of a group ideology or in the personified form of commitment to a charismatic leader, the individual resolves certain core narcissistic issues, secures a means for bolstering and sustaining self-esteem, and gains a vehicle that offers meaningful participation and purposefulness to his sense of self and his life. The idealizing tendencies of the ingroup formation, dispelling by projection undesirable or shameful attributes, create a context of self-enhancement and justification. Since truth and virtue reside within the group and are achieved through adherence to the group values and the leader, discomforting and disabling negative attitudes (particularly toward oneself) can be disregarded and submerged. The basic motivating force behind those processes is the fundamental need to gain a coherent and acceptable sense of self that will allow the salvaging of self-esteem and the achievement of a sense of meaningfulness and purpose through adherence to and participation in the religious group. Salvation is sought at the sacrifice of independence and autonomy.

The basic needs reflected in these dynamics can be satisfied effectively either through adherence to established and traditional religions or through the CP. The CP comes into play, according to this analysis, when basic needs, having to do with the inner need to attain and sustain a sufficient degree of narcissistic balance and integrity in reference to the organization of the individual self structure, remain unanswered and unattended. When the social influences of the traditional religious structures no longer fulfill that need, other resources are sought and come into being. The CP can thus be envisioned as resting on and deriving from basic human motivations and psychological processes. From the point of view of understanding the relationship of social structures and human dynamics, social processes arise out of individual dynamics in some fundamental sense, and provide the meaningful context and vehicle not only for the satisfaction of individual needs but for individual dynamics that undergird both social integration and deviance.

BIBLIOGRAPHY

GERTH, H. H., & MILLS, C. W., eds. (1946). *From Max Weber: Essays in Sociology*. New York: Oxford University Press.

JOHNSON, B. (1963). On church and sect. *Amer. Soc. Rev.*, 28:539–549.

MEISSNER, W. W. (1978). *The Paranoid Process*. New York: Aronson.

—— (1984). The cult phenomenon: Psychoanalytic perspective. *The Psychoanalytic Study of Society*, 10:91–111. New Haven: Yale University Press.

—— (1986). *Psychotherapy and the Paranoid Process*. New York: Aronson.

NIEBUHR, H. R. (1929). *The Social Sources of Denominationalism*. New York: Holt.

STARK, R., & BAINBRIDGE, W. W. (1979). Of churches, sects and cults: Preliminary concepts for a theory of religious movements. *J. for the Sci. Study of Relig.*, 18:117–133.

TROELTSCH, E. (1931). *The Social Teaching of the Christian Churches*. New York: Macmillan.

WILSON, B. R. (1959). An analysis of sect development. *Amer. Soc. Rev.*, 24:3–15.

YINGER, J. M. (1957). *Religion, Society and the Individual*. New York: Macmillan.

YINGER, J. M. (1970). *The Scientific Study of Religion*. London: Macmillan.

4

The Ego and the Mechanism of Adaptation*

PAUL PARIN
(Translated by Eva J. Meyer)

The title of this paper is to remind us of two works that are of undisputed importance to the development of psychoanalysis: Anna Freud's *The Ego and the Mechanism of Defense* (1936) and Heinz Hartmann's *Ego Psychology and the Problems of Adaptation* (1939). I hasten to add that neither the scope of this article nor the relevance of our consideration warrants any comparison with the two cited works. The relationship to Anna Freud's book is by analogy: I describe mechanisms, and call them mechanisms of adaptation, that are more or less firmly established in the ego of an adult and always run the same course unconsciously, just as Anna Freud describes the defense mechanisms. While the latter, however, are established in the ego to defend against undesired or disturbing drives, wishes and affects, the adaptation mechanisms I am talking about are meant to cope with active influences of the social environment. You will also find some analogies to Anna Freud's approaches in my arguments, and especially to her objectives. We have learned to understand the various defense organizations of the ego as an idiosyncratic form, even as the most important dynamically effective substratum of the ego; similarly the mechanisms of adaptation also seem to group themselves as an organization, which leads to idiosyncratic characteristics of social behavior, something like culture-specific ego variants.

POSING THE QUESTION

I have touched on the work of Heinz Hartmann because I want to provide a kind of sequel. Since 1939, after all, two very different uses of the concept "adaptation" have evolved in psychoanalysis from his discussion of the adaptational capacity of the ego.

---

*This chapter was originally published in *Der Widerspruch im Subjekt. Ethnopsychoanalytische Studien. (Contradiction in the Subject. Ethnopsychoanalytic Studies.)* Frankfurt: Syndikat, 1978.

"Adaptation" or "adaptational," first of all, is a point of view from which every psychic phenomenon can be considered, as it can also be explained genetically (from its origin), structurally (depending on its place in the structural scheme of the psychic apparatus), and so on. This adaptive point of view is of course also extended to the mechanisms established in the ego.

Second, adaptation is also conceived as a very specific process and its results. This usage starts from the task of the ego to mediate between the inner world and its surroundings, which is its origin and which determines its most important function. Ego psychology used a theoretical artifact to mark the course of adaptation to the environment, which from the very beginning was defined as social, the world of the respective person, and also measured the degree of adaptation achieved. This environment was reduced to that which could, on the average, be expected; that is, it was conceived as a constant. Now the study of the ego could blossom, its origin be studied, its structure develop until finally the apparatus of adaptation was also described, even though early psychoanalytic studies showed little interest in it. Now it would have been proper to drop this parameter and pursue the powerful and often violent effects of the varying social conditions on the structure and function of the ego. Hartmann was aware of this problem but did not pursue it further. Since, after all, people are biological creatures and in all animaldom adaptation as a means of survival is one of the chief characteristics of every species, adaptation seemed to be a goal; deviations were interesting only as disturbances, as a misstep in normal development, or as a lack of some functions. An examination of changes in the substrata "social environment" seemed superfluous.

I have tried to nullify this artifact, to absolve the social conditions of the fictitious status of an assumed average to observe what measures the ego takes and how it is equipped to counter these forces. In this respect, I am continuing where Hartmann stopped.

There are several reasons why I discovered a few new territories and why, for example, mechanisms of adaptation of the ego have hardly been noticed and have been studied even less, even though we are dealing with everyday observations. Many analysts still hold on to the biological concept that views the environment as a "natural given" and sees the individual as the only changeable element—a concept that does not hold for society as an environment. Another reason for this neglect may lie in the fact that psychoanalysis has had mostly bad experiences in referring to effects of the outer environment, rather than choosing the inner, or psychic, reality as a point of reference. The best-known example is Freud's supposition that sexual seduction by adults resulted in traumatic fixation on sexual childhood experiences. He soon had to recognize that it was the imagination of the child that reshaped harmless outside events into life-destroying inner dramas. Psychic reality, even if juxtaposed with a practical or, as Freud called it, objective reality, was and remains the main territory of psychoanalytic research.

I wish to emphasize that I follow the same direction. Who would dispute that psychic reality gives the real content to the abstract concept "ego"? However, if we want to examine which powers of the id evoke the defenses and demand the erection of defense mechanisms, we cannot ignore the drives. It is well known how the defenses differ depending on whether the libidinous drives demand satisfaction out of their oral or anal developmental phases. In an analogous manner, we must consider the forces of the environment when we want to define the ego structure in the service of adaptation, whether we are dealing with a passive autoplastic adaptation or an active alloplastic one or a mixture of both.

The objection that psychoanalysis began this step long ago is justified. What, after all, is the research on the early relationship of the infant to the mother (e.g., Spitz, 1965) and what else are the descriptions of early childhood (A. Freud, 1965; Mahler, 1975), what is the entire revision of ego formation in the light of preoedipal object relations, if not research into a person's adaptation to the environment? And is not the observation of modes of communication, of language, of interaction with family or groups the best way to trace the adaptation of the ego in great detail?

Another direction of research emanated especially from the Freud-Institut Frankfurt, where multiple examinations and applications of psychoanalytic knowledge are being undertaken in the light of historic processes and a critical examination of society.

Today, we know a great deal more about the psychology of social relationships than we did in 1939, when Hartmann began to examine the structure of the ego more closely from the vantage point of adaptation. One might wait until the results of the research on interactions and on the psychoanalytic social psychology have given us sufficient information to define the function of the ego in a changing environment which influences it.

My Method

Instead of waiting, however, my interest in trying to understand social behavior from an analytic point of view, impelled me to pursue another approach. I left the psychic development, the genetic point of view, aside for the time being, took note of the adaptation of the child to its familiar environment, but turned directly to the social behavior of the adult. Freud took this same path in his *Group Psychology and the Analysis of the Ego* (1921).

Based on the attitudes of the group and of the individual within the group[1] he arrived at interpretations and and reconstructions that are the foundation of all we know about the psychology of the individual vis-à-vis society. However, I was led to the point of view that I am presenting here by way of two seemingly quite different methodologies.

First of all, the psychoanalytic examination of members of tradition-bound nations, who live outside "Western civilization" and who use a precapitalistic form of economy, demanded a more exact understanding of the relationship of those ego structures (which are encountered immediately on beginning such a study) to the social system. Thus, one could not avoid questioning this adaptation analytically. We could describe idiosyncratic functions that apparently did not exist in European-American psychoanalyses or that received too little consideration. These studies led to the description of the "group ego," the "clan conscience," and the specific "modes of ego identification."

The second method, strongly influenced by the first, was that of classic psychoanalysis as practiced in Europe. Without changing the setting or the usual technique of interpretation, influences of the social environment on the analysand were included in the process of interpretation. This appeared to be necessary because many analysands were not able to perceive operative environmental influences; these were in the descriptive sense unconscious, while the ego had adapted itself to them structurally. For the time being, I have called this mechanism, which appeared most clearly during this process, "identification with the role." I have described my procedure in "Critique of Society in the Process of Interpretation," and have given my reasons for it there. (Parin, 1978, pp. 34–54). Here I will try to make the results of this method of analytic interpretation fruitful for ego psychological considerations and describe the clinical indications of automatic adaptation as parts of the ego.

If in the process of interpretation we begin with adaptive mechanisms of the analysand toward social influences, which are unknown to him (that is, unconscious in a descriptive sense) and proceed analogously with the interpretation of a resistance, a change frequently

---

1. Freud related his considerations mainoly to organized masses (e.g., the church or the military), which today we would call institutions.

occurs in the relationship to the analyst, such as a lowering of the transference resistance or a change of role assigned to the analyst in the transference situation.[2] Such interpretations result in intrastructural or even interstructural changes, that is, changes in the structure of the ego or those in the relationship between the ego and the superego, or the ego and the id. Here one can distinguish between two separate aspects. On the one side, mechanisms become clear that assure an automatic adaptation to certain social demands and forces, and that bestow a relative stability to the ego. The stabilizing function of those mechanisms may affect both the good, healthy, normal characteristics of the ego and the restricted pathological ones. At the same time, quite different changes in the ego are produced that range from a strengthening and improvement of all functions up to a thorough shattering of the systems of defense, to far-reaching regressions and the breakthrough of demands of drives against which defenses had been built up previously.

One can imagine that adaptation mechanisms free the ego from its steady conflicts with the environment, similarly to the way in which defense mechanisms work in relation to repressed demands of the drives. The other side of this unburdening is, however, rigidity and restriction. Whatever the ego has won in strength it loses in flexibility and elasticity.[3]

If there is no longer any forced automatic adaptation, the ego—after overcoming a phase of serious disruption—is presented with new possibilities of reorganization. It can assume a better, or at least a new, stance toward the environment, but especially towards the id and the superego. Practically speaking, the interpretation of unconscious adaptation appears to be followed most of the time by the uncovering of new material from the repressed unconscious. The relationship to the objects of love and aggression, as well as to the analyst is also affected and those parts of the superego related to social interactions are open to reworking. In other words, the analysis become deeper if through such interpretations one deprives the ego temporarily of the supporting function of its automatic adaptation.

DEMARCATION FROM OTHER PROCESSES OF ADAPTATION

Easily observed in children are several simple, one could even say primitive, mechanisms of adaptation, such as ritualization and imita-

---

2. Sandler (1974) differentiates clearly between the emotional attitude transferred to the analyst and the role that a child attributed to a parent and that also can be transferred.
3. ". . . every adaptation is a partial death, the giving up of a part of one's individuality . . ." (Ferenczi, 1931, p. 248; see also Ferenczi, 1927).

tion. These enable the ego to do justice to tasks of adaptation with much less energy than would otherwise be needed. If excessive ritualization shows up in childhood, or if imitative behavior substitutes for more mature processes of identification or learning, one can conclude that the ego is subject to conflicts originating in the sphere of the drives, especially great anxieties or failures of specific cathected objects. In the sense of an acute ego regression, the ego strives to balance its weakness by strengthening these measures. Both mechanisms are also available to the adult. It is well known that compulsive symptoms spread throughout the ego through ritualization or, better, that they force the ego to give in automatically to the demands of the incomprehensible compulsion. An excessive tendency to imitate is a conspicuous symptom in adults, indicating seriously disturbed object relations or a regressive detour to object relations less charged by conflicts. Of course, those and similar primitive mechanisms may continue to serve the adaptive process vis-à-vis the environment. We could hardly accomplish any task without the help of some routines, some adaptive ritualization; without imitation, we could hardly learn any new skills.

A housewife was undergoing analysis. She cooked three times daily, washed the dishes, shopped, served the meals. Everything was totally ritualized. Things ran like a charm. Still, she felt exhausted and took no pleasure in her work, and her family complained about the "loveless" preparation of the meals. Pointing out to her that her behavior was so ritualized that it not only spared her the trouble of personal initiative, but also excluded it, resulted in some disorder in this well-ordered household, but also enabled the patient to revise her attitude toward the members of her family, to realize, for instance, that she really did not like cooking for any of them, because she felt they gave her too little recognition and love. Exceptionally, in this case a primitive adaptive mechanism worked just as the more complex ones described below, by stabilizing the ego. When such additive mechanisms are no longer available, defense mechanisms are mobilized.

There is no doubt that adaptation to social demands included sublimated drive-discharge or gratification. The object of sublimated drives has been changed, and they can run their course with a displaced substitute. Even the aim, the gratification itself, has changed. Even though I do not share the opinion that sublimated actions have become "conflict free" (Hartmann, 1955) but instead suppose that the conflicts that are abreacted in this manner have been relaxed only partially, thus becoming easily displaceable or plastic, I cannot equate adaptation mechanisms with sublimation (Parin, 1978, pp. 20–33). If one actually interprets such adaptations, the difference soon becomes clear. The clarification of "genuine" sublimations, which are egosyntonic, permitting the nonconflictual discharge of aggression or libido, has no further consequences. However, if we interpret an automatic and unconsciously achieved social adaptation, a reorientation of the ego follows; frequently the activation of previously repressed material ensues, and not infrequently further processes of restructuring. If one did not wish to differentiate between sublimation and adaptation mechanisms—which to us seems fruitful both theoretically and therapeutically—one could say that in sublimations, synthetic and integrative functions of the ego are prominent; in other adaptations, social forces weigh more heavily, since isolation, loss of love, humiliations, and other punishments threaten if the ego does not adapt. The explanation of the fact that this adaptation is unconscious lies in the deficient perceptions of the "observing-ego," which needed to adapt itself so far-reachingly that it could no longer differentiate between its own interest and that of its social environment.

Sometimes one can see adaptive mechanisms in reaction formations that have lost their symptomatic character. The best-known example is personal grooming, which originates in the reaction to the anal pleasure of smearing; after "secondary autonomy" is achieved, it not only becomes an indispensible component of the libidinous cathexis of one's own body and one of the underpinnings of one's self-respect, but also serves as an adaptation to society. Neglect of the acquired habit of cleanliness can actually be used as a means of social protest. Obviously, reaction formations may also function as social adaptation. They are a lasting result of the education and socialization of the child. During an analysis, however, it becomes clear that these are genuine defense mechanisms; that is, without working through the resistances to some depth, they cannot be changed or given up. It would be useless to confuse their adaptive value and their importance to the culture-specific formation of the ego with the dynamic of their original functions, that is, the defense against drives. I believe that even if the borderline is not always clearly visible, one should subsume under the heading of adaptation only those other mechanisms that do not or no longer function as defenses against drives but that continue to confront demands and pressures of the environment, thus affording or maintain-

ing a relative stability of the ego.[4] That the ego contains a defense
system that represses impulses of the drives or allows them to appear
only in the form of symptom formations should be considered—as
indeed it has always been—solely in the light of the psychic reality of
fantasies, wishes, and anxieties, and not as related to the environment
and its influence.

MECHANISM OF ADAPTATION; COMMON CHARACTERISTICS

Characteristic of adaptive mechanisms is that they prove to be
stabilizers of the ego as long as the social conditions under which the
person lives do not change. Adaptive mechanisms function automatically and unconsciously, and they guarantee a relatively conflict-free
handling of very specific social institutions. Thus they have an economic advantage: They relieve other ego apparatuses and make it
easier to reach drive satisfactions that are offered within the framework
of the respective institutions. Narcissistic gratifications predominate
over object-related ones. At the same time, all adaptive mechanisms
restrict the ego's flexibility and prevent further adaptation of the
instinctive wishes to other or changing social conditions. Originally
they serve the precepts of the reality principle; thereafter, however,
they can limit the ego's functioning. I do not attribute to the adaptive
mechanisms any constant relationship to specific affects. If they function, they may, under certain circumstances, cause a sense of well-
being (Sandler, 1974); one cannot state, however, that they are always
accompanied by this state of well-being or even that producing that
state is their aim. When automatic adaptation fails, anxiety frequently
appears; adaptation, being a development beyond defense mechanisms, however, does not directly serve to avoid anxiety or to defend
against it.

Stated in brief: Defense mechanisms demand energy (counter-
cathexis) to free the ego from the demands of the drives, whereas
adaptive mechanisms relieve the ego of this task.

While one can view defense mechanisms as the remainder of childhood drive conflicts (or as their heritage, built into the ego), adaptive

---

4. According to Hartmann (1939), one could suppose that these adaptive mechanisms
"originally" were defense mechanisms that had become "conflict free," are now
attached with "neutralized" libido, and thus can be counted among the "secondarily
autonomous" functions of the ego. The evolution of these mechanisms and their
structure within the ego contradict such a supposition. A deeper discussion of the
concept of the neutralization of the libido would exceed the limitations of this study
(See Parin, 1978, pp. 20–33).

mechanisms are a much more direct expression of the encroachment of the social environment on the ego. They too have their beginnings in childhood,, but throughout life they remain subject to social forces. Concepts such as "The Individual and His Property" (Stirner, 1845) or the idea of self-determination of one's own behavior, which have been promulgated by the traditions of liberalism on through Sartre's (1953) existentialism and which are reflected in such psychoanalytic concepts as ego autonomy and ego dominance, are brought into further question by the existence of adaptive mechanisms.

In the following, I attempt to describe three mechanisms of adaptation, which I have derived in part from analytical conversations with Africans (Parin et al., 1963, 1971), but which also delineate the ego of European analysands. It should not be said that these three mechanisms are the only ones that exist. If my point of view proves to be correct, other modes of adaptation would probably be found or at least the third (identification with the role) would have to be split into several variants.

For each of these mechanisms I first review briefly: 1) the conditions under which they are "arranged" within the ego; 2) their dynamic and mode of operation; 3) the effects of each mechanism on social behavior.

The Group Ego[5]

OVERVIEW

We trace the origin of the group ego to relatively tension-free identificatory relationships that establish themselves during childhood and adolescence, preferably with youngsters of the same sex and age in "horizontal groups." If these relationships remain undisturbed by either frustration or aggression, and if certain "oral" ego qualities remain intact, the adult will always be ready to enter into such satisfying relationships again. If communities or groups exist in a social situation where mutual fraternal or sisterly identifications are possible because of these groups's special structure or the special psychology of their members, the group ego guarantees good social adaptation (as in the Dogon village) (Parin et al., 1963). This adaptive mechanism reflects the common structure of the society more accurately than others. It would be out of place in a nuclear family and it must fail in

---

5. The term "group ego" was coined by Paul Federn (1936), who, while speculating about earlier forms of civilization, indicated that the borderline of the ego used to be much less distinct, perhaps even nonexistent. We give a totally different meaning to this word (cf. Parin et al., 1971).

the public life of an urbanized industrial society, the ego structured in this manner is seriously weakened and becomes subject to pathological regression. Sometimes the group ego can serve adaptation even in our society, for example, within the framework of socially peripheral fraternal communities. Although it affords the participants some stability and an unaccustomed potential for action, it more likely corresponds to a desired utopian state than actually pressing for a changed society.

EXAMPLES

We first described the group ego in Africans. It was easily delineated, perhaps because the human environment is more important to these Africans than it is to us, in order to enable their ego to function relatively autonomously; perhaps, however, because their dependency on their environment became clearer to us than did that of our European analysands, whose dependencies are so similar to our own.

However, we also must ascribe a group ego to Europeans. Let us imagine a European scholar returning from a scientific colloquium with fellow specialists. Such occasions are important to him; his well-being depends on the satisfaction of aggressive and libidinous wishes, which can enter his ego only under these conditions. In this case, the necessary assumption, which determines the function of the ego as a whole, is that the ego is able to enjoy through these discussions gratifications that are subject to aim displacement and thus to secondary processes—only within a group (a manifestation of the group ego) whose structure permits scientific discussion and whose members have an ego with very similar capabilities (Parin et al., 1971, pp. 537ff.).

DYNAMIC AND FUNCTION

We understand the term group ego to be a specific mode of function that operates for the total ego, and a series of specific ego functions, manifestations of the group ego, that depend on the cooperation of a group of individuals in order to be and remain adequate. These groups must possess a specific structure, and their members must react in a specific way. The condition necessary for the group ego to become operational is their emotional readiness and capability to assume very specific roles. These ego functions rest on the acquired readiness of the ego to enter into very specific identificatory relationships. Thus, the group ego in principle is not a different structure from the ego described elsewhere, but neither is it an additional one (as if there were a properly delineated ego and an additional group ego).

Freud (1921) described such modes of identification. Participants in a group take the leader as their ego-ideal, thus becoming able to enter into relatively tension-free identifications with each other. Freud describes these identifications as a form of temporary relationship and suspects that cathexis of the participants with homosexual libido plays a role; he reminds us that heterosexual love relationships have a tendency to disturb the cohesiveness of the group or to break it up altogether.

Not everyone, however, becomes a total participant in the group. The strength of the inclination to make the leader or common ideals into the ego-ideal varies with the individual. Each person's ego lends itself very distinctively to structuring and retaining identificatory relationships. The African studies showed us that similar identificatory relationships may occur, without forming a group, without the existence of a leader or a leitmotif. This can happen under the following conditions:

1. The ego in its earlier development has gained the ability to identify with cathected individuals who awakened very particular feelings and who granted very specific satisfactions. I call this form of relationship fraternal, although the term is not to be taken literally.

2. The ego has retained the capability to regress to oral modes of cathexis and satisfaction, at least if the cathected person does not provoke aggression, for example as envy or rivalry. Fenichel (1945) believes this ability to regress to the oral stage to be the sine qua non for every new identification, based as it is on an act of introjection. The group ego does not always permit such regressions; it may even appear to be rigid. If, however, the individual group members behave cooperatively, like siblings, the group ego is ready to regress and to establish such identifications. The group as a whole then has a "maternal" effect, in the sense that the members find oral participation and mutual oral exchanges; this oral "nursing" may refer to any libidinous gratification. Oral is meant here to refer to the developmental stage of the ego and not to the level of libido development.

3. If identification is achieved, the ego is strengthened. It functions better as a whole, probably because aggressions are directed outward and not toward group members, who offer one another relatively frustration-free gratification. The group tie itself is maintained in this form by aim-deflected homosexual cathexes.

We trace the *formation of the group ego* to identifications in childhood and adolescence, which are not so-called identifications with the aggressor. Freud found that there are traces of all early object relations in the ego and that identifications are its building blocks. However, the outcome seems to vary: Sometimes it is forced through frustration and threats; at other times it is more peaceful, and attributes of the object are not internalized. However, the ego provides a structure that is always ready to repeat such a satisfying relationship, if it is offered by the environment. This structural track of satisfying identification may be compared to an electric plug, repeatedly delivering energy to the ego as long as a person or group exists that provides exactly the right current. It should be emphasized that this mechanism does not show any drive cathexis of its own. Defense mechanisms must be assumed to possess countercathectic drive energy. Plugs transmit energy; they do not contain their own.

Relationships to groups of the same sex and age, such as peer groups, fraternities, various gangs, and formal or informal youth organizations, are most likely to permit such identification. There are hierarchical (in sociological terms, vertical) group structures in contrast to egalitarian, or horizontal, ones. Within the latter, such tension-free identifications can take place only as long as the group behaves in a sufficiently motherly, permissive, caretaking, nurturing manner and is not too much disturbed by discord due, for example, to rivalries and envy in order to permit temporary "oral regressions." If during childhood and adolescence there is a balance between the vertical groups of individuals (according to the necessarily vertical model of the age-determined hierarchical family) and the horizontal ones—or better still if there is a harmonious back and forth movement between these two alternatives—then a well-functioning group ego is formed that facilitates later social adaptation.

In our society many groups seem to be organized horizontally, but they prove to have a vertical structure in their psychological effect: in the Boy Scouts and Girl Scouts, for example, there is leadership hierarchy and ideology. In the schools, the competitive pressure to achieve and the rivalry growing out of that pressure are more apt to outweigh the age-determined horizontalism of these groups. In such institutions, as a rule, identification with the aggressor develops, rather than a group ego.

On the other hand, some vertically organized groups, such as the matrilinear and age-hierarchical clan of the Agni, enforce an oral regression that assists in confronting even the most threatening objects symbolic of the assaultive, phallic mother, not by incorporating them in the typical manner of identification with the aggressor, but by using them to build up a readiness for identification.

In a *therapeutic analysis,* the group ego frequently makes the working relationship effective. Here the "good, cooperative, analytic work" enters into the ego ideal of the participants. The work is cathected, as is the leader in the formation of a group. This makes mutual identification easier. We may recall here that the formation of a common ideal, as the necessary basis for identification according to Freud's model of the formation of a mass, also occurs with the group ego. A mild homosexual transference, which is so beneficial for the working pact and for the progress of the analysis, can be traced back to the group ego. Object-displaced pregenital satisfactions, such as showing and looking of both partners, are perfectly permissible, and the ego, in spite of the regression, appears to be strengthened. The appearance of uninhibited sexualized or aggressivized transferences immediately damages the working partnership, as does the analyst's violation of his brotherly role. The group ego loses its automaticly adaptive function. The defense mechanism of the ego reassumes full power either with adequate or with symptom-forming characteristics. During training analyses, the group ego may mean belonging to the group of analysts. If this adaptation mechanism is sufficient, the ego becomes relatively conflict free, and the analytic process stops entirely. For such persons, the analysis may again proceed if they find it possible to experience how uncertain their group ego would become if they could not become psychoanalysts.

Frequently, the mechanism of adaptation solidifies attitudes of the analysand's ego and could thus be mistaken for a resistance. Consorting with drinking companions, participating in the ritual of invitations by a layer of society with an elegantly bourgeois life style, taking part in political groups are frequently ineffectively interpreted as acting out. If the analysand can be shown that his beloved drinking bouts with his pub pals only serve to spare him from the threatening humiliation of social or sexual failure that he might have to confront without his group, the mechanism can become transparent and the analysis of the corresponding symptoms can begin. The adapted ego has become stable; in the less well adapted one, conflicts become more vivid and may be more easily experienced as neurotic conflicts.

SPECIFIC EFFECTS

We have retraced the exemplary sense of community that creates in the traditional village of the Dogons a well-defined group ego (Parin, Morgenthaler, & Parin-Mattèy, 1963). This is formed in an effectively "motherly" group, into which a child enters in its fourth year of life after an extended period of nursing and symbiotic life as a twosome with its mother. The group ego is strengthened and renewed during adolescence, and later on during adulthood, in organized groups that consist of similarly socialized sex and age peers. The Dogon experience suggests that to achieve the educational goal of better social behavior, toward which so many utopian models of education strive, one might do well to give children and adolescents the opportunity to form a group ego.[6]

In the study of families, we might well ask whether adaptive mechanisms similar to the group ego might not play a role in patients with a specific form of schizophrenic development. Family researchers and family therapists (Stierlin, 1975) describe patients who have been socialized so invasively and one-sidedly that they can only live in a world that is totally circumscribed by the rules and expectations imparted to them by their mothers or other members of their families. Since this world does not correspond to the reality outside of the family, they are psychotic. We have observed that adult Dogons with good and stable ego functions, the result of a well-formed group ego, can suddenly enter into psychotic like states if they are suddenly transported to an environment structured differently from their own. Reconstitution is immediate when they return to their own village. Might it not be true that "delegating" mothers, by their spoiling attitude, further the formation of oral ego-qualities and that mutual identification with members of the family represents an irreplaceable ego stabilizer to the tied "delegate"? The concept of "delegation" has been related by family researchers (as have the modalities of interaction, or the so-called heritage) to the interpersonal process. Viewed metapsychologically (Hartmann, 1953), the psychotic ego should, however, also be described as structure. It appears to me that the ego of the "committed delegates" is not yet sufficiently characterized by its system of communication and interaction with objects largely involving splitting and introjection (Grotstein, 1982; Ogden, 1982; Boyer, 1983) and that it is distinguished by the establishment of a specific mechanism of adaptation.

The "Clan Conscience"

The most impressive adaptation to the demand of the social environment is, no doubt, the construction of the superego. This extraordinary process leads to a result that cannot just be called a mechanism; one is justified in speaking of a separate agency, a structure differentiated from the ego.

---

6. Murphy's (1974) hypothesis to explain the worldwide protest movement of the young would be quite compatible with the assumption of mechanism close to the group ego.

OVERVIEW

Still, the ego can develop and retain the ability to substitute extraneous authorities or institutions, intermittently or temporarily, for the internalized superego. These then are cathected with the same drive energies and have the same forbidding or approving effects on the ego. The ego is particularly inclined to establish this substitution as a mechanism, if during the years of childhood dependency educators, parents and family are especially highly subject to outer, macrosocietal influences. Extreme living conditions such as extreme privilege, ghettoization, impoverishment, and enforced or highly cathected ideologies, especially, for example, in the lower middle classes or in religious sects, favor such an ego development. In those cases, outer and inner introjected imperatives become one in the ego. In a classless society, in which ideological demands are relatively true mirrors of the interests of the individual in the society, the clan conscience not only has a stabilizing effect, but also furthers those interests that have any chance to be realized. However, if the ideological values and rules of the society are opposed to the needs of the individual—which is the case most of the time for our analysands, who do live in a class-determined society—the clan conscience frequently restricts the individual. The ego loses independence in the face of the social environment that it might have enjoyed after conquering guilt and shame vis-à-vis the internalized superego.

EXAMPLES

I am taking a simple example of the clan conscience from a conversation with a pious pagan Dogon. He says that he would pray according to the Islamic rite if he were in a Mohammedan village, "so that the elders there would not be sad if someone does not share their faith . . . it is not good for anyone if the village elders are depressed, then they cannot care properly for the common good." Religious ideas and rules, attributable to the superego, are delegated to external realms. From the point of view of the ego, relief is achieved if one can satisfy one's superego by adapting to the outer environment.

In our analysands, too, we can sometimes observe that the delegation of the superego to the environment can diminish ego conflicts without necessitating a total working through of the guilt or the loosening of the defense mechanism. The best-known examples are the confessions of faithful Catholics, or the soldier at war, who kills without suffering torments of conscience.

DYNAMIC AND FUNCTION

Freud (1921) distinguished very specifically between identification with an object that brought about pleasurable feelings and the embodiment of the ego ideal in an outer authority such as the church. Sandler (1964/1965) clarified this process and characterized it as an everyday event:

> The superego is being supported by the ego only as long as the superego also functions as support for the ego. There are, however, situations in which the ego can and will ignore the standards and rules of the superego altogether, i.e., if it can find sufficient narcissistic support elsewhere (p. 741) . . . in daily life there are many examples where the morals and the ideals of a group take the place of an individual's moral attitude, such as in religious conversions, in the forming of gangs, and the hero worship of adolescents (p. 742).

I speak of a clan conscience, however, only if the externalization becomes necessary, and therefore automatic, for the maintenance of the ego; for such persons no "other . . . narcissistic support" is necessary. Externalization itself is the support.

ON THE ORIGIN OF THE CLAN CONSCIENCE

In our culture parents take a back seat to the environment that they represent. They offer to the child values and ideologies that are not their own and that may not even determine their own behavior, which they may fail to live up to, or values they may even fear. If this happens during critical phases, the clan conscience becomes a permanent acquisition. Passive submission to the failing chief personage in the oedipal conflict seems, in our milieu, to be such a sensitive phase, especially if strong feelings of desertion, of not being loved, or a deficit in the narcissistic cathexis of the self result from the preoedipal phase.

Projections, or splitting processes, where the roles of a cruel superego or preautonomous superego nuclei are shifted to the external world, do not belong here. Those are emergency defenses through which the ego finds unreliable relief. Attempts at defense through primitive mechanisms have little value in adaptation, as do paranoid hallucinations.

On the other hand, during *therapeutic* analyses, we often overlook the fact that a patient's hyperidentification with the superego of a leader or a group has relieved his ego of conflict and even stabilized it.

The used car dealer who shares the business ethic of his colleagues follows his "clan conscience" just as closely as does the fanatic who fights ruthlessly for a good cause; but so does the analysand who makes the analyst who "understands everything" the bearer of the superego and who admits otherwise forbidden drive impulses. People who use this mechanism cannot by any psychiatric measure be considered delinquent or predelinquent personalities. It is exactly the well-adapted, good citizens with relatively sufficient ego functions who adjust to external powers, in order to begin to give their egos some strength.

The repetitive character of such actions indicates a transference situation, especially if the function of superego is attributed to the analyst. Surprisingly, an interpretation of the drive impulses against which the analysand believes his defenses to be intact, or of the transference, is impossible. The patient has no capacity to understand such interpretations. He says, "That's how it is, after all. Everybody does it, everyone demands it that way"; he means the group to which he allots his superego. If the analyst insists on his own interpretation, his person and his morality are put in question by the analysand, who may retreat in many ways, including aggressive withdrawal and submission. If one, however, proceeds in a way that allows the analysand to be the first to recognize whom and what he used as a superego substitute and to lay bare the morals of his clan conscience, then the ego can be relieved through adjustment of the superego to extraneous demands.

The ego of the young Agni woman Elisa who took first her mother, then the arbitrator Ibi, then the village chief, then the sorceress of Yosso as her "ideal," each time finding a sufficient discharge after being severely shattered by a revived oedipal conflict. There is no doubt that the borrowed "morals" were in most respects identical with her own (Parin et al., 1971). If in our analysands a corresponding correlation exists between their own and external moralities, it is hardly possible to unravel this mechanism analytically. If, however, the ideologically represented values are in opposition to the ego interest of the analysand, a revision of the mechanism can occur.

SPECIAL CONSEQUENCES

The clan conscience does not gain its importance so much from the projective identification that externalizes the introject with whose demand the ego identifies as through the opposite movement. If the demands and values of the external society change, a process that can be directed by means of power and propaganda, the ego must submit to the new ideology or use it to remain fully functional. This adaptation mechanism functions at the price of increased vulnerability of the subject to manipulation.

It might have to be examined whether those psychotic "delegates" that through their family carry along a kind of immunization against the individual conscience may own a clan conscience. The mechanism appears more clearly in the so-called torch bearer. Several generations of his family furnish him with a substratum for his clan conscience. When these values become ineffective in therapy, or when they diverge too far from the publicly held ones, there occurs a shock to the ego, which had depended on the narcissistic gains resulting from a good clan conscience.

"Identification with the Role"

PRELIMINARY

I assigned the term "identification with the role" to complex mechanisms of adaptation that establish themselves in the ego, temporarily or permanently. The delineation of these mechanisms from other functions is not a sharp one; their dynamic may not be uniform. Neither can I state their psychogenesis with absolute certainty. Nevertheless, I hold these mechanisms to be irreplaceable supplements to the psychology of the ego. In my own practice, I can no longer do without this concept; it permits a broad linkage between individual psychology and social psychology, our knowledge of behavior in small groups and in macrosociety.

I understand the term role as it is used in sociology: the desired and demanded attitudinal behavior, depending on sex, age, position in the family, occupation, and as a participant in various institutions. Attitudinal behavior specific to groups, castes, or social classes is included in this role concept.[7] Positively valued roles—the father figure in the family, the entrepreneur, the worker—or negatively valued ones—the criminal, the mentally ill, a ward—are considered equally. All these social roles are connected with social institutions. The ideological superstructure of these institutions contains the respective wishes and demands that have been directed to the real or presumptive role bearer by the narrower or broader societal unit. It does not matter here whether or not the society or the role bearer is conscious of this ideological content.

---

7. Identification with the role has little in common with the role playing in Moreno's psychodrama (Fromm-Reichmann and Moreno, 1956).

However, I do not include in my social role everything that can be subsumed in the term role in functionalistic sociology. Social behavior of any kind—whether desired, of no consequence, or despised by the society—if it is not defined by ideology, does not make identification with the role possible. The social behavior of an individual, whether, psychologically speaking, it follows the path of the reality principle or of a repetition compulsion, becomes role behavior only if it is predefined in an ideologic context. We are not yet making any statement about whether the person does or does not take on this role without identifying with it. Identification with the role is a process to be described in psychological terms, a step by which an "objective" role becomes a "subjective" one.

To give an example: The homosexual man has a specific social behavior pattern. He chooses only male sexual partners. This does not necessarily mean that he behaves in the manner dictated by the ideology of the system "homosexuality in an industrial society." If he does—frequents appropriate meeting places, wears homosexual clothes, and behaves in a manner corresponding to the expectations of society as a whole—he is playing the specific social role. But still we cannot conclude as yet whether or not he identifies with the role of the homosexual. If he does, which is a purely psychological process, there has been a change in his ego, which can be described psychologically and which can be clarified psychoanalytically.

OVERVIEW

During its development in childhood, the ego becomes able to take on various roles, assigned to it first by the family and later by the school and the wider public, and to behave according to these roles. Even though conflicts between the id and the demands of education are not totally resolved through this ability, identification does relieve the tension of many of these conflicts. Le Coultre (1970) emphasized that the ego of the adult is frequently "split": one is an able, adult man and, at the same time, a helpless little boy, or an aging woman of 55 and simultaneously an adolescent, whose life is still "ahead of her." The retention and splitting off of a childish role, according to Le Coultre, protect the adult ego against unresolved childhood conflicts—as a defense, after all. Other authors, such as Richter (1976), believe that the assumption of assigned roles alleviates or even avoids anxiety altogether, especially the anxiety of not being loved and being left alone and defenseless, which derives from the separation anxiety of the child.

We have seen that a passing or lasting identification with the role gives greater stability to the ego. In order to relax conflicts with the environment, simple assumption of role-determined behavior would be sufficient. How, then, can we explain the continuation of role playing when there are no longer any threatening outer conflicts? Even role identification does not resolve inner conflicts. However, two advantages result for the ego, if it does not merely assume roles but rather identifies with them. Outward adaption then occurs automatically; it does not demand the spending of energy or cathexis. Any ego split that might become necessary is seldom noticed and hardly decreases total functioning. Moreover, identification always offers a real or imagined libidinous or aggressive gratification, which is sometimes related to the role-conveyor. Additionally, it offers a narcissistic satisfaction because one fits one's role well.

As the identification with the role is the chief instrument of the adjustment of the adult to social demands and compulsions, so the analysis of these identifications (whether exchangeable and short-lived or lasting) is an irreplaceable instrument of emancipation. In other words: The person is not master of his own home. The analysis must make him aware not only of these forces from his repressed material to which he is subject, but also of the powers of his environment that automatically dominate him because his ego, mostly unconsciously and through diverse role models, has identified with them.

EXAMPLES

The identification with the role became particularly clear in Africans, in whose relatively simply structured environment the attributions are clearer and less numerous than with us.

In conversations with F. Morgenthaler (Parin, Morgenthaler, & Parin-Mattèy, 1971) Brou Koffi impressed him as an energetic, self-assured, and prudent man, as long as he spoke in his role as village chief. When he had to give up this role under the assault of unconscious material or through interpretations of his behavior, he became fraught with anxieties, perplexed, abjectly submissive; his self image was in disarray. When a new duty as village chief arose for him, he assumed the offered role, and his psychic equilibrium was restored immediately.

A case from my Zurich practice shows the effect of role identification:

During four preliminary interviews, a capable, intelligent, and seemingly articulate physician had expounded on his biography and the reasons for needing an analysis. He did this convincingly and with sufficient effect to evoke empathy. When I accepted his proposal—he wanted to begin to tell me what came to his mind without prior planning—he could not speak. This was an extremely mortifying experience for him, which repeated itself several times in spite of all attempts to help him over this obstacle. Every word he wanted to speak spontaneously, every feeling he wished to show was restricted by disabling anxiety or deathly shame.

During this period, he worked energetically and without complaint as chief physician of a complex medical institution and was seen as a rather cool, but friendly, accessible, and self-assured colleague. The identification with the allotted social role had been gained step by step and had substituted for otherwise deficient ego functions. At one point, he could not identify with the social role of a physician, when he accepted a position abroad, where the role expectations of him as a physician were totally different. There he suddenly became confused and wanted to commit suicide. He returned home just in time to find another placement as a physician.

In psychoanalytic theory and practice, one usually explains such a phenomenon without using the concept of identification with the role. I did likewise, and the analysis was successful in the end. Nevertheless, I believe that my interpretations, as well as my understanding of the patient, remained incomplete.

During the analysis, in addition to the well-known transference roles (Sandler, 1974) such as that of an educating mother during the anal phase, other role expectations are conferred on the analyst, attributed to him, or projected onto him. His own role identification has the effect of identifying the partner, alloplastically, with a corresponding role and treating him accordingly.

A young woman physician had in analysis a young man who came from a very wealthy family. The working alliance was a good one; the transference had a mildly eroticized, fraternal-positive coloration. In several of the last preceding hours, the patient had tried to clarify for himself the complicated, tormenting, neurotic entanglement in his parental family. Since he was unable to get a good grasp of the matter, the analyst sought to help him in his effort by summarizing what the patient had said about his family. Suddenly the patient lost his temper and berated the analyst, saying that she

had no right to discuss this and wondering what he still had to gain
through working with her. The analyst's first reactive thought was
that he was very rich, and then she became aware that he was
scolding her as if she were a maid. An appropriate intervention
made the patient conscious of his perception: "As long as I speak
to my physician, I have full confidence in her competence, and
she understands me like a sister. As soon as she discusses my
family, in which I am the 'son of a distinguished family,' (we
would say identify with that role), she turns into something like a
maid, whom we employ but who has no right to mix into family
affairs." After this interpretation, the favorable working alliance
was restored.

DEVELOPMENT OF ROLE IDENTIFICATION

The genetic steps leading to role identification probably coincide
with the development of the child's ego, which never occurs in an
unchanging environment: Just by growing older, the child encounters
steadily changing social situations relative to his role and must adapt to
them. Later role identifications are copied from those conveyed early
on and demanded by family and school; that is, they are drawn within
the same ego-contours.

Later on, social necessities and compulsions bring about an identification with a social role. The difference between need and compulsion
is not great. Both indicate that it is more advantageous to accept the
assigned role than to refuse it. If one does not accept the role, dangers
threaten; fear of real frustrations and punishments arises in the ego.
This does not exclude simultaneously arising neurotic anxieties. A
woman who marries to find her role as a wife and mother may be afraid
of the disadvantages and discrimination that await an unmarried
women in our society; a neurotic anxiety of being alone may codeter-
mine her decision. Anxieties triggered by real threats, as well as those
originating from drive conflicts, may be conscious or unconscious.

DYNAMICS AND FUNCTION

Identification with the social role is not meant simply to be behavior
in a prescribed manner, but the specific form in which the ego deals
with this assigned role. When examining this mechanism, we must give
weight to the fact that anxiety generally has the effect of a regulator;
but that the tracing of the anxiety signal in the ego will not help to
understand the processes within the ego further than recognizing that a

role has been assumed or that uncertainty and threatening dangers suggest some form of adaptation to the ego.[8]

One might deduce from observing families and groups that the fears of isolation, exclusion, or loss of love are the main or even the only determinants of role identification (Richter, 1976). However, conscious fears often can not be proven when multiple new roles are assumed in macrosocial institutions. On the contrary, it is just those role identifications that isolate the subject, distinguish and separate him from family or group, and frequently lend the ego particular stability so that the effectiveness of unconscious separation anxiety becomes improbable.

---

8. My concept of identification with a role is opposed by others, who commonly describe this mechanism as a defense mechanism, that is, as a defense against anxiety. That point is most clearly represented by the so-called English School, which is indebted to the thinking of Melanie Klein.

   I. Menzies (undated) examines "The functioning of social systems as a defense against anxiety," especially role distribution within an institution, a nursing school within a large London hospital. It is explained that the execution of the ascribed role always serves to defend against anxiety. It is said that reality (of the institution) acts as a symbol that triggers anxiety which originates from unconscious phantasies. When the symbol (i.e., the symbolic aspect of reality) is equated with the unconscious phantasy, unmanageable, acute anxiety arises. If real events as symbols only represent the unconscious content of the phantasies, then the anxiety can be conquered. The assumption that reality (e.g., working in that institution) in all cases triggers anxiety, theoretically permits the description of role identifications as a defense mechanism. In practice, they deduce from the fact that anxiety appears when a social role is given up that the function of the role is to defend against anxiety.

   Within the present framework, I naturally cannot present a sufficient appreciation or criticism of Melanie Klein's theory. For the theme of this paper, a clear delineation of my interpretation from that of the English school is, however, possible. Theirs has the advantage of furnishing a simpler model. Instead of assuming, as I do, a defense organization and separate adaptation mechanisms, they make do with the concept of defense alone.

   The mere fact, however, that anxiety appears if a situation changes does not lead me to conclude that the situation served to defend against anxiety; nor does the mere circumstance that a child shows anxiety as soon as the mother leaves lead to the conclusion that the presence of the mother functions as a defense against anxiety. Aside from the questionability of this theoretical reasoning, the model role/anxiety-defense is a closed one: The individual psyche needs the institution as a defense; the institution is organized in accordance with subjective (neurotic) needs. Thus one explains the conservative character of institutions, their tendency, contrary to a more reasonable arrangement, to remain always the same. They can be changed only through insight. My own model leaves open which conditions give stability to the institutions and the set roles within them: social conditions, economic and other interests and pressures. Insight into their psychological effect alone may well change the subjective experience of the role, but does not guarantee that the institution, which depends on other forces, together with its set roles, changes so readily.

The most important psychological predetermining factors to make role identifications possible are active adaptation to the social roles that must be assumed, and libidinous and aggressive experiences that are triggered in the individual by the role assignments and role expectations of the environment. For society offers each individual frustrations and seductions that are specific to his social situation and that advance the one-sided adaptation of his psychic structure. We might even suspect that the position of the individual within his class and his profession and his place in the power structure have a continuous influence on the cathexis of the self and thus determine the relationship of the psychic structures with each other.

Identification with social roles, no matter how dichotomous or frustrating they may be, always serves the process of social adaptation; without such identifications, the proper interaction with the environment would be most difficult. The roles themselves are derived from and defined by social institutions. Many of these institutions are arranged in such a way that they affect the individual like a defense mechanism that has been externalized. Freud (1913) uncovered this first in the "human penal system."

> If one person succeeds in gratifying the repressed desire, the same desire is bound to be kindled in all the other members of the community. In order to keep the temptation down, the envied transgressor must be deprived of the fruit of his enterprise; and the punishment will not infrequently give those who carry it out an opportunity of committing the same outrage under colour of an act of expiation. This is indeed one of the foundations of the human penal system and it is based, no doubt correctly, on the assumption that the prohibited impulses are present alike in the criminal and in the avenging community [p. 72].

We are still far from totally penetrating the effects of even the most important social institutions. The psychoanalytic illumination that Freud began again and again was stymied mostly by the fact that analysts, too, were identified with the same norms and value systems that legitimated the institutions under prevailing conditions, and they were not free to question them. Culturally constituted defensive systems, as Pollock (1972) calls them, are social structures, which relieve the individual of socially undesirable drive impulses and of the effort of defense or renunciation. Culture, which, in part, is based on the repression of drives, takes over a part of this effort through its institutions. The adapting ego is spared the effort of defence, as long as the person identifies, up to standard, with the role assigned to him by society. The finding that the ego does not need any energy for the identification with the role and that his defense system is actually relieved cannot be a surprise. It is true, however, that this economic gain brings with it a structural restriction.

Successful identifications with the role relieve the ego. Sometimes they help to bridge intrastructural conflicts in the ego, as between active and passive attitudes, where perhaps the role of an employee demands passivity vis-à-vis his superios and activity in his work or attitude vis-à-vis those below him in rank. The necessary outer-directedness may temporarily quiet uncomfortable affects. Demands of the id may also take a step backward, so that the distinction from a defense mechanism is not always easy. The most important difference from a complex defense mechanism, such as the narrowing of the ego, lies in the drive gratification that often follows the role identification. Here we can compare this mechanism with a symptom formation. However, while a symptom almost never brings about a secondary narcissistic satisfaction and a corresponding increase in self-respect, identification with the role is regularly accompanied by narcissistic satisfaction, even if only temporarily.

For both object-related ones and narcissistic gratification, we must consider that role identification frequently demands the renunciation of certain satisfactions (for example, he who drives should not drink) but that only the fewest social roles do not yield at least some gratification to the bearer from those who assign the roles.

The narcissistic gratification derived from role identification is most striking when the assumption of the role results in other massive frustrations. Recruits who have suffered deprivation of their rights and harassing treatment during military training, remember during their analysis how identification with their role brought them immediate relief. When part of the individual superego can be delegated to the authorities, passive, masochistic homosexual and other regressive satisfactions suddenly become possible. Here, and especially in less disagreeable role assignments, the narcissistic gain is achieved through being a recruit, a doctor, or a father, for example; if we are dealing with more or less permanent identification, the feeling of an identity of one's own is strengthened, no matter how much this identity is founded on unavoidable or even forced adaptation.

Under certain circumstances identification with the social role appears only temporarily, as an emergency mechanism. An otherwise kind man beats his children "as a father"; an honest merchant gets into trouble and takes unfair advantage of his friend and partner "as a businessman." The role model with which he identifies includes the motto that in business one's own advantage must be pursued above all else and that "friendship stops where business begins." Thus, a role identification may at times work like a manic mechanism by means of which the ego rids itself or otherwise valid demands of the superego.

The relationship of ego identity (Erikson, 1950) to the identification with the role is complex. To delineate these concepts from each other would take a more detailed discussion than we can present here. We must start from two statements that seem to contradict each other and that can be traced to psychoanalytic observation: On one hand, ego identity is built partly on role identification; on the other hand, the structure of a durable ego identity diminishes the tendency to identify with social roles.

In the "epigenetic crises," during which the identity of a person establishes itself (the most striking ones have been described by Erikson, 1950, 1959), assigned role models, which have been internalized through identification, connect—more or less modified—with other, previously internalized identifications. If the acquired ego identity is sufficiently strong and well-integrated into the psychic structure, it has the effect of an organizer, stabilizing the ego. Thereafter it is less dependent on identification with roles that social existence offers or presses on it. Clinically, it is sometimes difficult to distinguish between lasting identifications and the social role of ego identity. However, one really should speak of identity only when the sum of all self-representations is involved; a loss of identity is also accompanied by a shakeup and demands a psychic restructuring, while long-lasting role identifications are easily given up and exchanged against others when they no longer offer any advantages.

Many people are unable to identify with the roles offered to them. Their ego has suffered distortions during its development or is the steady locus of such conflicts that the person cannot behave according to the role model offered or cannot identify with this role. The ego of such persons, in fact, has an urgent need for such role identification, in order to retain sufficient stability, but cannot make use of the offering. Every psychiatrist is familiar with the following uncanny consequence of hospitalization: The offer of more and more restricted roles with which even a badly functioning or regressed ego can identify leads to a stabilization as demanded by these role-assigning institutions. Automatic adaptation under such circumstances leads to a result called hospitalism.

No doubt, there are persons who will not identify with any role model offered to them, no matter what kind it is. They are quite capable of behaving according to the dictates of one or another role. However, if the environment demands automatically conforming role behavior, which can be accomplished only by identifying with the total model, they prefer to change their social situation or leave it altogether, in order to oppose the identification offered or to avoid it. In very close or institutionally tightly structured social groups, such individuals become opponents of, or at least alienated from, society. But even if the social situation does not present such concrete disadvantages, the refusal of all role identifications takes a substantial psychic effort. Such individuals do not make life easy for themselves. Their ego renounces a stabilizer that, at least in our society, is more easily built-in than avoided. They decide to do without narcissistic gratification, which would automatically flow toward them through role identification. Their ego must, therefore, continue to work through various conflicts with both inner and outer authorities, without guarantee of the outcome, without any protection against upsetting its balance, but in danger of forfeiting gratification without compensation.

It is not clear which developmental steps of early childhood bring about such a character formation; there probably are very different constellations leading to the same result. Certainly all such persons have a strong ego identity into which further role models simply do not fit and into which nothing can be integrated that does not totally harmonize with it. Furthermore, one has the impression that the ego of such persons has somehow decided to follow the internalized ego ideal rather than to follow the demands of the external environment. Such an inner autonomy and external independence, which confronts all conflicts openly even in the face of danger, corresponds to the emancipatory aim of a psychoanalysis. However, we frequently see in therapeutic as well as in training analyses that the achieved relative ego autonomy may be sufficient for entering further identifications with the role not totally unconsciously, but that this autonomy alone is not a sufficient basis for refusing role identifications altogether.

SPECIAL CONSEQUENCES

Adulthood sees very deep psychological changes that are triggered by the environment. Psychoanalysis has paid little attention to them. They frequently do not run such a dramatic and life-determining course as the discovery of one's identity, which has been described by Erikson (1959) as the last step in the development at the end of adolescence, as adaptation to new tasks, and as inner restructuring. It appears, however, that later restructuring, which brings about great inner conflicts and a "new edition" of childhood conflicts, is introduced by changes in the role identifications. A role must be given up because of external circumstances. The ego loses its stability; narcissistic gratification, which the role had presented, is lost. Either new identifications are found or the ego must cope with the emerging conflicts without this support, which sometimes is successful only at the price of neurotic symptom formation. Conversely, diminished cathexis of the self and its subsequent impoverishment can force the ego to give up a role that demands much self-esteem, phallic exhibition, or similar qualities. Then the same process occurs.

The transformation of a human being through the assumption of power is an old psychological problem, which is clarified by close observation of role identification. It is true that only rarely will persons in positions of high political or economic power allow themselves to be observed psychoanalytically. But, given sufficient knowledge of the social relationships, one can delineate the position of power as a role assignment of those who outwardly seem to have little power, and make them conscious of it. It is obvious how little object-related satisfaction adheres to such roles and that the acting out and enjoyment of aggression appears only as a secondary gain. The narcissistic gain in self-cathexis—whether originating from the self-image, from the real or imagined admiration by less powerful individuals, or from the identification with more powerful persons in similar social positions—compensates for the effort necessary to reach this position of power and retain it. Many social roles confer power, but very few concrete material advantages. Still, people cling to such roles with great effort, because the narcissistic gain stems from the exercise of power. I could observe in several analysands that the narcissistic supply through the identification with a powerful role had replaced object-related ties step by step. In this sense, they followed the banal thesis that "power produces a lust for more power."

IN THE THERAPEUTIC ANALYSIS

During the analysis, I pay careful attention to the roles assigned to analysands and how far they identify with those roles. Sometimes the role identification can be observed easily, as in the earlier-mentioned young man who, as the son of a distinguished family, made a hired servant out of his woman analyst. The narcissistic satisfaction stemming from the aggressive or masochistic acting out of caste or class interests is easily overlooked if the analysand and the analyst belong to the same social layer and if the therapist does not have a special capacity to recognize and see through these social forces. As soon as the analysand is fully identified with his class role, the view of the analyst, who relies on the psychic reality of his patient, usually only reaches the line drawn by his patient's reality testing. To remain on the path of the analytic process, however, he must direct his constant attention beyond both lines of demarcation, that between conscious and unconscious and that between the conscious and unperceived social realities of the analysand.

When interpreting the identification with a role, it is wise to remember the old technical rule: to interpret regressive defense mechanisms first and only later on progressive ones, which give the ego a certain strength. Similarly, only after there is less readiness to regress and there is no further danger of unmanageable anxiety should one interpret role identifications that allow the ego more room to function and are linked with drive gratifications. Thereafter, however, the interpretation of identification with the role is absolutely necessary in order to make unconscious conflicts, which are far-reaching determinants of social behavior, accessible to a conscious working through.

Unconscious role identifications gain special importance at the beginning and at the end of analyses. The role of the patient can be conceived in such a way that the patient complains only about physical ailments to the physician, who is supposed to cure them. If one wanted to interpret this behavior during the analysis as resistance, then one would also have to guess what is being defended against with these complaints about physical frailties. It is not unusual to find that nothing has been defended against, that the temporary role identification was only intended to stabilize and strengthen the ego to enable it to stand up to fears and other burdens.

A student of architecture with whom I had started on a course of analytically oriented psychotherapy complained to me only about headaches. When I pointed out to him how he identified with the traditional role of a patient, he replied: "You, too, are wearing a white doctor's coat." (It was a hot summer's day, and I was wearing jeans and a shirt with an open collar.) During the course of the psychotherapy, which, with some interruption, lasted for two years, there was no further talk of headaches. This example shows us that, as frequently happens, a second "role assigning" person is also affected by this identification.

At the end of an analysis, identification with a newly attained social role sometimes simulates a cure, or at least a good narcissistic restitution. Ferenczi (1927) in his time and later Grunberger (1957) have described this restitution as characteristic for a resolution of childhood conflicts and for the "natural" end of the analysis. If the analyst realizes the true circumstances, he can easily bring the role identification into consciousness, without endangering the newly achieved social position. Then the analysis of those feelings can begin which the ego, now stronger by virtue of role identification through its defenses, had kept far away from consciousness.

ADAPTATION MECHANISMS AND "NARCISSISTIC" DISORDERS

The mechanisms of adaptation are able to accomplish much for the ego if it is to continue to be able to function under interfering or changing conditions of the outer environment. They assist the autonomy of the ego (Rapaport, 1951, 1957) but have a tendency to restrict independency from the environment. If they do function, the ego is discharged from drive conflicts, there is less anxiety, and the ego as a whole is stabilized. However, the environment interferes with its structure in a manner that cannot be controlled by the ego and that determines important ego functions.

Adaptation mechanisms cannot suffice in the adult whose psychic development has not led to a degree of socialization in which he finds himself in disagreement with his social environment. This does not happen only during transplantation to another cultural climate as in immigration; a change in the social situation (such as impoverishment, proletarization, or upward mobility) produces the same effect. Innumerable individuals are affected if the macrosociety changes rapidly, as in political upheavals, economic crises, urbanization, technological or power-related political and bureaucratic reorganizations of society. Because these mechanisms no longer relieve the ego, a deep restructuring of the person follows. Elsewhere (1978) I have expressed the suspicion that such "alienating" situations frequently permit neurotic fixations to become manifest, when they might otherwise have remained latent.

In the last few years, there have been assumptions from various sides that "narcissistic" personality disorders increasingly appear in Western industrialized countries (Kohut, 1971). We suspect that this is traceable less to changes in family structures or early childhood education, than to failure to adapt in an alienated social situation. By this I mean that although the ego has formed adaptation mechanisms to insure a sufficiently functional area under other circumstances, diminished gratifications cause regression or retreat to narcissistic modes of experience. Rapaport (1951, 1957) demonstrated convincingly that the ego not only is dependent on a sufficient delivery of drive energy from the id to retain a relative autonomy, which is diminished when the defense organization is neurotically frozen or distorted, but also needs a social environment in which it can function, which accepts it and nourishes it. In some analyses, I have found that the environment, when measured by the results of psychic development and socialization, was too frustrating, so that seemingly narcissistic personality disorders came about. Social adaptation was no longer successful. A narcissistic retreat ensued. This retreat did correspond to a regression to narcissistic modes of experiences of early childhood, but it could be relatively easily reversed as soon as active changes of the social situation or even a conscious confrontation with it became possible.[9]

In modern industrial society, socialization of the human being reaches a "higher" level, in the sense that the number of roles to be assumed, and the inevitability of their assignment, increases. Economic developments and crises entail a frequent and unpredictable change in the offering of roles. These conditions apparently lead to the ego's identification with an ever increasing number of roles that, in part, contradict each other. Thus, object-related satisfactions and conflicts retreat, are caught up by the role-identified ego in a compensatory way, and are replaced by narcissistic satisfactions and conflicts. In other words, the balance between narcissistic aggressive annd libidinous needs and object-related ones is disturbed; a shift ensues in favor of the narcissistic ones. The progressive marketization of the individual forces the ego to exchange the pleasurable gain of object-related wish fulfillment for narcissistic premiums, which are more easily compatible with the offered role identifications.

In principle, these are reversible processes. During analyses, one discovers repeatedly that once "scar tissue" has formed over narcissistic injuries, an improved self-image, resultant from cathexis of the self without conflict, makes automatic role identifications unnecessary and that seemingly lost object-related cathexes reappear.

But such a development is contrary to the social situation. Propaganda and advertising transmitted by mass media and the public consensus and directed by the marketplace (as well as by the morality of the so-called material compulsions) have the real aim of mobilizing narcissistic needs and offering means of narcissistic gratification (such as a new car for a narcissistic lack).[10]

Against propaganda and offers of that kind, the ego is relatively defenseless. Since no concrete opponent is available, it can neither

---

9. I would speak of "genuine" narcissistic neuroses if developmental disturbances of childhood weighed more heavily and if eternal life situations figured little.

10. Here I follow a hint from Pier Francesco Galli, Bologna (personal communication).

organize attacks against him (in the service of the ego) nor easily renounce its adapted formation: It would first be thoroughly shaken and confronted with inner conflicts and the frustration of object-related wishes. Frequently it happens that further narcissistic satisfactions are sought to balance the deficit of gratification. This may occur through new or strengthened role identification, which can then no longer be given up.

If one follows these considerations, one comes to the conclusion that the ever more frequent narcissistic personality disorders are structured like perversions (Morgenthaler, 1974). Defects in the cathexis of the self and of objects are compensated by hypercathexis of narcissistic needs. Such cathexes are necessary for the retention of some ability to function; without them, the ego would lose its stability. Since the social situation favors a narcissistic compensation of the frustrated ego and of the defective self, it is doubtful whether such narcissistic personality disorders may still be called pathological. Measured against a greater flexibility and tolerance of the ego for drive demands and an assumed harmony between narcissistic and object-related needs, we are dealing with serious disturbances. Measured against the obligatory integration into the managed world of technology, production, and capital, "narcissistic" developments are successful solutions that the ego has achieved after having become identical with its roles.

Poets of our time have described such conditions quite impressively. Bertold Brecht (1921) in his "In the Jungle of the Cities," shows a man who no longer can find anyone with whom he can experience anything, not even an opponent to fight, if no happier relationship is possible, and who despairs because of it. Samuel Beckett's (1954) Godot, for whom everyone is waiting, does not arrive; the waiting is filled by manifestations of narcissistic power. In Boris Vian's (1959) "Les Batisseurs d'Empire" no human being is expected any longer. Living space, represented by the meager apartment of the protagonist, becomes tighter, uninhabitable. At the end of each act, the threatened individual gives Schmuertz, a lifeless puppet standing in a corner, a tremendous slap in the face and then withdraws to the floor above by way of an evernarrowing circular staircase into an apartment exactly like the one below, again with a Schmuertz in the corner. This he does three times, in three acts. One does not know whether this flight upwards, step by step, will still continue after the play is over. Perhaps no way out is left.

In an extremely alienated social situation, possibilities of adaptation no longer work. Psychological collapse ensues; the dark visions of these poets realistically describe the effect of unbearable life situations on the soul. In psychoanalysis we try to make it possible for the ego to renounce its unconsciously functioning adaptation mechanisms, so that it becomes capable of actively changing its social situation. To strive actively to change unbearable social conditions is not only an ethical imperative or consequence of a political decision; this fight for a better life is also an irreplaceable function of the ego.

Freud, at the beginning of his psychoanalytic studies, took as his starting point the concept that living conditions are the producers of neuroses and that the therapist's task is to enable the patient to confront his environment actively. He wrote in 1895:

> No doubt, fate would find it easier than I do to relieve you of your illness, but you will be able to convince yourself that much will be gained if we succeed in transforming your hysterical misery into common unhappiness. With a mental life that has been restored to health, you will be better armed against that unhappiness [Breuer and Freud, 1893–1895, p. 305].

BIBLIOGRAPHY

BECKETT, S. (1954). *Waiting for Godot*. New York: Grove Press.
BOYER, L. B. (1983). Analytic experiences in working with regressed patients. In *Technical Factors in the Treatment of the Seriously Disturbed Patient*, eds. P. L. Giovacchini and L. B. Boyer. New York: Aronson, pp. 65–106.
BRECHT, B. (1921). *Im Dickicht der Städte*. Frankfurt a. M.: Surkamp.
BREUER, J., & FREUD, S. (1893–1895). The psychotherapy of hysteria. Studies in hysteria. *Standard Edition*, 2:255–305. London: Hogarth Press, 1955.
ERIKSON, E. H. (1950). *Childhood and Society*. New York: Norton.
———(1959). Identity and the life cycle. *Psychological Issues*, Mongr. No. 1. New York: International Universities Press.
FEDERN, P. (1936). Narcissism in the structure of the ego. In *Ego Psychology and the Psychoses*, ed. E. Weiss. New York: Basic Books, 1952, pp. 38–59.
FENICHEL, O. (1945). *The Psychoanalytic Theory of Neurosis*. London: Routledge & Kegan Paul.
FERENCZI, S. (1927). The problem of the termination of the analysis. *Final Contributions to the Problems and Methods of Psychoanalysis*, Vol. 3. New York: Basic Books, 1955, pp. 77–86.
———(1931). Aphoristisches zum Thema Totsein-Weibsen. *Bausteine zur Psychoanalyse*, Vol. 4. Bern: Huber, 1964.
FREUD, A. (1936). *The Ego and the Mechanisms of Defense*. New York: International Universities Press, 1946.
———(1965). *Normality and Pathology in Childhood*. New York: International Universities Press.
FREUD, S. (1913). Totem and taboo. *Standard Edition*, 13:1–164. London: Hogarth Press, 1955.
———(1921). Group psychology and the analysis of the ego. *Standard Edition*, 18:67–144. London: Hogarth Press, 1955.

FROMM-REICHMANN, F., & MORENO, J. L., eds. (1956). *Progress in Psychotherapy*. New York: Grune & Stratton.

GROTSTEIN, J. G. (1982). *Splitting and Projective Identification*. New York: Aronson.

HARTMANN, H. (1939). *Ego Psychology and the Problem of Adaptation*. New York: International Universities Press, 1958.

————(1953). Contribution to the metapsychology of schizophrenia. In *Essays on Ego Psychology: Selected Problems in Psychoanalytic Theory*. New York: International Universities Press, 1964, pp. 182–206.

————(1955). Notes on the theory of sublimation. *The Psychoanalytic Study of the Child*, 10:7–29. New York: International Universities Press.

LE COULTRE, R. (1976). Ichspaltung als zentrale neuroseerscheinung. *Psyche*, 24:405–422.

MAHLER, M. S. (1975). *The Psychological Birth of the Human Infant*. London: Hutchinson.

MENZIES, I. (undated). The Functioning of Social Systems as a Defense Against Anxiety. Tavistock Pamphlet No. 3. London: Tavistock.

MORGENTHALER, F. (1974). Die Stellung der Perversions in Metapsychologie und Technik. *Psyche*, 28:1077–1098.

MURPHY, H. B. M. (1974). Theories of youth unrest in cross cultural perspective. *Australian and New Zealand J. Psychiat.*, 8:31–40.

OGDEN, T. H. (1982). *Projective Identification and Psychoanalytic Technique*. New York: Aronson.

PARIN, P. (1978). *Der Widerspruch im Subjekt. Ethnopsychoanalytische Studien*. Frankfurt A. M.: Surkamp.

———— Morgenthaler, F., & Parin-Mattèy, G. (1963). *Die Weisse denken zuviel. Psychoanalytische Untersuchung bei den Dogon in West-Afrika*. Zurich: Atlantis & Munich: Kindler.

———— ———— ————(1971). *Fear Thy Neighbor as Thyself. Psychoanalysis and Society Among the Anyi of West Africa*. Chico, CA: University Press, 1980.

POLLOCK, G. W. (1972). On mourning and anniversaries. The relationship of culturally constituted defensive systems to intrapsychic adaptive processes. *Israel Annals of Psychiatry and Related Disciplines*, 10:9–40.

RAPAPORT, D. (1951). The autonomy of the ego. In *The Collected Papers of David Rapaport*, ed. M. Gill. New York: Basic Books, 1967, pp. 357–367.

————(1957). The theory of ego autonomy: a generalization. In *The Collected Papers of David Rapaport*, ed. M. Gill. New York: Basic Books, 1967, pp. 722–744.

RICHTER, H. E. (1976). *Fluchten oder Standhalten*. Reinbeck: Rowohlt.

SANDLER, J. (1964/65). Zum Begriff des Über-Ichs. *Psyche*, 17:721–743 and 812–828.

————(1976). The Importance of Countertransference in Current Psychoanalytic Practice. Published as Gegenübertragung und bereitschaft zur Rollenübernahme. *Psyche*, 30:297–305, 1976.

SARTRE, J. P. (1953). *Existential Psychoanalysis*. New York: Philosophical Library.

SPITZ, R. (1965). *The First Year of Life*. New York: International Universities Press.

STIERLIN, H. (1975). *Von der Psychoanalyse zur Familientherapie*. Stuttgart: Klett.

STIRNER, M. (pseudonym for Johann Kaspar Schmidt) (1845). *The Ego and His Own*. Trans. S. T. Hyington. New York: B. R. Tucker, 1907.

VIAN, B. (1959). *Les bâtisseurs d'empire*. Charleville: originale du Collège de Pataphysique.

5

Male Adolescent Initiation Rituals: Whiting's Hypothesis Revisited

LEORA N. ROSEN

It is now more than a quarter of a century since the first publication of Whiting, Kluckhorn, and Anthony's (1958) hypothesis concerning the relationship between harsh puberty rites and mother–infant sleeping arrangements. Historically speaking, it was a landmark in the development of attempts to validate psychoanalytic theory cross-culturally. During the subsequent two decades, owing to a changing theoretical orientation, few anthropologists tried to build on Whiting's theory or to explore his insights any further. It became increasingly unacceptable to draw on facts or theories about the psychology of the individual to explain social phenomena; the former were considered irrelevant to the understanding of the latter (see Leach, 1959). In recent years, however, a new generation of anthropologists has begun to revive interest in psychodynamic issues and in the importance of individual psychology to the understanding of social and cultural phenomena (Tuzin, 1980; Herdt, 1981, 1982). It therefore seems appropriate at this time to reexamine Whiting's hypothesis and consider its current usefulness in providing a theoretical link between the psychological and the social.

Attempts to explain social facts in terms of psychoanalytic theory began with the publication of *Totem and Taboo,* wherein Freud (1913) sought to explain the origins of culture through his theory of the primal parricide. Even at that time, anthropologists described as unacceptable "the crude transfer of a novel, one-sided method, of psychological investigation of the individual to social phenomena" (Boas, 1920, p. 289). Aspects of Freud's theory were nevertheless intriguing, and the debate that ensued immediately following the publication of *Totem and Taboo* centered on the validity of Freud's libido theory and particularly the Oedipus complex as the postulated cornerstone of family relationships and possibly of human culture itself (Jones, 1925; Malinowski,

1927). Though Malinowski argued against the universality of the Oedipus complex, later anthropologists have disagreed with his conclusions—specifically those based on evidence drawn from Trobriand society (e.g., Parsons, 1964; Spiro, 1982).

Scholars of the 1930s and 1940s continued to grapple with the problem of seeking universal psychodynamic processes in diverse cultures. Roheim (1932, 1945, 1949, 1950), who adhered most closely to Freud's original theories, has been criticized for what Harris (1968) termed his "obsessional search" for oedipal symbols in various aspects of primitive cultures.

It was Kardiner (1939) who moved furthest away from Freud's original theory, dispensing with its instinctual aspects and emphasizing psychocultural adaptation. Kardiner postulated that members of a given culture develop certain common personality characteristics by adapting to specific sets of environmental conditions. These common characteristics he referred to as "basic personality," which is shaped in childhood by a set of childrearing practices within the context of a specific family organization. Together these comprise "primary institutions." Kardiner also postulated the existence of "secondary institutions," which develop to satisfy the needs and tensions created by the primary institutions and typically comprise systems of religion, ritual and taboo (p. 476).

Whiting (1964; Whiting et al., 1964) adopted Kardiner's scheme and sought to demonstrate cross-culturally a relationship between specific types of primary institutions (child-rearing practices) and secondary institutions (ritual), relating both to environmental and ecological factors. Whiting and his colleagues (1958) also modified Freud's oedipal theory, hypothesizing that oedipal rivalry is not uniform throughout all cultures and that it may be strong or weak depending on the specific relationship between father, mother, and son. In societies where infants sleep exclusively with their mothers for prolonged periods, there is likely to be a greater dependency of sons on their mothers and a correspondingly greater rivalry between father and son. He postulated further that severe male puberty rites would be found in those societies wherein a prolonged nursing period resulted in particularly intense dependency of sons on their mothers and, consequently, greater hostility toward the father. If, in addition, there is a long postpartum taboo on intercourse, the mother–child relationship is also likely to be exclusive, which would further intensify father–son rivalry and hostility. The psychological function of initiation rites, according to Whiting, is to prevent boys from openly rebelling against parental authority and making incestuous advances toward their mothers at a time when physical maturity would make such behavior socially disruptive. He added that even a moderate or weak degree of emotional dependence on the mother and rivalry with the father will be dangerous at adolescence if the father does not exercise authority over his son in childhood (pp. 369–370).

While it is true that most of the 56 societies he examined conformed to this pattern, there were several that did not. Among the Trobriand Islanders, for example, the combination of a long postpartum taboo, a long exclusive mother–son relationship and lack of disciplinary authority of the father are factors that should lead to harsh puberty rits, but do not. Whiting (p. 366) explained the absence of these rites in Trobriand society by postulating that a change of residence at adolescence serves the same function as puberty rites, establishing male authority and breaking the bond with the mother. By contrast, the absence of rites among the patrilineal Tallensi, who also have a long postpartum taboo, is explained by the fact that open and conscious hostility between father and son is an accepted part of Tallensi life and therefore presumably does not require ritual expression (p. 368).

Whiting was criticized largely on methodological grounds. A major problem seemed to be the questionable accuracy of some of his sources (Norbeck et al., 1962). Another problem was his narrow focus on certain sets of variables out of a wide range of possible variables, and the fact that his type of survey deals only with fragments of culture wrenched out of context (Norbeck et al., 1962; Harris, 1968, p. 452). Thus, examining mother–infant sleeping arrangements without taking into account other aspects of the mother–child relationship, or focusing on certain features of puberty rites to the exclusion of others, may have resulted in only a partial understanding of the interrelationship between ritual and childrearing. If Whiting had adopted a more holistic approach—involving an in-depth examination of puberty rites in their specific context—he might not have had the problem of creating special categories for each exception to the rule.

A few years after the first publication of his hypothesis, Whiting moved away from his original neo-Freudian position to a learning/socialization model (Burton and Whiting, 1961). According to this view, the boy's emotional dependence on the mother leads to identification with her, and initiation is seen as a way of dealing with the problem of cross-sex identity conflict. A further development took place a few years later with the accumulation of a large body of data from several independent studies establishing a link between prolonged infant nursing, severe puberty rites, polygyny, and patrilocality (Whiting, 1964). All this was further linked to tropical climate and kwashiorkor, a disease associated with protein deficiency during child-hood. Whiting explained this chain of correlations as follows: Protein deficient tropical diets place a premium on prolonged lactation for maintaining an infant's protein intake during a critical period of development. Interruption of lactation by the demands of a second infant is prevented by a prolonged postpartum taboo on intercourse, which places a premium on a second wife. The husband in a polygynous household sleeps separately from his wives; hence exclusive mother–infant sleeping arrangements is the byproduct. Polygyny makes patrilo-cality more convenient and patrilocality is associated with patriliny. With a strong patrilineal/patrilocal emphasis, boys who have spent prolonged periods with a nursing mother are subject to intense pressure to assume a normative male role identity. The function of initiation rites is to facilitate the adoption of this identity (Whiting, 1964).

In a later cross-cultural study, Whiting and Whiting (1975) explained the trait of masculine hyperaggressiveness as a psychological mechanism for dealing with the cross-sex identity conflict resulting from sons' being reared in exclusive mother–child households. They describe this pattern as the indirect though adaptive consequence of certain environmental factors, such as the need for men to be prepared for war and agricultural practices that make polygyny profitable. Since puberty rites are not mentioned anywhere in this paper, their relationship to the development of masculine hyperaggressiveness is not addressed. We are left wondering whether hyperaggressiveness is a "natural," "automatic" response to cross-sex identity conflict or whether it must be imposed through ritual mechanisms.

Whiting's shift from a psychodynamic to a technoenvironmental approach was consistent with the waning interest at that time in psychodynamic issues in anthropology. The growing emphasis on the Durkheimian sociological approach, and on environmental determinism, received its most extreme expression in Harris's writing (1968, 1979). In Harris's (1979) modification of Whiting's scheme, ecological factors play an even more central role: Ecological stress (protein deficiency—which necessitates prolonged nursing and a postpartum taboo on intercourse—is also regarded as responsible for the presence of warfare, and, consequently, for male superordination and patrilocality, all of which require special aggression training for males (i.e., harsh puberty rites). In Harris's view, the mother–infant relationship is only spuriously related to harsh puberty rites; in fact both phenomena are caused by ecological stress (1979, p. 295–296). Harris sees no conflict in the fact that women train infants and small children. Such conflict would exist, he says, only if women did not treat little boys and girls differently. According to Harris's view, then, gender identity is simply a result of a conditioning process in which identification with adult objects plays no part.

Langness (1974), like Harris, emphasized ecology in his interpretation of initiation cults, but he also included a psychodynamic perspective. Building on the theories of Murphy (1959) and Allen (1967), Langness proposed that in a social order in which male loyalty to fellow males is the foundation for warfare and the solidarity of the local group, and in which male prestige quests depend on the appropriation of women's labor by men, ties with women pose the greatest threat to male solidarity both from within and without. If left unchecked, the bond between young men and their wives could divide men from one another and align them with their affines, who could be enemies of the group. Male initiation cults serve to break the bond with the mother and establish male dominance over women as well as solidarity among residential males.

Although male cultism in New Guinea has been linked in many studies to the presence of warfare, Keesing (1982) cautions against basing explanations on the "Unseen Hand of Ecological Wisdom," which treats the human response to environmental exigencies as reactive rather than creative and which furthermore does not account for why some responses are actually maladaptive (pp. 17–24). Keesing's criticism is directed against partial modes of interpretation that analyze a set of customs either as functionally interlocking elements or as adaptations to ecological circumstances or manifestations of innate cognitive structures. Not only have anthropologists failed to put these partial modes of explanation together, but they have also dealt with the problem of personality and subjective experience by ignoring them (pp. 2–3). This is particularly true of those anthropologists during the last two or three decades who tended to treat psychodynamic issues as, at best, irrelevant to the understanding of social realities (cf. Leach, 1959).

In all fairness it must be stated that many of the objections of anthropologists to the use of psychological explanations were in response to the early, naive, psychodynamic reductionist interpretations propounded by certain scholars—notably Roheim—who treated institutionalized ritual and myth as if they were productions of the individual human psyche (Kracke, 1979). Whereas in general anthropologists studying ritual tended to shy away from psychological explanations, there have been a couple of exceptions. Murphy (1959) pointed out that although not all societies allow for the expression of unconscious psychological conflict in ritual form, those that do may have special characteristics. Turner (1970, p. 46) argued that symbols have a spectrum of meanings ranging from the purely social to the deeply unconscious.

The beginning of the 1980s seems to have marked a changing attitude toward psychodynamic issues in anthropology, with the emergence of a new generation of anthropologist who are showing a renewed interest in the psychological perspective of ritual particularly with regard to the study of initiation cults (Barry and Schlegal, 1980; Crapanzano, 1980; Herdt, 1981, 1982; Tuzin, 1980, 1982; Keesing, 1982; Poole, 1982).

In a cross-cultural study of 182 societies, Barry and Schlegal (1980) concluded that adolescent initiation is part of the socialization process, helping to ameliorate biological discontinuity in the transition from childhood to adulthood. Herdt (1981) similarly emphasizes the psychological impact of ritual practices and procedures on young boys undergoing the arduous and lengthy induction into manhood among the Sambia of New Guinea. He regards initiation ritual as part of the actual process of gender identity formation—a task that was not fully accomplished through child-training methods during infancy and early childhood. Ritual, in fact, eradicates unacceptable personality traits and behaviors acquired during that time, "Like a primitive form of behavior surgery" (p. 305). Herdt suggests a reformulation and expansion of Whiting's hypothesis, taking into account theoretical developments in areas such as infant dependency and gender identity. In addition he draws attention to significant features of initiation ritual that Whiting does not deal with, notably, that in many tribes initiation takes place before puberty and the presence of ritual secrecy and ritual homosexual contacts (pp. 308–318).

It might be useful, therefore, at this time to critically reexamine Whiting's hypothesis with some of these issues in mind. Also of interest is Whiting's shift from a neo-Freudian to a learning theory position over the course of a few years and in light of additional information. An important question here is whether this shift was really justified in terms of providing a better interpretation of the facts or whether the same issues could have been more adequately explained by a more subtle application of psychodynamic theory.

For the purposes of this analysis, I will compare two societies that have male adolescent initiation rituals that include circumcision but are very different with regard to sociopolitical and economic organization. They are the Aranda of Central Australia and the Ndembu of Zambia in Southern Africa. I shall begin by outlining some important background features of these two societies, particularly those which Whiting regarded as significant to an understanding of initiation ritual.

PATRILOCALITY AND SOCIOECONOMIC ORGANIZATION

The Aranda

The Aranda are a hunter-gatherer tribe of the inhospitable central Australian desert. Even under the best of circumstances, their existence is extremely precarious with no guaranteed food supply for most of the year. Rights to food and other resources (particularly water) in a given area are vested in the local clan, which is patrilineal, patrilocal, and exogamous (Elkin, 1935, pp. 76–80).

Patriliny for the Aranda and other Aboriginal tribes involves an intimate, mystical bond between a group of male agnates and the territory they inhabit, sometimes referred to in the literature as "ancestral estates." These estates are the homes not only of living clan members but also of ancestral spirits that dwell in special spirit centers awaiting reincarnation. The location of these centers may be marked by a heap of stones, waterholes, or other natural objects; the centers are believed to be the places where culture heroes stopped to rest or visit during the course of their mythological journeys (pp. 176–177; Strehlow, 1968, pp. 88–89). Furthermore, the actual paths followed by these heroes during the course of their travels have a special importance in cult life. It is significant that ancestral paths traverse the territories of different clans and tribes and, in doing so, bind these local groups by obligations of mutual protection and hospitality. The emphasis on paths in South and Central Australia has been linked to the dry nature of the country and the scarcity of readily accessible water, since for most of the year the natives are not free to roam too far from the shortest routes between two available sources of water. The demarcation of ancestral territories has also been linked to the availability of food resources, since there is often no precise claim to ownership of land in which there are few resources, resulting in a vague definition of tribal boundaries (Elkin, 1935, p. 177). In other words, the spiritual tie between the Aborigines and their patrilineal clans and ancestral lands has strong economic underpinnings.

The precarious nature of existence among the Aborigines necessitated the development of social mechanisms for promoting intergroup cooperation. Included among these mechanisms are totemic cults, the intertribal nature of sacred paths, and the subsection system. This system, which is superimposed on that of local patrilineal clans, is based on the maternal tie. Though mother and child do not belong to the same subsection, a mother's membership in a particular subsection will determine her child's placement in one of the other seven in the tribe. The main role of the subsection system is to summarize kinship relationships and regulate marriage choices and relationships at inter-tribal gatherings (p. 138). The larger and more complex the subsection system, the greater the number of categories of women who are forbidden in marriage. This means that men must go far beyond the local group to seek wives, thus extending ties of kinship and mutual obligation over a wide area.

Aboriginal social structure nevertheless emphasizes the father–son relationship above all others. Unlike the mother–child relationship, which is thought of as having a purely biological basis, this relationship is believed to have a spiritual basis. The Aborgines believe that a woman becomes pregnant when the spirit of one of her husband's ancestors enters her body in order to be reincarnated. This moment is identified by a sudden stab of pain, which is regarded as the first sign of pregnancy. Hiatt (1971) has suggested that although the Aborigines certainly recognize the physiological role of the father in procreation, they regard this aspect as being of minor importance in comparison with the spiritual nature of the father–son bond. Furthermore, a son is believed to be a reincarnation of his father's patrilineal great-great-great-grandfather, which means that a son is his father's own great-great-great-grandfather (Roheim, 1950). This in no way implies, how-ever, an egalitarian relationship between father and son. Aboriginal communities are strongly gerontocratic, power in the local group being firmly vested in male elders, while respect for seniority is entrenched in the value system.

The Ndembu

The Ndembu occupy a well-wooded plateau where they practice a form of subsistence cultivation together with hunting (cf. Turner, 1968a). Cassava, the main subsistence crop, is grown according to the method of shifting cultivation. This involves the clearing of an area of bush, which is then cultivated, producing crops for about four years. After that the land must be left fallow for about 30 years to regenerate. This means that village settlements disband from time to time, and people move on to new areas. The Ndembu, therefore, unlike the Aranda, do not have strong ties to the land.

Cultivated fields are owned by people individually. Most agricultural work is done by women and requires steady and continuous labor and little mobility from place to place. Men's agricultural work, on the other hand, is sporadic, occurring only when land has to be cleared.

For the rest of the time men occupy themselves with hunting, which is associated with high status rather than the need for food. Furthermore, since hunting may take men away from home for days at a time, male economic pursuits are of an individualistic nature and are relatively unstable in time and space.

Since the mother is the more stable influence in a child's environment, in Ndembu society the mother–child tie is given more structural importance than the father–child tie. According to a folktale, matriliny became established when, during an enemy raid, a certain man ran to save his hunting equipment, whereas his wife's first thought was for their child, with whom she fled to a safe place. Later, when a marital separation took place, the wife was granted custody of the child because she had saved his life, whereas the husband's only concern had been for his hunting gear (Turner, 1968a, p. 27).

The father–son tie is, however, not unimportant. Hunting is a highly esteemed male occupation. It is individualistic and competitive in nature, and men take great pride in teaching their secret hunting skills to their sons. Furthermore, although descent is matrilineal, residence after marriage is patrilocal, and children grow up in their fathers' local group. On reaching adulthood, men should leave their fathers' villages and move back to their mothers' villages, where they are subject to the authority of their maternal uncles. Legally, nephews are entitled to succeed their maternal uncles to headmanship. Since villages are not enduring structures, and since people are periodically on the move, it would be difficult to enforce this rule, and in practice people may choose where they want to live. Thus headmen have ample opportunity to compete for power. A man will encourage his sister and her children to come and live in his village, while at the same time trying to win his sons over from their mother's brother. If he is divorced from his wife, this will be difficult, since sons will tend to follow their mothers.

A symbol that often appears in Ndembu ritual is the "milk" tree (mudyi), which when cut exudes a white milky latex. This tree stands for breast milk, the maternal breast, the mother–child bond, matriliny, and tribal custom itself. Turner (1970) writes: "It is as though the infantile experience of breast-feeding were associated with the correct performance of ones duties as an Ndembu tribesman or member of a matrilineage" (p. 19). Therefore, just as the spiritual bond between father and child defines membership of the social group among the Aranda, so the physical bond between mother and child defines this membership among the Ndembu.

Patrilocality and the Male Principle in Sociopolitical Organization

It is evident from the foregoing account that the relative importance of the paternal tie in social organization differs in these two societies and that the difference can, in part, be related to economic factors. It is important to note that despite the subsection system among the Aranda, the paternal tie is still the uncontested basis of sociopolitical organization. By contrast, the conflict between the principles of matrilineal descent and patrilocal residence among the Ndembu has been well documented (Turner, 1968a, 1970).

Whiting (1964) made a global generalization that patrilocality leads to an emphasis on male gender identity. As I have shown, however, patrilocality is not necessarily an indicator of the relative importance of the male principle in sociopolitical organization. This highlights a problem of generalizing about a single principle in a large number of societies. Though it is important to know that a rule exists, it is more important to know how strictly it is observed and what rationale underlies it.

Another global generalization made by Whiting concerned the role of the mother–infant relationship in gender identity formation. With this in mind, we turn again to the Ndembu and the Aranda.

Infant Nutrition and Oedipal Rivalry in the Aranda and Ndembu Family

Both the Ndembu and the Aranda nurse their infants for prolonged periods—approximately two to three years—although nursing often goes on even longer among the Aranda (Berndt and Berndt, 1964, p. 130–131). A major difference between the two societies is the presence of a postpartum taboo on intercourse among the Ndembu and the strict separation of the sexual activities of parents and children. Until a Ndembu child is weaned, he sleeps with his mother and has exclusive access to her while the father sleeps elsewhere. After weaning, however, the father returns to the mother's hut and the child is sent to live with grandparents, because it is thought improper that an older child should share a hut with sexually active parents (Turner, 1968b, p. 245). Grandparents and grandchildren, on the other hand, are permitted to witness one another's sexual activities and may even engage in sex play together. These may not be real,, but classificatory grandparents or cross-cousins. Hence, children in Ndembu society learn about sex from their grandparents, not their parents, owing to the fundamental rule that the sexual activities of parents and children must be kept strictly separate.

Similarly, the Aranda child sleeps with his mother until he is weaned. However, there is no postpartum taboo on intercourse between the parents, who remain sexually active, and the child is not sent to live elsewhere until he is much older. Berndt and Berndt (1964) write that there is very little privacy in an Aboriginal camp, and children often witness the sexual act. In fact, as they get older, this may become an absorbing pastime (p. 134). Aranda parents, Roheim (1932) says, simply wait until they think their children are asleep before proceeding to have intercourse (p. 89).

Because their dwellings are single rooms shared by entire families, it seems likely that the witnessing of parental intercourse is a common childhood experience. Thus, although the Ndembu boy may feel enraged at being superceded by his father at his mother's side, his removal from the parental hut shields him from direct confrontation with the primal scene. It may also be important that this transition occurs before the onset of the oedipal stage of development or in its incipient stages. The Aranda boy, on the other hand, experiences a more direct kind of rivalry with his father over access to his mother, particularly while he is still nursing, which sometimes continues into the oedipal stage of development.

IMPLICATIONS FOR WHITING'S THEORY

Whiting and his associates' (1958) earlier hypothesis was that prolonged and exclusive contact with the mother fosters intense oedipal rivalry between father and son, which is ultimately dealt with through puberty rites. According to Whiting's later hypothesis (Burton and Whiting, 1961; Whiting, 1964) this type of mother–son relationship results in cross-sex identity conflict, which is resolved through puberty rites.

In terms of Whiting's earlier hypothesis, the absence of the postpartum taboo among the Aranda should reduce oedipal rivalry. However, the fact that Aranda children share sleeping quarters with sexually active parents may actually increase it. Therefore, by narrowly focusing on the postpartum taboo alone, Whiting failed to recognize that there may be other aspects of parent–child interaction that could affect the intensity of oedipal rivalry.

Another major conceptual problem with Whiting's first hypothesis is that he does not explain if and how oedipal feelings are resolved. His suggestion that oedipal feelings would actually lead to sons' making

incestuous advances towards their mothers implies that society's incest prohibitions are maintained largely through external restraints.

Whiting never had to address this issue, because he changed his
explanation from the oedipal theory to that of cross-sex identification
(Burton and Whiting, 1961; Whiting, 1964). Yet even with this theory
there are problems explaining those cases which do not fit the model
despite the impressive statistical correlation. Indeed, using classical
oedipal theory, a satisfactory explanation could be found for the
absence of puberty rites among the Tallensi, whereas there is no
reasonable explanation for this using the theory of cross-sex identification. In certain Aboriginal tribes, the absence of the postpartum taboo
and the presence of the father in the household should result in an
absence of puberty rites, yet they have some of the most stringent
puberty rites anywhere in the tribal world.

Whiting's main problem lies in his limited and rather naive conceptualization of the Oedipus complex and its resolution. Though he
moved away from the oedipal theory to one of cross-sex identification,
the latter theory is not incompatible with a psychoanalytic orientation.
Indeed, it has been postulated by more recent psychoanalytic theorists
that the preoedipal boy identifies with his mother (A. Freud, 1936;
Jacobsen, 1964; Blos, 1962, 1979), from whom he must first separate
before he can enter the oedipal stage proper.

THE OEDIPUS COMPLEX, ADOLESCENCE, AND INITIATION

The resolution of the Oedipus complex and the formation of the
superego and enduring identifications are processes that Freud originally associated with childhood. Subsequent theorists, notably Anna
Freud, Edith Jacobson, and Peter Blos, have pointed out that oedipal
conflicts re-emerge at adolescence and must be resolved once again as
part of the process of adult gender identity formation. Jacobson (1964)
writes: "In adolescence sexual maturation leads to a revival of the
oedipal infantile sexual strivings, but now the incestuous sexual and
hostile wishes must finally be relinquished. The superego must once
more enforce the incest taboo, yet must allow for the expression of
mature sexuality" (p. 173). She goes on to say that probably the most
incisive and difficult step is the gradual establishment of enduring
identifications with the parents as sexually active persons, who will
ultimately grant the adolescent the right to engage in sexual and other
adult activities (p. 175).

Blos has also written extensively on the re-emergence of a second oedipal situation during puberty, a developmental process he refers to as the "second individuation process." According to Blos (1979), whereas the first individuation process constitutes the establishment of independence from the concrete physical presence of the mother, the second phase, at puberty, establishes independence from internalized infantile objects (p. 483). Its purpose is psychological weaning and the establishment of extrafamilial love objects. The resolution of infantile conflict during childhood, according to Blos, takes place in two stages. The first stage involves the resolution of the "negative passive oedipal position," when the child still identifies with the mother, while his passive receptive libido is attached to his father (Blos, 1962, p. 26). This view is in accordance with Freud's that boys do not merely have ambivalent attitudes toward their fathers; they also behave like girls, displaying affectionate feminine attitude toward them (Freud, 1923, p. 23). The "positive aggressive" oedipal phase begins, according to Blos, when the boy realizes that the female has no penis. Libidinal drive is now directed toward possessing the mother, and the well-known triangular relationship emerges, in which the father is seen as the son's rival and competitor. For the son, this leads to castration anxiety, which, if appropriately resolved, should lead to identification with the father and a desire to become like him.

The negative oedipal position re-emerges at puberty, when the adolescent attempts to break away from the preoedipal archaic mother, who now represents the castration threat, and move toward the father, from whom he seeks nurturance and protection. This phase is also characterized by homosexual or bisexual libido organization (Blos, 1962, p. 221; 1979, p. 479). Gradually the establishment of a heterosexual orientation leads once more to the emergence of the "positive" phase of the Oedipus complex, in which sexual attraction turns to the mother, and fear and hostility are aimed at the father. The resolution of the positive Oedipus complex is a major developmental task of advanced adolescence and is a prerequisite for progression into adulthood. Blos repeatedly emphasizes the important role played by regression during adolescence. He draws a distinction between regression as a defense mechanism and normative regression, which operates in service of development, following Hartmann's (1939) formulation of "regressive adaptation" and Geleerd's (1961, 1964) view of the adaptational role of regression during adolescence. Essentially, he maintains that it is only through regression at adolescence that residues of infantile trauma, conflict, and fixation can be modified so that ego maturation takes place. Blos (1979) writes:

Ego regression is, for example, to be found in the re-experiencing of traumatic states, of which no childhood was ever wanting. In self-contrived confrontations with miniature editions or proxy representations of the original trauma in real life situations, the ego gradually acquires mastery over prototypical danger situations [p. 155].

It is my contention that rituals performed at adolescence are an institutionalized form of normative regression designed to facilitate this second individuation process. If we examine these rituals carefully, we find that their dramatic components are symbolic reenactments of infantile conflicts and traumas. They are the miniature editions or proxy presentations that Blos refers to. These conflicts will vary from one society to another according to the different kinds of culturally determined childhood experiences. Puberty rites will take these into account, and ritual mechanisms for resolving conflict will be based on two factors: the first is the nature of the childhood conflict situation; the second is the society's ego ideal of adult gender characteristics. I shall return to this point later.

The idea of a parallel between adolescent initiation ritual and the resolution of adolescent conflict is not new. Roheim (1950) went to great lengths to demonstrate that the various stages of Aranda initiation are dramatizations of the stages of adolescent psychological development, including the resolution of oedipal conflicts and superego development. Roheim quotes Anna Freud (1936) who, in her psychology of puberty, characterizes the behavior of adolescents as showing two trends in dealing with id impulses. One is the tendency to self-deprivation or asceticism, whereby the ego tries to inhibit the maturationally reinforced id; the other is to intellectualization. Roheim detected parallel themes in Aboriginal puberty rites. Asceticism is evident in cicitrization and deprivation; intellectualization is evident in the avid acquisition of knowledge of ceremonial life and mythological tradition, as well as hunting techniques (Roheim, 1950, p. 87).

Muensterberger (1961) characterizes the role of adolescent initiation as follows: "Initiation rituals are aimed at helping the new generation attain adult status and prerogatives: in other words, these rites stress the social side of psychosexual developments in young men and women and deal, in a culturally prescribed manner, with both the oedipal rebellion of the adolescents and the ambivalent response of the older generation" (p. 352). Muensterberger goes on to say that the main function of the rites is to substitute identification for antagonism and rivalry toward parents of the same sex. Using the Gusii as an example, he also points to such rites as the separation from the mother and notes the castration symbolism in circumcision. Muensterberger sees the painful aspects of ritual as checking the aggression of the novices, as well as helping the older men and women to express and partially satisfy their hostile impulses (p. 355). Brain (1977) has suggested that puberty rites have a number of psychological functions: helping to establish sexual identity, easing the transition from an asexual to a sexual role, satisfying unconscious envy of the opposite sex, and resolving unconscious conflicts regarding sexuality, incest, excrement, and death.

While many of the parallel symbolisms between initiation rites and adolescent conflict resolution seem self-evident, several important questions need to be addressed. Roheim (1950) dismisses the possibility that the absence of rites among certain tribes indicates the absence of conflicts. However, he does not address the issue of why some people have rites and others do not (see also Schlegal, 1977). Another question relates to the fact that while common themes are often evident in the rituals of various societies, such differences as the presence versus the absence of circumcision must also be accounted for. Some of this variation may correspond to variations in childrearing practices, which would lead to greater or lesser intensities of certain universal conflicts. For example, childrearing in certain societies may involve practices which intensify oedipal rivalry, or which encourage maximum dependency on the mother, in comparison with other societies. If this is the case, then adolescents in these societies may need some assistance—in the form of ritual—in finally resolving these conflicts and progressing into adulthood. But childrearing alone does not account for all the variations in ritual forms. It is perhaps just as important to take into account certain structural principles on which the society is based, and that determine the form that adult roles should take. Does the society dictate that there should be a close bond of cooperation among male agnatic kin or that the relationship among male kinsfolk should be competitive? Is extreme respect and obedience due to elders, or is the system one in which sons can and should break away from their fathers and establish their own independence? Although many of these rules will be learned in childhood, it is now recognized that adolescence is a critical stage of human development, particularly with regard to the formation of gender identity. During initiation, the ritual itself works toward establishing this identity, which may account for the fact that in certain societies so-called puberty rites do not take place at puberty. Rather, initiation may begin during the latency stage, or even during the oedipal stage of childhood, and

continue in successive stages over several years until adult identifications are finally established (Herdt, 1981). Initiation means that the
individual's psychological development is not left to chance. A very
specific outcome is ensured through the manipulation of experiences
involving well-known conflict situations. While initiation may be seen
as a kind of conditioning, it cannot be understood through a learning-
theory model, which does not explain the complex symbolism of
circumcision, subincision, the imitation of female biological functions
by men, and homosexuality and bisexuality. In the following sections, I
shall attempt to identify some of the developmental processes that take
place during initiation, with reference to the Aranda and the Ndembu.

Adolescent Initiation: Its Function and Symbolism with Reference to
the Aranda and the Ndembu

Both Aranda and Ndembu initiation can be said to exhibit roughly
the three stages that Van Gennep (1960) first identified as being
characteristic of rites of passage. These are: 1) Rites of separation, in
which the novice's old object ties are severed; 2) a liminal period, in
which new social identifications are formed and the novice is prepared
for the assumption of a new status and responsibilities; and 3) rites of
return, in which the novice is returned to society with his or her newly
conferred status and role. These stages are not necessarily always
marked by a single distinct ceremony. Each may involve several
ceremonies or ritual procedures extending over several years. Spencer
and Gillen (1899, pp. 214–272) described Aranda initiation as exhibiting
four phases. The first marks the occasion when a boy is told that he
must forsake the collective company of women and children and
instead join the men; this phase takes place between the ages of ten and
twelve. Second, several years later, he is circumcised; and third,
subincised. In the final phase, full adult status is conferred on him.
    Among the Ndembu, the entire sequence of initiation takes about a
year and involves the participation of a large group of boys, who
experience the entire process together. Among the Aranda, boys
undergo initiation either individually or in pairs (Elkin, 1935, p. 207).
My purpose here is not to document the long and complex ritual
sequences others have dealt with comprehensively (Roheim, 1945,
1950; Spencer and Gillen, 1927; Turner, 1968b, 1970), but rather to
draw attention to categories of symbolism that prominently unite these
rituals. These themes are: 1) castration symbolism, 2) homosexual and
transsexual symbolism, and 3) secrecy themes.

Castration Symbolism

The association between circumcision and castration is evident in both societies. Among the Ndembu, songs sung at circumcision make open reference to castration; in Aranda mythology, circumcision originated from an earlier rite that involved castration. There are some notable differences, however, between these two societies in the way the rites are performed.

In both societies, circumcisers are represented as terrifying figures who come to "kill" and "devour" the novices. Ndembu circumcisers merely threaten the novices, whereas among the Aranda they may actually bite the novices on the head and draw blood. Ndembu circumcisers are highly skilled specialists who have undergone a long apprenticeship and are expected to operate with speed and dexterity. It is said that at one time a boy's father would stand behind the circumciser with an axe, ready to wound him if he made a mistake during the operation. Ndembu boys are even legitimately entitled to beat the circumcisers after the operation—if the circumcisers dare to come near them. Among the Aranda, however, the circumciser is the boy's future father-in-law and thus comes much closer to representing a father figure.

Each Aranda boy is circumcised in a separate ceremony. The most important relationship emphasized throughout the ritual is that between the boy and his elders, toward whom he owes complete obedience. If the novice falls to the ground during the ceremony, the elders may beat him till he bleeds. Among the Ndembu, on the other hand, boys are circumcised in groups, and there is considerably less emphasis on the authority of elders. Equality and competitiveness among the participants is evident throughout the ritual, as is some expression of aggression toward authority figures. Symbols and symbolic actions in Aranda initiation more closely approximate the actual castration threat than do those in Ndembu ritual, which are more obscure. There is, for example, more emphasis on pain and mutilation in Aranda circumcision. Furthermore, in addition to circumcision, the Aranda have a subsequent ceremony involving subincision—an operation in which the urethra is slit up to the scrotum.

Even myths about circumcision are more brutal among the Aranda—who believe that in mythical times the foreskin was burned off and later bitten off, until, eventually, knives were invented. According to Ndembu myth, on the other hand, circumcision was invented when a boy was trying to follow his mother into a field and was "accidentally

circumcised by a blade of grass" (Turner, 1970, p. 153). The incest
theme suggested in this myth is also evident during initiation. Songs are
sung during which the Ndembu mother is referred to as "forbidden
fruit." Among the Aranda, during the subincision ritual, novices are
actually accused of sleeping with their mother and mother-in-law. It
may seem that the greater emphasis on castration symbolism among
the Aranda is related to the relatively greater authority of male elders
in that society, so that "castration" rites may be regarded as impress-
ing on the novice the necessity of submitting to their authority. Yet
circumcision and subincision are paradoxically seen as conferring adult
status and elevating the novice to the same structural level as the older
men.

If circumcision makes men out of boys, are the Aranda more
"manly" because of the greater pain and mutilation they have to
endure? To answer this question it is necessary to understand the
function of castration anxiety that these rites may be said to promote.
Freud (1923) originally proposed that the overcoming of castration
anxiety propels identification with the father and the normative formation of the superego (p. 23). If this is so, then the greater intensity of
castration anxiety among the Aranda may propel a more vigorous
identification with the father than it does among the Ndembu. This
would be appropriate in a social organization based on the paternal tie
but not in one where this tie plays a secondary role.

Homosexual and Bisexual Symbolism, and the Theme of Secrecy

Thus far I have discussed only those aspects of the rituals that are
concerned with the "positive aggressive" phase of the Oedipus complex and that focus on competition and rivalry between father and son.
There is also the "negative passive" phase, in which the boy attempts
to separate from the archaic preoedipal mother and seeks nurturance
and protection from the father. An important feature of this phase,
according to Blos (1979), is the boy's fear of being overpowered by the
phallic mother. "The fear revolves around surrender to the archaic
mother, and the wildly aggressive impulses are directed towards the
overwhelming and ominous woman giant" (pp. 120–121). At this stage,
the boy's feelings toward the mother are ambivalent. On one hand, he
feels overpowered and robbed of masculinity; on the other, he enjoys
the "passive reclining blissful state of being an appendix to her" (p.
124). Fixation at this stage would lead to the development of a
personality that was passive, dependent, and easily dominated. It is

also during the "negative" oedipal phase that a boy must come to terms with emerging homosexual feelings (p. 479).

My hypothesis is that elements of initiation rituals involving homosexual and transsexual symbolism and secrecy themes help boys to deal with the conflicts and problems associated with the "negative" oedipal phase. While it is difficult to test these assumptions in the absence of specific psychological data, there are numerous interesting features to these initiation rituals that lend support to my theory.

It is interesting, for example, that among the Ndembu, the word for "novice" is the same as that for "senior wife." Both the Aranda and Ndembu circumcisers perform dances in which they mime copulation, and in both cases symbolic dramas involve younger men crawling between the legs of older men. In both societies, symbolic acts suggest that older men are offering themselves to the boys as mother substitutes. Among the Ndembu, immediately following circumcision fathers feed their sons as if the latter were infants. Turner (1970) observed this to be an emotionally charged period when rules about orderliness were broken and fathers almost tumbled over themselves in their efforts to get food to their sons (p. 217). A similar theme is evident in the final rite of Aranda initiation, in which the novices are "reborn" from a hole in the ground representing the womb. They are painted with blood contributed by initiated men and are held over a smoking fire as a mother and her newborn child would be. They are also fed on bread made of crushed seeds and mother's milk (Roheim, 1945, pp. 102–117).

In another ritual sequence performed during this stage of initiation, some of the older men may resubincise themselves (Roheim, 1950, p. 94). Later they reveal their subincision wounds to the novices, although they keep them strictly hidden from women and the uninitiated. Roheim interpreted this part of the ritual as the substitution of the father's penis for the nipple (p. 90). He also noted that the subincision wound is referred to as a vagina in mythical songs, and the blood of subincision is likened to milk (Roheim, 1949, pp. 321, 324). The aim of the ceremony, Roheim suggests, is to separate the young men from their mothers and aggregate them with their fathers, who are offering an artificial vagina as a substitute for the real one (p. 321).

According to Aranda mythology, the blood of circumcision and the blood of menstruation both originated from a serpent that was half male and half female; among the Ndembu, the blood of circumcision is openly referred to as menstrual blood. Bettelheim (1955) interpreted rites such as these in terms of envy of the opposite sex. Hiatt (1971), however, disagrees with this interpretation and attempts to demonstrate that what the men are really doing is transforming boys into men by "reproducing" them using a female generative model. The aim of simulating the genitals of the opposite sex, he says, is an attempt to break the bond between sons and mothers and to extend male mastery into areas in which women have a natural advantage.

Hiatt's theory about the extension of male mastery appears to be supported by some particularly striking examples of transsexual symbolism in recent accounts of male initiation rituals of certain New Guinea tribes. Among the Illahita Arapesh novices are gorged on pork as a method of transforming them into whole men and severing once and for all the ties of affection and substance that bind them to women. Tuzin (1982) writes: "Men may easily perform both sides of the division of labor and surrogate women (i.e., pigs) are available in profusion. If women are absolutely needed to partner a marriage or to sing the high harmony of a song, a man simply plays the part" (p. 344).

Particular attention should be drawn to the homosexual and nurturant themes evident in Sambia initiation, in which the ingestion of semen through homosexual fellatio is believed to be essential to the growth of masculinity (Herdt, 1981, 1982). The Sambia believe that masculinization is impossible without semen ingestion, which is consciously compared to a form of "male breast feeding" (p. 302).

I submit that homosexual and transsexual features of initiation rites capitalize on the specific needs and vulnerabilities experienced by boys during the "negative" oedipal phase, thereby directing and manipulating the outcome of adolescent psychosexual development. Ritualized homosexual contacts may help boys to come to terms with homosexual feelings experienced during this phase, while the imitation of maternal functions by men satisfies the need for nurturance from the father. But perhaps the most important task to be accomplished during this phase is the nullifying of the power of the preoedipal archaic mother, with whom the boy has hitherto identified and who threatens to rob him of his masculinity. While nurturance from the father facilitates the transfer of the boy's emotional attachments from mother to father, the perceived power of the archaic mother is neutralized by more radical measures, such as isolation from women and ritual secrecy. Ritual themes involving the actual physical separation of boys from their mothers and the exclusion of women from sharing in cult secrets are present to a greater or lesser degree in most male initiation cults. The most striking examples of cult secrecy come from New Guinea, where the constant threat of warfare required that men develop fierce, warriorlike temperaments in order to be prepared for war. Paradoxically, in these societies boys spend prolonged periods enjoying a close warm relationship with their mothers (Herdt, 1981, pp. 303–304; Langness, 1974).

If, psychodynamically speaking, failure to break loose from the power of the archaic mother would lead to the development of a passive, easily dominated personality, it follows that in societies where such temperaments in men would by dysfunctional steps must be taken to ensure the development of an appropriately masculine temperament. Different societies give varying emphases to particular ritual themes because they require different outcomes. Among the patrilineal Aranda, pseudoprocreative and secrecy themes are prominent features of initiation ritual; this emphasis may be due to the structural importance of the father–son bond in that society and the consequent need for sons to identify strongly with their fathers. By comparison, transsexual and secrecy themes are less evident among the matrilineal Ndembu, perhaps attesting to the fact that in this society the bond between mother and son should never be fully broken.

Summary and Conclusion

This paper has reconsidered Whiting's hypothesis concerning the relationship between prolonged nursing and exclusive mother–infant sleeping arrangements, on one hand, and harsh male puberty rites, on the other. I have pointed out that Whiting's earlier hypothesis that puberty rites are a way of dealing with oedipal rivalry, and his later hypothesis that they are a way of breaking identification with the mother, are complementary and not mutually exclusive. I have discussed the views proposed by many post Freudian theorists that oedipal feelings are revived at adolescence and must be worked through once again. Blos (1962, 1979) in particular, has emphasized that the "negative oedipal position," which involves such preoedipal issues as separation from the mother, must also be dealt with at adolescence. Thus, rituals in which fathers play a maternal role may facilitate the transfer of emotional attachments from mother to father, thereby diminishing the power of the preoedipal mother, while rituals that involve "castration" symbolism may help in the resolution of the "positive" oedipal position through mastery of the traumatic situation.

I have suggested that Whiting's focus on specific elements of culture, such as the postpartum taboo on intercourse, and patrilocality, was too narrow, and that by adopting a more holistic approach we are able to see how these elements of culture affect psychological development and determine the society's ideals regarding gender characteristics. I have also indicated that initiation rituals may actually be a way of manipulating psychological development to ensure that culture appropriate identifications are formed when adulthood is reached. It is for this reason that initiation rituals vary in form and content from one society to another or may be absent altogether. Although universal themes may be detected in all initiation rituals, they receive different emphases from one society to another and do not necessarily follow the same sequence. I have shown, for example, that "homosexual" and "castration" themes may be maximized or minimized, depending on the specific developmental outcome required by the society.

Before concluding, I would like to draw attention to two paradoxes evident in the major symbolic themes I have discussed. The first question that needs to be addressed is how circumcision and subincision can serve different symbolic functions in the same ritual sequence. At one point, they represent the castration threat; at another, they become symbols of female reproductive functions, particularly in the case of voluntary subincision. Since castration represents the opposite of masculinization—the withdrawal of maleness—it could also aptly represent feminization, which in another way is also the opposite of masculinization. This explanation is in accordance with Freud's observation that the absence of the penis in females is perceived by children as having resulted from castration.

The second question relates to the fact that among both the Aranda and the Ndembu rites dealing with castration symbolism actually precede those dealing with the nurturant role of the father, even though, developmentally speaking, the "negative" oedipal position is supposedly earlier. This paradox may be explained by my suggestion that rites do not merely mirror developmental sequences, but actually direct and manipulate them. By receiving nurturance from their fathers after mastery of the castration trauma, the novices are, in effect, being told by their fathers that the conflict that divided them is over but the final outcome should be dependency on the *father* rather than total independence, which would be an appropriate adjustment in other societies but not in these. Interestingly, Herdt (1981, p. 310) has pointed out that the consequence of Sambia initiation is not the dismissal of masculine dependency but rather the redirection of attachment behavior towards masculine figures.

In conclusion, I would like to suggest a possible direction for future research on gender identity and initiation. This approach would compare those societies that emphasize both oedipal (castration) symbolism and preoedipal (homosexual) symbolism with those that emphasize preoedipal symbolism alone. An example of the latter would be the Sambia of New Guinea. It is interesting that in this society, which does not practice circumcision, mention of the incest theme is rare, which led Herdt (1981) to question the validity of the psychoanalytic argument about the oedipal conflict (p. 323). It would be interesting to examine the psychological and adaptational consequences of initiation rituals in which the oedipal theme is central as compared with those in which it is virtually absent. To do this, though, anthropologists will have to be considerably more attentive to collecting data on individuals and their emotional responses. Without this type of data, theoretical speculation about the psychodynamic significance of ritual remains conjectural and incomplete.

BIBLIOGRAPHY

ALLEN, M. R. (1967). *Male Cults and Secret Initiation in Melanesia.* Melbourne: Melbourne University Press.

BARRY, H., & SCHLEGAL, A. (1980). Early childhood precursors of adolescent initiation ceremonies. *Ethos,* 8:132–145.

BERNDT, R. M., & BERNDT, C. H. (1964). *The World of the First Australians.* Chicago: University of Chicago Press.

BETTELHEIM, B. (1955). *Symbolic Wounds.* New York: Free Press.

BLOS, P. (1962). *On Adolescence: A Psychoanalytic Interpretation.* New York: Free Press.

———(1970). *The Young Adolescent: Clinical Studies.* New York: Free Press.

———(1979). *The Young Adolescent: Clinical Studies.* New York: International Universities Press.

BOAS, F. (1920). The methods of ethnology. In *Race Language and Culture,* ed. F. Boas. New York: Free Press, 1966, pp. 281–289.

BRAIN, J. L. (1977). Sex, incest and death: Initiation rites reconsidered. *Current Anthropology,* 18:191–208.

BURTON, R. V., & WHITING, J. W. M. (1961). The absent father and cross-sex identity. *Merrill-Palmer Quart.,* 7:85–95.

CRAPANZANO, V. (1981). Rites of return: Circumcision in Morocco. *The Psychoanalytic Study of Society,* 9:15–36. New Haven: Yale University Press.

ELKIN, A. P. (1935). *The Australian Aborigines: How to Understand Them.* Sydney: Angus & Robertson, 1966.

FREUD, A. (1936). *The Ego and the Mechanisms of Defense. The Writings of Anna Freud 2.* New York: International Universities Press, 1966.

FREUD, S. (1913). *Totem and Taboo. Standard Edition,* 13:1–161. London: Hogarth Press, 1953.

———(1923). *The Ego and the Id.* New York: W. W. Norton, 1962.

GELEERD, E. R. (1961). Some aspects of ego vicissitude in adolescence. *J. Amer. Psychoanal. Assn.,* 9:394–405.

———(1964). Adolescence and adaptive regression. *Bull. Menn. Clin.,* 28:302–308.

HARRIS, M. (1968). *The Rise of Anthropological Theory.* New York: Crowell.

———(1979). *Cultural Materialism.* New York: Random House.

HARTMANN, H. (1939). *Ego Psychology and the Problem of Adaptation.* New York: International Universities Press, 1958.

HERDT, G. H. (1981). *Guardians of the Flutes: Idioms of Masculinity*. New York: McGraw Hill.

———(1982). Fetish and fantasy in Sambia. In *Rituals of Manhood*, ed. G. H. Herdt. Berkeley: University of California Press.

HIATT, L. R. (1971). Secret pseudo-procreation rites among the Australian Aborigines. In *Anthropology in Oceania: Essays Presented to Ian Hogbin*, ed. L. R. Hiatt & C. Jayawardena. Sydney: Angus and Robertson, pp. 77–88.

JACOBSON, E. (1964). The self and the object world. *J. Amer. Psychoanal. Assn. Monogr. 2*. New York: International Universities Press, 1977.

JONES, A. (1925). Mother-right and the sexual ignorance of savages. In *Psycho-Myth, Psycho-History, Vol. II*. New York: Stonehill, 1974, pp. 145–173.

KARDINER, A. (1939). *The Individual and His Society*. New York: Columbia University Press, 1961.

KEESING, R. M. (1982). Introduction, *Rituals of Manhood*, ed. G. H. Herdt. Berkeley: University of California Press.

KRACKE, W. H. (1979). Review of Roheim's *Children of the Desert. J. Amer. Psychoanal. Assn.*, 27:223–231.

LANGNESS, L. L. (1974). Ritual power and male domination in the New Guinea highlands. *Ethos*, 2:189–212.

LEACH, E. R. (1959). Magical hair. *J. Royal Anthrop, Inst.*, 88:147–164.

MALINOWSKI, B. (1927). *Sex and Repression in Savage Society*. London: Routledge & Kegan Paul, 1953.

MUENSTERBERGER, W. (1961). The adolescent in society. In *Adolescents*, ed. S. Lorand and H. I. Schneer. New York: Harper & Row.

MURPHY, R. F. (1959). Social structure and sex antagonism. *Southwest. J. Anthrop.*, 15:89–98.

NORBECK, E., WALKER, D. E., & COHEN, M. (1962). The interpretation of data: Puberty rites. *Amer. Anthropolog.*, 64:463–485.

PARSONS, A. (1964). Is the Oedipus complex universal? The Jones-Malinowski debate revisited and a south Italian "nuclear complex." *The Psychoanalytic Study of Society*, 3:278–328. New Haven: Yale University Press.

POOLE, FITZ JOHN P. (1982). The ritual forging of identity: Aspects of person and self in Bimin-Kuskusmin male initiation. In *Rituals of Manhood*, ed. G. H. Herdt. Berkeley: University of California Press.

ROHEIM, G. (1932). The psychology of the Central Australian culture area. *Internat. J. Psycho-Anal.*, 13:74–120.

———(1945). *The Eternal Ones of the Dream: A Psychoanalytic Interpretation of Australian Myth and Ritual*. New York: International Universities Press.

———(1949). The symbolism of subincision. *Amer. Imago*, 6:321–328.

———(1950). *Psychoanalysis and Anthropology: Culture, Personality and the Unconscious*. New York: International Universities Press.

SCHLEGAL, A. (1977). Comments. *Curr. Anthrop.*, 18:204.

SPENCER, W. B., & GILLEN, F. J. (1899). *The Native Tribes of Central Australia*. London: Macmillan.

——— ———(1927). *The Arunta*. London:

SPIRO, M. E. (1982). *Oedipus in the Trobriands*. Chicago: University of Chicago Press.

STREHLOW, T. G. H. (1968). *Aranda Tradition*. Melbourne: Melbourne University Press.

TURNER, V. W. (1968a). *Schism and Continuity is an African Society: A Study of Ndembu Village Life*. Manchester: Manchester University Press.

————(1968b). *Drums of Affliction: A Study of Religious Processes Among the Ndembu of Zambia*. Oxford: Clarendon Press.

————(1970). *Forest of Symbols: Aspects of Ndembu Ritual*. Ithaca, NY: Cornell University Press.

TUZIN, D. F. (1980). *The Voice of the Tamberan: Truth and Illusion in Inlahita Arapesh Religion*. Berkeley: University of California Press.

————(1982). Ritual violence among the Ilahita Arapesh. In *Rituals of Manhood*, ed. G. H. Herdt. Berkeley: University of California Press.

VAN GENNEP, A. (1960). *The Rites of Passage*. Chicago: University of Chicago Press.

WHITING, J. W. M. (1964). Effects of climate on certain cultural practices. In *Explorations in Cultural Anthropology*, ed. N. Goodenough. New York: McGraw Hill, pp. 511–544.

————, KLUCKHORN, R., & ANTHONY, A. (1958). The function of male initiation ceremonies at puberty. In *Readings in Social Psychology*, ed. E. E. Maccoby, T. M. Newcomb, & E. L. Hartley. New York: Holt, pp. 359–370.

———— & WHITING, B. B. (1975). Aloofness and intimacy of husbands and wives: A cross-cultural study. *Ethos*, 3:183–207.

6

The Bimin-Kuskusmin: A Discussion of Fitz John Porter Poole's Ethnographic Observations of Gender Identity Formation in a New Guinea People

EDWARD F. FOULKS

Fitz John Porter Poole has captured the essence of the psychological frameworks of the Bimin-Kuskusmin by richly detailing their own theoretical explanations. His exegeses during the Colloquium on Psychoanalytic Methods and Questions in Anthropological Fieldwork demonstrate the difference between superficial observation and interpretation of behavior manifest in a foreign society versus obtaining an insider's understanding of that behavior. Poole presented an epistemology of Bimin-Kuskusmin morality, history, ontogeny, disease theory, socialization theory and psychology that will be the basis of the discussion in this paper. The principles organizing Bimin-Kuskusmin thought and action represent the outcome of tensions between evenly polarized forces, which Poole reported in the numerous publications cited in the Appendix and read by Colloquium participants. Bimin-Kuskusmin ethnopsychological theories include notions of intrapsychic conflict between male and female forces in the mind and body of each person, reminiscent of Freudian psychoanalytic theories of conscious and unconscious conflict as well as those described by Lévi-Strauss (1966) and others.

COSMOLOGICAL PRINCIPLES

In the Bimin-Kuskusmin cosmological system, maleness is manifest in stoicism, orderliness, control of emotions, knowledge of rituals, and

Presented to the Colloquium on Psychoanalytic Methods and Questions in Anthropological Field Work of the American Psychoanalytic Association, New York, December 1983, chaired by Daniel M. A. Freeman, M.D. and Ruth M. Boyer, Ph.D.

the exercise of willpower; in body parts, including the heart, bones, sense organs, brain, hard muscle, and semen; in the colors red and white; and in the direction right. Maleness is reinforced by white taro and the pandanus nut and is expressed in the mythological and spiritual entities of the *Yomok-Echidna* and *Finiik*. Maleness is also expressed in the confraternity of the men's houses. In contrast and in opposition to maleness are the essences of femaleness whose regressive pull requires males to be ever vigilant and prepared. Femaleness is manifest in Khaapkhabuurien, the unruly, emotional aspects of personality, where anger, tantrums, weakness of will, and violation of ritual are acted out. Female bodily essences include stomach, diaphragm, black blood, soft tissues, menstrual fluid, soft parts of the body, as well as the left side or left direction and the color black. In their ethnopsychological systems, the figures of the Afek-Cassowary and the *Khaapkhabuurien* are female forces, as are all the "people of the women's houses."

Bimin-Kuskusmin ontogenetic theory proposes that as the infant grows up to become a man, the personality loses its femaleness and relinquishes the power of the Afek spirit to the power of maleness. There is a movement from the left to the right. The *Khaapkhabuurien* is decreased, and the *Finiik* is increased. Implicit in their theory is that this transformation is never complete, that there is an ongoing tension between male principles and female principles throughout life.

A notable feature of the Bimin-Kuskusmin's gender ideology is the poetic, symbolic representation of beliefs about the androgynous embryonic origins of each child. The fetus is said to be composed of a central mass of *yemor*—a mix of fertile fluids and agnatic blood from the mother's body—which is surrounded by menstrual blood and then further surrounded by a masculine substance that the male contributes through frequent intercourse. A small opening in the outer layer determines the sex of the baby: if it faces the vagina, the child will be female; if it faces the uterus, the child will be male. The mass of substance revolves many times during pregnancy, and it is the very last position before birth that determines the final result. Males and females try to influence the child's sex by standing in certain locations or having more frequent sex; however, these procedures are considered only mildly helpful. The Bimin-Kuskusmin conclude that a mere last minute orientation of the fetus dictates the child's sex. Indeed men advise other men to treat their sisters well, for they might have been their brothers. The theory of the androgynous fetus is reminiscent of Stoller's (1968) discussion of the male and female aspects of the central nervous systems' role in regulating sexual behavior. During development, one aspect comes to predominate, and the other subsides.

However, the secondary sex system is present, and no human is exclusively masculine or feminine. The Bimin-Kuskusmin believe that the sexual characteristics of the sex not "chosen" dissolves into the placenta.

MALE AND FEMALE ESSENCES

Central to an understanding of gender conceptions among the Bimin-Kuskusmin is their idea of "natural substances"—fluids and spirits present in males and females that ordain the strength and characteristics of the individual. Among spiritual substances are the finiik and the Khaapkhabuurien. The former characterizes males and comprises the controlled, ordered, and moral aspects of personhood. The latter exemplifies women—it is the foundation for the weak, unpredictable, and irrational aspects of personhood as built up through personal experiences. Both types of spirits exist in all human beings, but the development of gender identity is hinged on developing the gender-appropriate spirit. These spirits are held within the fertile fluids of males and females respectively. Thus, the manipulation of gender revolves around the flow of natural substance, and all of life is a regulating of this substance: the draining of "menstrual blood" from boys, the tubes of menstrual blood and semen planted in female sweet potato gardens and male taro gardens respectively, the eating of certain foods, and the taboos surrounding others that fortify particular sex-related characteristics. By eating only female foods and imbuing himself with female natural substances, the male will never become female, for the two sexes differ in their physical and psychological capacities to receive, transform, and transmit these substances. However, it is believed that a peerson can temporarily alter his nature. The Bimin-Kuskusmin also believe that males and females create different body parts: the men create the long-lasting, hard, and internal body parts, and the female fertile fluids (except menstrual blood) as well as semen. Women produce weak, external, and soft elements, which decay soon after death. Similarly, male knowledge is more powerful than female knowledge.

The importance of these concepts lies in how they affect action, taboo,, and concept of self and other. Symbolically, the draining of female menstrual blood or the ingestion of foods that augment male characteristics are the cultural manifestations directing gender-identity formation. The female child not only has certain characteristics based on her anatomy (in this case extended to the menstrual blood, fertile fluids, and predominance of Khaapkhabuurien within her), but as she augments these natural substances through female food, she correspondingly increases her female activity.

DEVELOPMENTAL THEORY

The theory of androgyny is applied not only to fetuses, but to the most respected and powerful adult members of the community. While abnormal babies are killed at birth because they are thought to be infertile, "pseudo-hermaphroditic males" are regarded with reverence and elevated to the highest position among males, implying an ideal of male and female unity within one being. Similarly, certain postmenopausal, no longer married, and asexual women are chosen as the *waneng aiyem ser,* the prominent female "androgynous" beings who represent the ancestor Afek. The *waneng aiyem ser,* immune to most pollution, participates in both male and female rituals and possesses some of the properties of initiated males. In addition, the presence of overinclusion can be seen in the *couvade* (birth procedure) whereby the father squats on the ground and simulates giving birth. Furthermore, the semen of men is regarded as the essence of fertile fluids in women.

According to Bimin-Kuskusmin ideology, uninitiated males are weak, vulnerable, irrational, and composed of female substance; they are appropriately called "people of the women's houses." During the Colloquium Poole stated:

The ritual operations of the initiation cycle in general and the *ais am* rite in particular are a recognition among Bimin-Kuskusmin that manhood does *not* follow naturally as a continuous development out of childhood. Instead, the personhood and selfhood of novices must be ritually disassembled and transformed in an elaborate male act of the creation of manhood.

Of significance is the late age (9–12) at which the ceremony takes place. For women, the initiation procedure is individual and centers around natural bodily events, such as the onset of menstruation. Girls are seen as developing naturally, in contrast to males, who require physical precautions to insure biological maturity, such as the stretching of their penises during initiation rites.

Another aspect of Bimin-Kuskusmin behavior examined by Poole is the infant–parent relationship. One short but fascinating essay discusses the sexual relationships between mother and infant boy. Babies nurse for three to four years. The mother has the duty of pulling her baby boy's penis so that it becomes strong and grows. She often allows the child to suck and play with her breast at the same time as she caresses his penis, thus associating genital sexual stimulation with maternal oral gratification. The mother may have particular incentive to engage in such activities because of the postpartum sex taboo imposed on married couples in order to insure the channeling of natural substances to nutritious breast milk for the baby rather than to fertile fluids during intercourse; thus a mother, after months of frequent sexual encounters to promote a healthy baby, is suddenly deprived and may use the baby to fulfill her sexual drives.

The incidence of this type of mother–child relationship bears significant similarities to the occurrence of transsexualism described by Stoller (1968). In both cases the father is absent and thus is unable either to intercede between mother and child or to provide a presence for masculine identification. In fact, the child, while anatomically recognized as male, is largely regarded as female and thereby receives encouragement to manifest female characteristics, which are considered his normal state (at weaning he will receive a female name).

When the child grows slightly older, his father will begin to tantalize him with the privileges of manhood, for example, the ritual of "seeing the men's houses." However, the possibilities of severe and overly programed attachment to mother and the presence of feminine characteristics remain. The long processes of ritual by which boys become men paradoxically entails the learning and achieving of mechanisms to ward off female forces while at the same time becoming increasingly cognizant that femaleness is in fact the essence of all real power. The Bimin-Kuskusmin have a theory of the bisexual nature of human beings reminiscent of our own. The ultimate secret of life—the secret that is embedded intricately in all their rituals, the secret that is increasingly revealed in the progression rituals—is that *boys and young men are unaware, are unconscious of the pervasive female elements and power that is the basic essence of all men!* Once the masculine *Finiik* spirit forces of each man are brought together with the *Khaapkhabuurien* female forces *Krisem*, "the whole person," is obtained.

With this inadequate and all too late base of gender-identity for boys, ultimate gender-identity formation centers on how well male initiation rites transform the boys into the Bimin-Kuskusmin masculine ideal. In ritual context, the processes of delimitation, differentiation, separation, identification, and cultural influence are blown up into monstrous symbolic scale. The men use many tactics to accomplish these goals. Their aim is to affect the boys psychologically so as to destroy the bonds to their mothers and the woman's world to which the boys are attached. Through deception, physical lacerations, burning, secrets, sudden attacks, isolation, deprivation, and threats, the men create a temporal and special discontinuity with the boys' feminine world of the past.

Bimin-Kuskusmin ritual stresses the experiential, not the intellectual, as a way to embed gender identity. With the physiological events come emotional adjustments and memories, which can have a lasting effect. The very physical effects begin to convince boys they are men: flat stomachs, stoicism in the face of pain, and courage are examples of the physical transformation. Furthermore, the boys have no other choice but to undergo physical attack, and male initiation is the route to all privileges provided by living in the male society.

Initiation ritual progresses from the degradation and elimination of women to accentuation of the masculine. For instance, during some rites, the boys are forced to eat female foods and then vomit; in others, they are bled to remove the female menstrual blood within them. Women strip the boys and crudely scrub them, teasing them about their small genitals. Thus boys learn that they can no longer associate women with kindness. The dramatic effect of role reversal is also demonstrated by the men's becoming kind at the end of the initiation ritual. The social significance of the male initiation is that it creates strong, courageous, angry warriors, unifies the men, and creates order for the community. Poole stated that "the more dangerous the climate of raiding and warfare, the wider is the gulf between boys growing up in a world of women and shaped by female gender roles and identities, and the men they must eventually join and emulate." The rigorous ordeals produce angry men. But the internal gender identity formed at infancy most likely remains feminine. Indeed, it emerges in the tender relationships men have with their close female relatives. Poole remarks that elaborated ritual symbols of androgyny and complex symbols suggesting ambivalent and fragile gender identity may indicate that the transformation is not complete, due to the very late start in masculine identification.

Colloquium Participants' Discussion of Fitz John Porter Poole's Presentation of The Bimin-Kuskusmin

GILBERT HERDT: I never really understood the status of women among the Telefomen people in New Guinea. Poole's presentation clarifies much for me regarding the tales of females' relationship to males and children. The exclusive mother–child sleeping arrangements and prolonged breast feeding might predictably result in problems in separation-individuation. However, Poole tells us that young boys seem secure and happy in their exclusive male peer groups even shortly after separation from their mothers. We should differentiate the conscious, overt behavioral displays of male self-sufficiency from potential massive repression and denial of their attachment to mother. Remember that these people have institutionalized a powerful female gerontocracy that has a major influence on the elaborate male initiation rituals.

HERMAN ROIPHE: I wonder about the degree of child abuse, particularly mothers' toward their sons. Many who have worked in New Guinea have pointed out the poor quality of male–female relationships and the fact that males are extremely sensitive to contradiction and punishment. There does not seem to be very much sexual interest between adult males and females. In our society, this situation provides fertile ground for child abuse. Also, among the Bimin-Kuskusmin there is a high level of sexual stimulation of children. Women simultaneously stimulate the penis of their young sons and their own nipples.

GILBERT HERDT: This fact and the observation that the Bimin-Kuskusmin children are not weaned until two to four years old no doubt delays the separation-individuation process and interferes with the nature of the self object boundaries. Among males there is a sense of incompleteness of core gender identity. There is also difficulty in expressing anger appropriately among males in many New Guinea societies. Masculine protest thus may be turned toward abusing women. Their belief systems attribute the cause of anger to outside spiritual agents. The true underlying psychodynamic tensions of masculine insecurity are revealed in the irony of the extremes of the male cults, which reflect the androgyny of preoedipal maternal attachments.

CLARA AISENSTEIN: These men seem to be extremely brutal. I believe that their lack of secure self-image is a result of their inability to individuate from the object at critical periods in their early development.

GILBERT HERDT: Males seem to be obsessed with their body and their body's image. Symbols of femaleness are painted on the body.

JOSEPH LUBART: I wonder whether this preoccupation with body integrity is a defensive response to prevent disintegration of self-boundaries such as is seen in borderline personalities in our own society.

RUTH BOYER: In contrast, it appears that the females have good self-image and strong self-esteem. This might be expected inasmuch as the little girl is unambivalently socialized to the female's role of having babies and tending gardens. They observe their role models from infancy on in a steady consistent manner. On the other hand, young boys have no idea about masculine roles until about age 9, when their long process of initiation begins.

GILBERT HERDT: I would like to propose two hypotheses to explain the relationship between childhood development among the Bimin-Kuskusmin and images of masculinity and femininity, with particular focus on the reasons for the harsher initiation rites and higher suicide rates among males in that society. First, among the Bimin-Kuskusmin there is a lower relevance of father in the household than among other New Guinea societies. Before the child is age 5, father's physical proximity and symbolic presence is normally not part of the child's life. Second, mothers offer more negative images of males and actively discourage separation, exploration, and motoric activity. They also present verbally negative images of father, and men in general, by saying such things as father is stupid, angry, aggressive, does not bring enough food, and the like. These factors result in a somewhat schizoidal quality in males. Remarkably, homosexuality seems to be absent among the Bimin-Kuskusmin. At least, it is not institutionalized, as it is in a number of other New Guinea societies. Among the Bimin-Kuskusmin, male solidarity is not as intense and their prowess as warriors is not as aggressive or proficient as in other New Guinea societies. It seems possible, then, that poor father–child relationships, in addition to the mother's offering negative images of males, results in difficulties in separation-individuation and poor male identity formation for little boys.

THEODORE LIDZ: Among the Bimin-Kuskusmin men are frightened of females and of female substances. Menstruation and menstrual fluids are considered by males to be grievous dangers. Men are reminded of the mother's power over them in early life, of her dominance and her ability to give life. I suspect that menstrual blood is so dangerous for several reasons. It is "dead" womb blood—the antithesis of life, and it is also a "filtrate," so to speak, of the dangerous female secretion and emanations of the female libido. Men also envy the women's capacity for self-purification by menstruation, whereas males must purify themselves ritually.

JEAN BRIGGS: The symbolic emphasis on menstrual fluid, semen, and liquids in the body may relate to the problems of self-object boundaries. It is as if each sex in each person could flow into the other and the degree of flow becomes dangerous because the shell of the self can be inundated.

WALTER SLOTE: Regarding the degree of masculine stoicism exhibited by the Bimin-Kuskusmin, I am curious about their ability to withstand the pain of initiation. My own experiences of people in several primitive societies indicates that the ability to withstand extreme pain without crying out or showing emotion is an expression of male pride and their sense of masculinity.

DAVID FORREST: The conjunction of our viewpoints from psychoanalysis and anthropology permits us to look at the needs of the whole society, within which the psychodynamics of individual development produce more or less successful adults. Here we have a society that is successful in defending its territory but at a cost borne by the men, who are warriors and must renounce intimacy as feminine and inferior, and by the women, whose status as nurturers is demeaned and subordinated by a structure of myths that is highly organized and elaborated. Males in this society and in many other societies seem to have ways of contending with pain and suffering; they have come to expect it in war and in hard physical work.

DANIEL M. A. FREEMAN: I believe that among the Bimin-Kuskusmin there are many ego-splitting mechanisms and borderline traits in both males and females. At the Colloquium, Poole reported that half of the deaths in the field among males were due to suicide. He also reported a much greater degree of empathy, relatedness, and mutuality in later life than in early adult life. Splitting mechanisms are also evidenced in the ambiguous image of the female, who can be, on one hand, an evil witch and, on the other, can look seductive. I believe that we can gain an undertanding of aspects of adult personality by observing the processes of separation-individuation in early childhood among these people. By now we well understand the child's reaction to rejection and loss of the mother. The child is at first hyperactive and angry. Ultimately, however, the child gives up, which produces a marasmus, a failure to thrive, a collapse of the biological systems, and even death. Perhaps with the first child the Bimin-Kuskusmin mothers are not well prepared for the emotional demands that children will press on them. These mothers may withdraw from their children's demands or express sadomasochistic rage in response. Thus, they may further interfere with the child's urges toward separation-individuation.

THEODORE LIDZ: The mother–child symbiosis is, I believe, unusually strong. The Bimin-Kuskusmin have a word to designate the mother and child as a unit. The boy becomes resentful that the mother abandons him to the male cult at the age of 7 to 10. However, I take issue with Dr. Freeman's hypothesis. These women, even at the birth of their first child, are 19 to 20 years old. They are not adolescents as they might be considered in our own society. The average life span for these people is about 35 years. Therefore, when they have their first child they are essentially halfway through their lives. I am impressed that rather than having sadomasochistic urges toward their children these women seem to care well for their infants. They are concerned with how much the child is supposed to eat and what it is to eat. The care of their child is well formulated.

CHARLES SARNOFF: It would be fascinating to contrast the child-rearing attitudes and behaviors of the younger with those of the older mothers. Differentiation from the object may be a problem generated more by younger mothers toward their first children than by older mothers toward later children. Thus, we may find different personality styles generated in this society, which are determined by demographic characteristics rather than overall model child-rearing patterns. During the Colloquium Poole pointed out that the first menses in this society is between 16 and 18 years. it is at that time that the female initiation rites are held. Although females are betrothed in infancy, they do not start bearing children until age 19 through 22.

THEODORE LIDZ: Many of us, including Pearl Katz and Ruth Boyer, are also interested in the vicissitudes of the mother–daughter bond, how girls learn female roles and caring for a baby. This process contrasts starkly with that undergone by young men, who must disidentify with their mothers to become male. The process of disidentification with the mother and the acquisition of a firm masculine identity is certainly a primary function of the initiation ritual, as is the removal of adolescents from the presence of all women, not only their mothers. In many New Guinea societies, boys cannot become men without being inseminated repeatedly to attain a store of semen. In other societies, boys must be rid of the womb blood that goes into their makeup. The Bimin-Kuskusmin do not provide adolescents with a homosexual outlet that helps differentiate them from the women; but they do remove the mother's blood by cutting the navel, and they provide semen through the taro fertilized with semen and by making the boys eat "pus" from the taro, which they equate with semen.

RUTH BOYER: I think our discussion has generated a number of hypotheses, most especially concerning patterns of older women versus younger women and their respective child-rearing attitudes and practices.

JEAN BRIGGS: The complex question that needs to be addressed is how these children integrate various fragments of Bimin-Kuskusmin reality. How do they learn the nature of masculinity? Like other children, they make judgments by what others tell them and what their own senses tell them. Illusion often undercuts obvious appearance, and the notions of what it is to be a male are clouded in the mysteries of ritual and lore.

WAUD KRACKE: I agree that we must elaborate our studies of affect through psychoanalytic observations of the concrete aspects of emotion and how it is applied among these people. We must investigate the ideology and semantics of emotional material, particularly that which is produced by the boys 8 years old and younger.

JOSEPH LUBART: We must also attend more to female attitudes particularly toward themselves. Here the focus would be on mother–daughter relationships. I am impressed with implied attitudes of women that state "Let men have their rituals. We have the things that count, that is, producing babies, raising pigs and tending gardens." I am also impressed with the intense rage of men toward women. In considering this, I have to wonder what holds these people together? Why doesn't their society disintegrate? With all the repressed hostility, what keeps these people functioning together? I wonder whether there is any affection, any warmth, any joy, any fun in this society.

L. BRYCE BOYER: In treating borderline and other regressed patients, therapists often find that strongly cathected derivatives of triadic relationships (revived, unresolved oedipal problems) appear early in the development of the transference–countertransference relationship. If the psychoanalyst or other therapist interprets such material on an oedipal level, the treatment process is stalled or harmed. The preoedipal, diadic conflicts must be treated before one can deal effectively with the oedipal problems that were presented initially in the service of defense. In the case of the Bimin-Kuskusmin, the ritual polarities, seemingly representing more oedipal than preoedipal issues, may also be seen as serving defensive functions, just as their early presentation does in the treatment situation. This interpretation would be consistent with this group's apparent borderline personality modal personality structure.

EDWARD FOULKS: I am intrigued with the question of influence exerted by first-born males on Bimin-Kuskusmin society. It appears that most Bimin-Kuskusmin are relatively healthy, physically and psychologically. Poole reported that mothers closely attend to their plump happy babies. The availability of mother's brother and grandparents also undoubtedly plays a major role in helping develop masculine identifications. He also reports that young boys comfortably leave their homes and play in groups with outgoing displays of affect toward their peers. In the Bimin-Kuskusmin rituals there also seems to be a sensitive awareness of balance between good and bad, masculine and feminine. Such behaviors appear relatively neither nondefensive nor brittle, stressing neither masculinity nor femininity, but rather integrating both aspects within each individual. This, in fact, is the ultimate secret of human life as revealed in the rituals.

On the other hand, we do have evidence of sadomasochistic acting out in Bimin-Kuskusmin executions: in the "roasting" of a scapegoated boy and in the unusually brutal torture and execution of both male and female enemies. We also observe the strictness of the dichotomy of goodness–badness and health–sickness in the masculine–feminine mythological characters of the *Finiik* and the *Khaapkhabuu-rien*. These projective systems may symbolically portray aspects of splitting. I wonder if this cosmological system is one that meets the needs of the least psychologically healthy of the society—those first-born males who have endured trauma during their early life.

DANIEL M. A. FREEMAN: It is noteworthy that the affective experiences of particularly the first borns in this society reveal sequences of development that are similar, if not identical, to those recorded by psychoanalytic observers in our own society. This indicates to me that psychoanalytic theory and scientific method have application in all human cultures. Our universal theory can be advanced, however, only by the recording and analysis of the kind of rich clinical and ethnographic detail provided to us by anthropologists like Fitz John Porter Poole. Our colloquium membership and our science of psychoanalysis are forever grateful to him.

BIBLIOGRAPHY

LEVI-STRAUSS, C. (1966). *The Savage Mind*. Chicago: University of Chicago Press.
STOLLER, R. J. (1968). *Sex and Gender: On the Development of Masculinity and Feminity*. London: Hogarth Press.

APPENDIX

The following works of Fitz John Porter Poole were distributed to the participants and used as a basis for discussion at the Colloquium.

Symbols of substance: Bimin-Kuskusmin model of procreation, death, and personhood. Unpublished manuscript in author's possession.
The Ais Am, unpublished doctoral dissertation, Cornell University, 1975.
Transforming "natural" women: Female ritual leaders and gender ideology among Bimin-Kuskusmin. In *Sexual Meanings*, ed. S. B. Ortner & H. Whitehead. Cambridge: Cambridge University Press, 1981.

Cultural significance of "drunken comportment" in a non-drinking society: The case of the Bimin-Kuskusmin of Papua, New Guinea. In *Alcohol Use and Abuse in Papua New Guinea,* ed. M. Marshall. Boroko: Papua New Guinea Institute of Applied Social and Economic Research, 1981.

Taman: Ideological and sociological configurations of "witchcraft" among Bimin-Kuskusmin. *Social Analysis,* 8:58–76, 1981.

Couvade and clinic in a New Guinea society. In *The Use and Abuse of Medicine,* ed. M. W. de Vries, R. L. Berg, & M. Lipkin, Jr. New York: Praeger, 1982.

Folk models of eroticism in mothers and sons: Aspects of sexuality among Bimin-Kuskusmin. Presented at 82nd annual meeting of American Anthropological Association, Chicago, IL, November, 1983.

Morality, personhood, tricksters and youths: Some narrative images of ethics among Bimin-Kuskusmin. In *Anthropology in the High Valleys: Essays on the New Guinea Highlands in Honor of Kenneth E. Read,* ed. L. L. Largness & T. E. Hays. Novato: Chandler & Sharp, 1986.

"Knowledge rests in the heart": Bimin-Kuskusmin meta-communications on meaning, tacit knowledge, and field research. Presented at annual meeting of the American Anthropological Association, Washington, DC, 1986 (mimeographed).

7

Cultural History and the Film *Cabaret*: A Study in Psychoanalytic Criticism

STEPHEN F. BAUER

Forgetting impressions, scenes or experiences nearly always reduces itself to shutting them off. When the patient talks about these 'forgotten' things he seldom fails to add: 'As a matter of fact I've always known it; only I've never thought of it.'
—S. Freud (1914)

I am a camera with its shutter open, quite passive, recording, not thinking. Recording the man shaving at the window opposite and the woman in the kimono washing her hair. Some day, all this will have to be developed, carefully printed, fixed.
—C. Isherwood (1937)

Meine Damen und Herren, Mesdames et Messieurs, Ladies and Gentlemen: Where are your troubles now? Forgotten! I told you so. We have no troubles here. Here life is beautiful! The girls are beautiful. Even the orchestra is beautiful!
—Master of Ceremonies in "Cabaret" (1972)

In his discussions of the compulsion to repeat, Freud (1914, 1920) calls to our attention the relationship of remembering (and forgetting) to our actions, to conflict, and to trauma ("real" and fantasied) and to the role of working through in establishing genuine insight and conviction in a psychoanalysis.

In his literary work, Christopher Isherwood (1939) has returned again and again to the same themes in fiction (for example, *Goodbye to Berlin*), autobiographical novels and, more recently, frank autobiography. One might say, using Isherwood's own words, that the themes concern ". . . a lifelong education—the education of a novelist. A young man living at a certain period in a certain European country, is subjected to a certain kind of environment, certain stimuli, certain influences (from the Preface, 1938). In the 1977 revision, referring specifically to *Lions and Shadows* but applicable to his work in general, he added that it is about

> . . . the predicament of being young. It is about rage against the dictatorship, no matter how benevolent, of your elders; about enthusiasms you are shy of confessing to, because they are so passionate; about escapes from your anxieties into frantic bodily action, intoxication, noise; about roles which you and your friends play to reassure each other that your lives are significant [from the Foreword].

These books engage the curiosity of the reader; they invite us to peek into the interior world of the characters and their author: indeed at times we are hard pressed to know which is character, which is author. By combining an expository style written in the first person, yet naming the narrator Christopher Isherwood, the author (Isherwood) creates tension through ambiguity. Is this fact? Is this fiction?

But in addition to the exquisite focus on the individual author/ character in these works, we cannot avoid seeing, just off-stage, on the periphery of the experiences of the main characters, the demise of the Weimar Republic in Germany, the rise of Hitler, and the coming second world war. Indeed, the interplay of the two—the post-World War I coming of age of alienated English youth juxtaposed against the developments in Germany during the late twenties and early thirties— contributes to the powerful evocativeness of these works.

It was Santayana, I believe, who suggested that those who do not learn from history are doomed to repeat it. His remarks recall Freud's statements noted earlier. A culture "remembers" through its literary, historical, and literary-historical works as well as through its oral tradition. Indeed, it may be that cultural "memory" is insured far more through such works than through journalism. After all, nothing is an dead as yesterday's news. Chroniclers rarely have the force of writers of literary and related works. We need only compare the impact of Shakespeare with that of Elizabethan journalists to confirm this.

When Freud described the patient's compulsion to repeat in the transference, he suggested that it is the patient's way of remembering. Since *Goodbye to Berlin* appeared in 1939, other artists have reinterpreted Isherwood's novel as a stage play, movie, stage musical, and most recently as a controversial movie musical, *Cabaret*. When our most popular are forms (theater, movies) insistently present revisions of the same work, we may recall Freud's comments and attempt to remember what we are forgetting. But here we enter the complex and murky territory of applied psychoanalysis, with the multiple risks of speculative and wild analysis of an author, of literary, or other texts and of history.

History considers a society as a whole: sequences of political and economic events, developments in institutions, its popular culture and art, its science. The same factors are at work in an individual's history. We may think of the politics of the family, the transmission of values across generations, as well as rebellion against those values. The individual in a sense is a reflection of his family, his culture. But it is a reflection integrated with and modified by his own biology—drives, development, unconscious wishes and fantasies, defenses. *Oedipus Rex* maintains its hold on us because of its art and because of the universality of the Oedipus complex. The universality of the Oedipus complex as perceived by Sophocles was recorded indelibly in literary form, transforming the personal—the story of Laius, Jocasta and Oedipus—into the universal through a shattering drama. The narrative action and drama in all lives makes the historical side of the books and movie considered here *intrinsic* rather than a mere contributor to understanding. The lives we are concerned with here are played out in an historical context; but the historical context can also be seen as the creation of those lives. In the movie, the film *is* memory, but also the recounting of the movement of world and personal histories. Personal history and world history lend each other meaning. Memory makes such meaning possible. As it is for Oedipus himself, memory is intrinsic to truth-seeking and meaningfulness, no matter what the consequences.

Reed (1982) has discussed and summarized the methodological problems of psychoanalytic literary criticism in detail. She reminds us of the "important tradition in literary criticism which considers the text itself paramount" (p. 20) and which had led psychoanalytically informed literary critics to concentrate on the text, taking into account psychoanalytic knowledge, and to "trace psychoanalytic patterns discernible from manifest content" (p. 20). Her approach takes into account the reader's (in the instance given, the literary critic's) response to the text as one part of the method of the psychoanalytic study of a text. That is, the reader's response may be seen as an unconscious enactment of an organized fantasy embedded in the text, and that helps illuminate the original text, which, in turn, can be restudied in light of the critical response.

Here my approach is similar but takes into account wider cultural issues. Authors writing and working in the "lively" arts (stage, screen) are seen as responding to an original text taking into account what will appeal to the audience for whom they are writing and performing. These later interpreters, then, are responding to something in the previously written text that leads them to believe that a popular success is likely. That is, they intuit that a play or movie based on an earlier work will have strong appeal to the present-day audience for which the revised work is intended. I suggest that there is something universal in such a work's being revised, something close to the bone of author and audience, that also specifically meets the needs of and resonates with the historical moment. The playwright correctly senses what the audience wishes and needs to see performed. These ideas are close to those that Erikson (1950) presented when he spoke of "relevance and relativity in the case history" (p. 19).

This study considers one work in particular, the film *Cabaret*, along with Isherwood's original *Goodbye to Berlin* and later sequences of his autobiographical writings.

HISTORICAL CONTEXT AND SETTING

Consider the following. After a world war, a proud nation teeters. A powerful demagogic figure proclaims that a conspiracy of communists has invaded the highest offices of the nation, even the departments of state and army; no one can be trusted. Impassioned speeches inflame the populace and endanger freedom. The liberal ranks are shaken, and there is a yearning to unite behind a strong paternal figure. An aging general, an heroic figure of the recent war begins tó emerge as a symbol of unity.

The place is the United States. The year is 1951, a scant six years after the end of World War II. The Alger Hiss affair and the Rosenberg trial have embarrassed the Truman administration, which, one year before a national election, finds itself mired in Korea. Senator Joseph McCarthy mounts an increasingly shrill campaign, finding communists under (and in) every bed. The frightened Democratic and Republican parties both scramble to curry favor with the war hero General Eisenhower, now serving as president of Columbia University. It is Eisenhower to whom the nation will turn in the following year to extricate it from the Korean Conflict and to respond to Senator McCarthy's predictions of a communist takeover.

It was in this context that John van Druten prepared a play (*I am a Camera*), produced in November of 1951, based on Christopher Isherwood's *Goodbye to Berlin*. It is interesting to compare the times.

Isherwood's novel, published in 1939, evoked the final years of the Weimar Republic (1930–1932). Germany had turned to its aging hero of the first World War, Hindenburg.

In the Germany of the Kaisers at the turn of the century "Jews, democrats, socialists, in a word, outsiders, were kept from the sacred precincts of higher learning" (Gay, 1968, p. 3). Artists like Kathe Kollwitz, Kandinsky, and Marc were reviled. Literary works were described by Imperial statesmen (in one example) as a "monstrous wretched piece of work, social-democratic-realistic, at the same time full of sickly, sentimental mysticism, nerve-racking, in general abominable" (p. 3). With the defeat of Germany in 1918, revolution erupted; the philistine and oppressive, although not dictatorial, Germany of the Kaisers was turned out of power and the short-lived Weimar Republic instituted, a total rejection of the old order. Weimar was associated with "modernity in art, literature and thought . . . rebellion of sons against fathers; Dadaists against art; Berliners against beefy philistines; libertines against moralists . . ." (xiii). But bloody civil war, political assassination, the imposition of the Versailles Treaty, economic collapse, and astronomical inflation spurred the hopes of monarchists and militarists. And so, through political compromise and timidity the country turned to Hindenburg, the aged "hero of Tannenberg." Gay points out: "Hindenburg smelled of the old order; he had been sold to the public in a demagogic campaign as the great man above parties, as the near mystical representative of the German Soul, the very embodiment of traditional values—in a word, as a sturdy paternal figure" (p. 118). Hitler and the Nazis relentlessly manipulated the public and gained votes. The Brown shirts and the Black shirts were in bloody battles with the communists and espoused a virulent antisemitic program. Eventually, at the end of 1932, Hindenburg, now aged and senile, was persuaded to accept Hitler as Chancellor in a ruthlessly cynical maneuver by Vice Chancellor Franz von Papen and others. Hitler would get rid of the communists; the rest of the cabinet would contain Hitler. History has taught us differently.

Although the comparison between Hindenburg and Hitler, on one hand, and Eisenhower and McCarthy, on the other, may seem far fetched, we may profit from considering similarities. The power of the demagogic right to frighten and intimidate centrists, themselves frightened by the left, through innuendo and propaganda—the "big lie," the popular fear of what is novel, the suspicion of rebellious youth (recall the "beats" of the early fifties)—these all lead centrists to seek the old order to reduce unrest. At a time when government is particularly suspect, when a generation of a nation's young men have been killed and mutilated in a great war, a country will turn to its heroes for restraint and calm. No matter that these heroes were previously associated with the very death and destruction now feared, they are recalled as men responsible for the resolution of terrible times in the past. If the "old order" can be restored, then rebellion will end and all will be right. But from another point of view, young people will identify with the struggle against that very "old order," which they associate with destruction through narrowmindedness, arrogance, and stolidity. At this level *Goodbye to Berlin,* with its emphasis on the passion, sexuality, and apolitical youthful self-concern of the early thirties, especially as embodied in the character of Sally Bowles, had the right psychological fit for the United States in the early fifties.

But there are additional vicissitudes of the presentation of the Isherwood stories: the theater musical *Cabaret* of 1966 and the movie musical based on it in 1972. The two productions virtually embrace the American adventure in Vietnam, a war that led one president (Johnson) to withdraw from seeking reelection. His successor, Nixon, finally resigned his office in disgrace. It was also a period characterized by unrest, assassination (John Kennedy, Robert Kennedy, Martin Luther King), youth in revolt, drugs, decadence, and cynicism about the established order.

THE CONTEXTS OF GROUP AND INDIVIDUAL MEANING

I have said that when our most popular art forms—theater and film— insistently present to us revisions of the same work, we may suppose that there is a preoccupation, conscious and unconscious, with themes that the artist correctly senses will excite the interest of the audience. It is of some interest that artistically successful plays and movies tend to have popular success in their own time. For example, we may think of the plays of Aeschylus and Shakespeare. In contrast, more abstract art forms, such as painting and music, are often "discovered" generations later. Think of the work of Van Gogh or the late sonatas and quartets of Beethoven. One explanation of this tendency, akin to Arlow's (1961) ideas about myth, follows: The theatrical event presents and enacts an action version of unconscious fantasy in culturally acceptable form. The fantasy produced by the artist and shared by the audience, in the same sense that we share a good joke, allows the expression of wishes without fear, ultimately without fear of retribution. We may identify with the characters and work over the conflict repeatedly. When the lights go on in movie house or theater there is applause and then a gradual return to reality, much as occurs when awakening from a dream. A quality of ineffability may linger until some member of the group of theater goers ventures a comment. Frequently, however, after an affecting play or movie, pro forma statements are made and the evening, or day, gone on.

Repeated revisions of a work of art from written fragments, to a novel, to plays, musical plays, movies, and movie musicals represent a preoccupation, an effort by an artist or a group of artists to present what the audience is prepared to see and hear and to help that audience overcome a traumatic situation. And the audience needs to hear what it needs to remember in a form remote enough from the central conflict and traumatic situation to be safe, but close enough to be experienced and worked through.

What is the central conflict referred to in the works under consideration? It is the rebellion of sons against their fathers, traditional values, and fatherland under conditions in which the worst wishes and fears of young boys (i.e., parricidal fantasies) are fulfilled: the destruction of a generation of fathers (including one's own father) by war (i.e., devastating trauma). And how is the rebellion expressed? Through the repudiation of the ideals of their fathers and dashing the hopes and desires of their mothers. There will be no wives, no children, no grandchildren. There may be disengagement and a search for meaning; or there may be worship of "life," free love, love of one's own body.

This repudiation of the ideals of the previous generation becomes an ideal in its own right. In *Goodbye to Berlin,* such ideals are reflected in the character Christopher Isherwood who, like a camera, is merely a medium that records, isolated, uninvolved, and homosexual to boot. No children will issue from him to continue any "line." In contrast, the character Sally Bowles, in her fashion, portrays an immersion in life and "living."

EXPLORATION OF THE TEXT:
GOODBYE TO BERLIN AND *CABARET*

It is of interest that despite major surface differences, *Goodbye to Berlin* and *Cabaret* have identical formal structures. They are both extremely symmetrical works. For example, *Goodbye to Berlin* begins and ends with a diary; the interior sections include polar contrasts— heterosexuality/homosexuality, poverty/wealth, Jew/Gentile, fascism/ communism, isolation/involvement (Hynes, 1977). The movie *Cabaret* begins and ends with protracted silence; a drum roll introduces the film and ends it; there is a parallel introduction by the Master of Ceremonies and a farewell. The same inner polarities are presented as in the novel—heterosexuality/homosexuality, poverty/wealth, Jew/Gentile, and so on. Characters are rearranged in the movie, thus obscuring the similarity to the novel. Some are eliminated entirely (e.g., Otto and the Nowaks); some are retained (e.g., Sally Bowles, Natalia, Fritz); some are renamed (e.g., Christopher Isherwood is now called Brian Roberts); others appear to be condensed (e.g., Maximillian comprises the unlikely combination of qualities of Clive from the "Sally Bowles" chapter with Bernhard from the "Landauers" chapter).

THE FILM

The story itself is simple. A young English doctoral candidate from Cambridge (Brian Roberts) arrives in Berlin in 1930 to complete research necessary for his degree. He is to support himself by giving English lessons. He is a diffident outsider, alienated from his own sexuality. He tells us that he has attempted sex with three girls and that all attempts have been failures. He obtains a room in a rooming house populated by a street walker, a writer of pornographic novels, a "yodeler," and a young American singer-entertainer, all presided over by Frl. Schneider, a down-at-the-heels Berliner.

The movie is dominated by three major plots and subplots: Brian's relationship with the young American singer, Sally Bowles, which culminates in an affair; Sally's affair with the wealthy German aristocrat Maximillian, which culminates in a three-way ménage (Sally/Maximillian, Maximillian/Brian, Sally/Brian), a troika of sorts (an important scene of three-way sexuality in *Goodbye to Berlin* takes place in a dive called the Troika); the love story and eventual marriage between Fritz, the gigolo who has concealed his Jewishness, and Natalia, the Jewish heiress. The musical elements in the film emerge out of scenes in the Kit Kat Klub—Auden and Isherwood's favorite boy-bar in Berlin was the Cosy Corner—in which the songs comment on both the characters and the times. During the film, Maximillian seduces both Sally and Brian and leaves both after the promise of a trip to Africa. Sally becomes pregnant, possibly by Brian. This could never have happened in the novel, where Christopher's (the Brian character) homosexuality, not bisexuality, is implied throughout. The weakwilled Fritz reveals his Jewishness and convinces Natalia to marry him. Although when he first learns that Sally is pregnant Brian asks her to marry him, he is unable to commit himself to her and she aborts the pregnancy. Brian leaves Berlin and Germany for home, leaving Sally behind with her dreams of "amounting to something as an actress."

During the film, Naziism becomes an increasingly ominous and violent presence through an almost tachistoscopic viewing of beatings, of murders, of screams, "Juden! Juden!" These were the years (1930–32)—following the death of Stresemann, a powerful German republican leader, and at the time of final imposition of humiliating war reparations—when Hitler, through strident and vehement denunciations, gained greater and greater power. Again, as in the novel, such scenes are presented with descriptive clarity, virtually without comment.

Quite different from the novel and of particular interest is the introduction into the movie of the Master of Ceremonies of the Kit Kat Klub as a character of central significance.

Let us consider the opening of the film. The screen is grey-black. There is silence. Credits begin to appear. As the title, *Cabaret*, appears, a barely audible mumbling of conversation is heard, gradually increasing in intensity. There is laughter. Instruments begin to tune up. We have begun to see vague images on the screen that slowly become clearer. The movie audience is becoming the audience in the cabaret. We have moved from the outside ("outsiders") inside. There is a long drum roll and finally a smash of cymbals. The distorted face of the Master of Ceremonies appears on the screen—a spectacle, shocking, as though out of an expressionist[1] painting (Otto Dix, George Grosz, or Emil Nolde come to mind). As the camera moves, we realize that this first image of the garishly made up face was a reflection in a distorting mirror along a stage. An atmosphere of uncertainty, close to unreality, has been established.

The Master of Ceremonies sings, "Welcome, stranger . . .," asking the cabaret audience to ". . . leave your troubles outside!" His delivery is hard, mocking, leering, ironic; his expression and made-up face decadent. But most of all, he is knowing. He seems to say: "You, ladies and gentlemen, think yourselves to know reality. I am a clown, a brief distraction. We'll see." We in the movie audience are now the strangers, part of the cabaret audience, part of the film. But the film cuts back and forth to another stranger. The film, through its Master of Ceremonies, is welcoming him to Berlin. It is the character we know from *Goodbye to Berlin* as Christopher Isherwood, here called Brian Roberts.

---

1. German expressionist art developed at the turn of the century as part of the evolving modernist movement, a revolution against the stifling artistic climate of the time. These artistic "secessions" eventually led to the formation of revolutionary associations. Dix, Grosz, and others were part of a later development, the Neue Sachlichkeit (the "new objectivity"), whose works of social criticism often had a bizarre and fantastic quality (Hirschfeld, 1980).

CONTEXT: FILM AND NOVEL

Isherwood, the author, is one of our most intensely autobiographical writers. Through the device of calling his main character Christopher Isherwood in *Goodbye to Berlin* and in his use of semi-autobiographical fiction in his autobiographical works, he intrigues us. We become intensely curious and are made to wonder about those people who were transformed into his fictional characters.

Isherwood (1976) has written about Jean Ross, the woman who forms the basis of the character Sally Bowles: "I wish I could remember what impression Jean Ross . . . made on Christopher when they first met. But I can't. Art has transfigured life and other people's art has transfigured Christopher's art" (p. 59). This is a complex, confusing, and artful statement. The continual shift from first to third person (I, Christopher) including a reference to Christopher's art—Is he referring to the author as a young man or to the character?—confuses. Isherwood continues:

What remains with me from those early years is almost entirely Sally. Beside her, like a reproachful elder sister, stands the figure of Jean as I knew her much later. And both Sally and Jean keep being jostled to one side of my memory to make way for the actresses who have played the part of Sally on stage and screen . . . Sally Bowles's second name was chosen for her by Christopher because he liked the sound of it and also the looks of its owner, a 20 year old American whom he met in Berlin in 1931. The American thought Christopher treated him with "good humored condescension"; Christopher wasn't then aware that this young man was in the process of becoming a composer and novelist who would need nobody's fiction character to help him make his second name famous. His first name was Paul.

Studying early photographs of Jean—that long thin handsome white face, that aristocratic nose, that glossy dark hair, those large brown eyes—I can see that she was full of fun and quite conscious of herself as a comic character. Once a few years later she told Christopher that she was going to Ostende for the weekend. He asked: "Why on earth—?" She answered with her brilliant grin: "So I can come back here and be the Woman from Ostende." I wouldn't care to risk letting Sally say that line [pp. 59–60].

It is intriguing to think that Sally is exciting because she reminds Christopher of a boy. We might consider the presentation of Sally in the film as the embodiment of both heterosexual and homosexual desire. To extend the thesis stated earlier: Boys who have been abandoned by their father through death in war and then claimed by their mother may seek young boys to love so that they may feel loved and desired themselves; in short, a classic, disappointing search for the narcissistic object. Again, recall the bewildering shifts back and forth from the first person (I) to the third person (he, Christopher), from the involved to the observer and back. The passage teases us, implies, leaves us unsatisfied.

An additional perspective about Sally (Jean Ross) comes from Stephen Spender (1980) in a letter written to Isherwood:

> Jean . . . is very well and having an affair with a BBC man. His wife asked her to sleep with him. His wife, like Hindenburg with Hitler, imagined that Jean's attraction would not last, but it has now lasted the amazingly long time of a month so she—the wife— is getting alarmed. Knowing that Jean is attracted to giants she has been giving her a series of tea parties for people not under 6 ft. 5 in. in order to seduce her from her husband [p. 59].

Here, as in the film, is an embedded reference to the times—the hoped for marriage of convenience between Hindenburg and Hitler, which leads instead to betrayal and the final disaster, the end of Weimar and the elevation of Hitler.

Because Isherwood promotes ambiguity, we cannot extricate ourselves from it, for example, the ambiguous reality of the times, the real conflicts of real people (Jean Ross, Isherwood, Spender and others), the imagined conflict of fictional characters. Indeed, "art has transfigured life and other people's art," including the art of moviemakers, "has transfigured Christopher's art." History, art, the interpersonal, and, as we shall see, the intrapsychic become inseparable and lend meaning to each other.

The character Christopher in *Goodbye to Berlin* has often been described as the consummate observer: detached, disinterested, uninvolved. This description has often been extended to indicate that the author, Christopher Isherwood, is himself the character. But this is an oversimplification that cannot stand. In the previously quoted passages, the juxtapositions of "I" and "Christopher," that is, the constant shifting from the first to the third person, is designed to promote uncertainty. There is an "I," an author, who is involved, selecting what to record, a "cameraman"; there is "Christopher," a fictional character, recording, in conflict but trying to keep his distance, a "camera." I suggest here that the two are, in fact, presented to us explicitly in the film: the "I," knowing, involved, beckoning, snickering, teasing—in short, our Master of Ceremonies; and "Christopher," observing, alienated, "outside," and unable to become an "insider"[2]— in short, Brian Roberts.

FORM: NOVEL AND FILM

The shift in presentation from the novel to the movie is important. In the novel, Christopher remains the observing recorder. Behind him rests Isherwood, the author, selecting what is recorded, his involvement and knowingness left implicit. The descriptions of the developing Nazi menace throughout the novel are offstage, never dealt with other than descriptively. The same is true of the major human conflicts portrayed: love, betrayal, sexuality, poverty. Christopher to the end observes, describes, records. But in the movie, from the outset the Master of Ceremonies is a Greek chorus. He sees things as they are. He is decadent, leering, above all, ironic. He teases us with his knowledge of reality and our lack of it. His garish makeup gives him a disturbing, almost uncanny appearance, like a primal scene figure. In short, the embedded author, hidden in *Goodbye to Berlin,* has beeen revealed in the film.

How this disclosure is achieved is of interest. As the Master of Ceremonies greets the audience of the cabaret, we too in the audience are so greeted. The film shifts from the cabaret, and we watch the stranger, Brian, arrive at Sally Bowles's pension. But simultaneously the Master of Ceremonies introduces Sally Bowles in the cabaret to the cabaret audience. What might have been a naturalistic device has become a theatrical device, with the cabaret serving as a counterpart to and commentator upon life. And the Master of Ceremonies is its host, its director.

In an essay about *Cabaret,* Balter (1981) discusses in detail the device of the play within a play, the dream within a dream. He discusses this "framing" and the conventions of the film text, comparing this movie musical with other musicals and opera. The characters, their relationships, and the cabaret as a defense against reality ("It's

---

2. My use of the terms "outsider" and "insider" is intended to evoke the atmosphere of Weimar Germany as elucidated in Peter Gay's cultural history and encapsulated in his title, *Weimar Culture: The Outsider as Insider.* Irreverent and modernist artists and thinkers who were outsiders and rebels in Imperial Germany later became insiders of the Weimar Republic. Ironically, they once again became outsiders following the Nazi takeover.

only a dream") is a central focus of his. His ideas help illuminate what is being presented here. The presence of the Master of Ceremonies only as part of the cabaret, not as part of life itself, is explained in part by Balter's thesis. It also represents the transformation of the implicit author/Christopher split of the novel into the explicit Master of Ceremonies/Brian split of the film.

Every song introduced by the Master of Ceremonies emphasizes the harsh underbelly of life: those things we need to know about ourselves, but don't want to, that we deal with by denial and derisive laughter. Each of these songs comments ironically and indirectly on the events and characters: the Nazi menace; Sally and Brian; Maximillian; the marriage of the Jews, Fritz and Natalia. The Master of Ceremonies and Sally are the principal characters in the cabaret. Sally is a member of the "chorus," whose other main voice is that of its director, the Master of Ceremonies.

Only once does Sally introduce a song herself, and she does that *outside* of the cabaret. She has just gone to meet her father, who characteristically has not shown up. Brian returns to the rooming house to find Sally sitting in the dark. She tells him what has happened. Brian comforts her. The scene becomes sexual. They make love. Sally sings an intensely romantic song, a song with none of the harshness or satire that characterizes those introduced by the Master of Ceremonies ("maybe this time, I'll be lucky . . ."). The scene shifts from the room with Brian to the cabaret. But it is a very different cabaret from the one we have seen, practically empty; the Master of Ceremonies not present. During the song, at one point the camera focuses on Brian, who is flexing his biceps and saying, "Doesn't my body drive you wild with desire?", taking one of Sally's old lines. This scene specifically evokes a passage in one of Isherwood's later autobiographical writings, one that will be referred to later. Here it is sufficient to mention that the linkage is to Isherwood and his father, paralleling those between Sally and her father, sexuality and love.

Thus, the movie presents to us from its first minutes the central situation: the involved, titillating, excited, frightened, degraded Author/Master of Ceremonies juxtaposed with the alienated, observing, difficult to involve Brian (i.e., Christopher). By bringing the now less implicit "author" onstage in the film through the masquerade of the Master of Ceremonies, the film establishes a convention through which the conflicts of the characters may be highlighted, even commented upon. Yet the concealment of the novel persists, the film paralleling the novel. The Christopher character (Brian Roberts) struggles with the problem of engagement versus alienation, observer versus participant, and, of course, homosexuality versus heterosexuality.

The problem of what is really going on about him and in him includes the rise of Naziism and antisemitism. Is Brian, an Englishman, involved? Or is this a "German" problem? In the film, he questions Maximillian, "Who will control them?" when they ride past a stark scene of murder in the streets. Much later there is a beer garden scene, a scene that powerfully—and painfully—evokes the quintessence of the Nazi appeal. For there a scene that begins innocently with a handsome, even pretty, young man singing what seems to be a pastoral lyric turns into one in which a Brown Shirt transforms a group of country people into a zealously patriotic crowd singing a powerful militaristic anthem.

Here the external world has intruded completely. This song is neither introduced by the Master of Ceremonies, nor sung by Sally. It is from outside, outside the frame of the fictional characters, outside the frame of the cabaret, outside the convention of the film. It is reality that can no longer be warded off (Balter, 1981). It is the only sustained presence of the external world (the Germany of 1932) in the entire film—this despite the relentless undercurrent of its presence throughout. After the scene, Brian asks Maximillian, "Do you still think you can control them?" He has excluded himself. This is a German problem. The same can be said of the way he handles his relationship with Sally and, in the final analysis, his intrapsychic conflict.

Gay (1968) has sought the historical roots of Weimar in the Germany of Bismark and then the Kaisers. He has noted that modernism and expressionism in art and culture reflected a rebellion against a strongly paternalistic culture, a revolt of sons against fathers. But under the influence of worldwide economic depression, joblessness, and political ferment, the youth of Weimar Germany thought of these rebels, their fathers, as "middle-aged, not only in years but in ways of thinking" (p. 139). Hitler and the Nazis recognized the importance of youth, who might enslave themselves, "not merely to political adventurers and psychotic idealogues, but to the old industrial-military-bureaucratic machine disguised in new form" (p. 139). Gay terms this "the revenge of the father" (p. 119); that is, a return to paternalism.

In the end Brian (Christopher) leaves Germany and Berlin. The scene is not unlike his arrival, despite his struggles during the film, although it is somewhat more somber at the end than at the beginning. Despite the abortion, despite his own beating at the hands of the Nazis he remains bemused and detached, perhaps like the German people in general. He and Sally shake hands. Sally walks off toward her next adventure, one of her "interviews" with a producer. Not looking back, she signals a goodbye with her "divinely decadent" green nail-polished fingers. Their goodbye restores the balance of their first meeting. No tears, no feeling expressed, as though nothing has really happened. Brian's departure evokes the end of the novel:

> Today the sun is brilliantly shining; it is quite mild and warm. I go out for my last morning walk, without an overcoat or hat. The sun shines, and Hitler is master of this city . . . I catch sight of my face in the mirror of a shop and am shocked to see that I am smiling. You can't help smiling in such beautiful weather. . . . The people on the pavement, and the teacosy dome of the Nollendorfplatz station have an air of curious familiarity, of striking resemblance to something one remembers as normal and pleasant in the past— like a very good photograph.
>   No. Even now I can't altogether believe that any of this has really happened . . ." [Sherwood, 1939, p. 207].

This ending recalls the beginning of the novel: "I am a camera with its shutter open . . ." (p. 1). But the movie does not end where the novel does, for its coda is different from the novel's.

The scene shifts abruptly from the railroad station to the Kit Kat Klub and the Master of Ceremonies introducing Sally. She is back in the cabaret. This final song is a last gasp of denial, a desperate attempt to deal with reality ("Life is a cabaret, old chum"), abandoning and abandonment, pregnancy and abortion, life and death. In the end the Master of Ceremonies comes forward.

He says farewell (this time only in German and French—the Englishman is gone), not goodbye, and disappears. The music becomes discordant and ends, its final ascending chords unresolved. There is a very long, mournful, ominous drum roll, and the camera pans across the same expanse of mirror it did in the beginning of the film. The room is now filled with Nazis, and with a cymbal smash the camera settles on the Nazis in a kind of stop-motion. In contrast to the beginning of the film, this time there is no feeling of confusion. Confusion has been replaced by a feeling of dread; something awful is about to happen. The film ends with an extensive list of credits, the Nazis in the background, the silence total. The authors and filmmakers, through the Master of Ceremonies, have made explicit all that was implicit in the book.

FURTHER EXPLORATION OF BACKGROUND AND CONTEXT:
CHRISTOPHER ISHERWOOD

In 1951 Stephen Spender described the Christopher Isherwood of
1930:

> Isherwood, according to Auden, held no opinions whatsoever
> about anything. He was wholly and simply interested in people.
> He did not like or dislike them, judge them favorably or unfavor-
> ably. He simply regarded them as material for his Work. At the
> same time he was the Critic in whom Auden had absolute trust. If
> Isherwood disliked a poem, Auden destroyed it without demur [p.
> 92].

> I entered so completely into Christopher's moods that although
> I was in part entertained by [his] pronouncements, they also filled
> me with a certain apprehension, and, as we went down the stairs
> into the street, I felt the oppression of the silence which follows
> fateful news. Secretly I was disappointed that Christopher's dra-
> mas rarely ended with a complete catharsis. ("Do you know what
> that bitch Sally said to me last night?" "No." "Perhaps, one day,
> Christopher darling, you will write something really great, like
> Noel Coward.") All the people who had fallen into disgrace were
> sooner or later taken back into favor, for Christopher, so far from
> being the self-effacing spectator he depicts in his novels, was
> really the center of his characters, and neither could they exist
> without him or he without them [p. 112].

> . . . About three years of my life, I realize now, were lived
> precariously off the excitement of being with Isherwood. I told
> him everything, I showed him every letter of any interest I
> received. I looked to his judgement of my friends and activities
> . . . [p. 115].

So Isherwood himself was something of a Master of Ceremonies—
Mentor was his own word (1976, p. 54)—for a small but significant
group, Auden and Spender among them. The similarity to the Master
of Ceremonies in the film becomes evident in the following passage,
published four years *after* the film was produced, describing him with
his "pupil" Spender:

> The Pupil, striding along beside the brisk, large-headed little figure
> of the Mentor, keeps bending his beautiful scarlet face, lest he
> shall miss a word, laughing in anticipation as he does so. There are
> four and a half years between their ages and at least seven inches

between their heights. The Pupil already has a stoop, as tall people must who are eager to hear what the rest of the world is saying. And maybe the Mentor, that little tormentor, actually lowers his voice at times, to make the Pupil bend even lower [Isherwood, 1976, p. 55].

We will be interested in important "facts" of Isherwood's life and imagination, not to explain his art nor to have his art explain him, but because they bring a different reality, context, and meaning to it and to the subsequent "transfigurations" of that art by others.

Christopher Isherwood was born into a middle-class family. His father's side of the family is described as "verging on the aristocratic" (Finney, 1979, p. 19). His father, Frank, was the second son and thus by tradition had to find "aristocratic" work to do so that the entire estate could eventually pass on to his elder brother. Being "in trade" would never do. Such men in England were limited to selected professions, such as law or medicine, or soldiering. Like his own father, he became a professional soldier, rising eventually to the rank of Lt. Colonel. Although an adequate soldier, he was never at ease with it. He was described as "reticent and sensitive [preferring] to spend his spare time reading, painting and playing music, rather than drinking and exchanging dirty stories in the officer's mess" (p. 19). Frank's marriage to Kathleen, Christopher's mother, was delayed by her father because of Frank's impecunious situation. It was her father's revenge on the class system that had made the impoverished Frank an aristocrat by birth and had relegated him, a wealthy wine merchant, to the lower classes, "in trade." After her marriage to Frank at 35, Kathleen became "more upper class than the upper class family into which she married" (p. 20). It is ironic and very significant that Kathleen's efforts to uphold English class distinctions occurred at the very time when such values were disintegrating.

It was Christopher's father who introduced him to fantasy as his diary-keeping mother initiated him into journal-keeping. Frank taught six-year-old Christopher reading and writing by compiling an illustrated daily called the *Toy-Drawer Times,* which was kept up intermittently until Christopher went to boarding school at age ten. There were many home theatricals. When he was seven years old, Christopher's father gave him a toy theater, which enthralled the boy. At age ten, as typical for upper class English boys, Christopher was sent to boarding school, where he eventually met Auden. It was at school that first year, just short of his 11th birthday in May of 1915, that his father was killed in the second battle of Ypres.

Isherwood (1971) wrote in detail about that time:

> When Christopher came back to St. Edmund's [boarding school]
> in September 1915, after his summer of convalescence, he wore a
> black crepe band around his sleeve. He had now acquired a social
> status which was respected by everybody in wartime England,
> including the crown, the church and the press: he was an Orphan
> of a Dead Hero. At St. Edmund's there were only two or three
> others who shared this distinction, and at first he was vain of it; it
> made you, or rather your mourning-armband, slightly sacred. . . .
> However, Christopher soon found that being a Sacred Orphan had
> grave disadvantages—that it was indeed a kind of curse which was
> going to be upon him, seemingly, for the rest of his life. Hence-
> forward, he was under an obligation to be worthy of Frank, his
> Hero-Father, at all times and in all ways. [The headmasters] were
> the first to make him aware of this obligation. Later there were
> many more who tried to do so: people he actually met, and
> disembodied voices from pulpits, newspapers, books. He began
> to think of them collectively as The Others [pp. 501–502].

A secret, at first, and passionate rage welled up in young Isherwood
against "The Others" who had conjured up the "Hero-Father," that is,
schoolmasters, ministers, newspapers, books—in short, society. The
Hero-Father had come between him and Frank, who had told stories
and drawn pictures.

> He hadn't grieved much for Frank in 1915, but that was because
> he had then regarded Frank's death chiefly as an injury done to
> Kathleen [i.e., his mother]. He had also been jealous of Frank
> when he came between him and Kathleen by dying and thus
> monopolizing her emotions. And then the "Hero-Father" had
> come between him and Frank [p. 503].

He rejected the Hero-Father. But by denying duty to the Hero-Father a
far greater rejection occurs: "Flag, Old School Tie, The Unknown
Soldier, The Land That Bore You, The God of Battles," (p. 502) that is,
traditional values.

And so a fantasy, an absurdist fantasy, of an "Anti-Heroic Hero"
was evolved by the young Isherwood:

> The Anti-Heroic Hero always appears in uniform, because this is
> his disguise; he isn't really a soldier. He is an artist who has

renounced his painting, music and writing in order to dedicate his life to antimilitary masquerade. He lives this masquerade right through, day by day to the end, and crowns his performance by actually getting himself killed in battle. By thus fooling everybody (except Christopher) into believing he is the Hero-Father, he demonstrates the absurdity of the military mystique and its solemn cult of War and Death. . . . He shows his contempt for Army documents by doing comic sketches of them, and for his dignity as an officer by knitting in the midst of a bombardment. He tells Christopher that his sword is useless except for toasting bread and that he never fires his revolver because he can't hit anything with it and hates the bang it makes. There was a report, which Christopher accepted because he wanted to believe it, that Frank had last been seen signaling directions to his men with a short swagger cane as he led them into action. Christopher made this symbolic: The Anti-Heroic Hero mocks the loud Wagnerian Hero-Death by flourishing a stick like a baton at it, as if conducting an opera [pp. 503–504].

It is not hard for us to see in this sardonic, teasing, satirical, witty, self-sacrificing fantasied Anti-Hero the human and loving Frank. Perhaps we may also see elements of the Master of Ceremonies and the author himself.

We may also see in the idea "he isn't *really* a soldier" a classic defense against anxiety. Frank is not a dangerous man, and neither is Christopher. Frank need not fear Christopher's parricidal tendencies, nor Christopher any reprisal from Frank. It's only a masquerade. The masquerade may then be seen as related to the familiar dream content, "It's only a dream!"

Isherwood recalled parts of his father's last letters:

I don't think it matters very much what Christopher learns as long as he remains himself and develops along his own lines. . . . The whole point of sending him to school was to flatten him out, so to speak, and to make him like other boys and, when all is said and done, I don't know that it is at all desirable or necessary, and I for one would much rather have him as he is [p. 505].

It is interesting to hear Frank's voice. It may remind us of Isherwood's ambiguous reference to himself, sometimes as "I," sometimes as "Christopher." When we hear the author speak of himself as Christopher, it may be that we are hearing the author identified with his dead father (or his image of him as the Anti-Hero), carrying him along with him, a constant companion.

We mentioned earlier a scene in the movie where Brian flexes his muscles after making love to Sally. The scene calls up an autobiographical passage. Isherwood (1971) recalls that at about age six he used to watch his father doing exercises every morning, naked except for his undershorts. He remembers taking a definitely erotic pleasure "in the sight of his father's muscles tensing and bulging within his well knit body, and in the virile smell of his sweat" (p. 350). This may be seen as a screen memory, whose contents call forth the visual imagery of a primal scene. He then recalls his later masturbatory fantasies:

> But when Christopher began masturbating, his fantasies weren't about Frank. He imagined himself lying wounded on a battlefield with his clothes partly torn off him, being tended by a woman; Kathleen, no doubt, in disguise. The mood of this fantasy was exhibitionistic; Christopher's own nakedness was what excited him. His wounds were painless [p. 350].

Although it would be unusual to interpret the manifest content of a fantasy, we do have some associations. The image of the woman reminds him of his mother. Frank is brought in through a negation. A few further remarks are possible. The wounded soldier, however painless his wounds, is tended by a woman. The conditions for sexual excitement are masochistic and submissive. The image of himself as a wounded soldier could easily remind us of the image of his soldier-father, Frank. The excitement in his own nakedness also recalls his excitement in looking at his father's virile body. The wounds suggest castration anxiety (related to an erotic interest in both mother and father) and the defense against that anxiety, that is, the wounds are painless. As in the playful naming of Sally Bowles for Paul Bowles, heterosexuality and homosexuality are combined in a single image. These childhood memories and masturbatory fantasies remind us of Isherwood's later (1976) descriptions of his adult sexual preferences:

> . . . arm twisting, sparring and wrestling half naked. . . . What excited Christopher most, a struggle which turned gradually into a sex act, seemed perfectly natural to these German boys; indeed it excited them too. . . . This rough athletic sexmaking was excellent isometric exercise. It strengthened Christopher's muscles more than all his years of joyless compulsory games at school. He felt grateful to his partners for his new strength. There was much love

in his contact with their sturdy bodies; love which made no demands beyond the pleasure of the moment [p. 31].

Christopher more or less took up a crusade, the crusade of the Anti-Son, allying himself with the Anti-Heroic Hero against The Others, the Hero-Father and the Holy-Widow, a role The Others forced upon Kathleen. His mother's feminine patriotism (of the Holy-Widow) disgusted him with her and with England (the Motherland) and attracted him to Germany (the Fatherland), which had killed the Hero-Father. Later, Isherwood's adolescent fantasies were filled with such images as "The Test" (an imagined challenge he might meet by performing an heroic act), "The Enemy," the "truly strong the the truly weak man." Unwittingly and unconsciously, he was attempting in fantasy to meet the demands of "The Others," (society), to live up to his "Hero-Father" (Isherwood, 1938, 1971).

The death of his father—who at one time had been derogated as a dreamer, a second son, a ne'er do well—combined with his mother's pressure for him to take his father's place and to support the values of the English Aristocracy threw him into a rebellion. His fury toward his mother could not be better demonstrated than by this passage written in 1976, in which he describes himself at age 25, just about the time of his Berlin experience. He had just completed his only full sexual experience with a woman, which had been intensely pleasurable:

Couldn't you get yourself excited by the shape of girls too—if you worked hard at it? Perhaps. And couldn't you invent another myth—to put girls into? Why the hell should I? Well, it would be a lot more convenient for you if you did. Then you wouldn't have all these problems. Society would accept you. You wouldn't be out of step with nearly everybody else. It was at this point in his self-examination that Christopher would become suddenly, blindly furious. Damn Nearly Everybody. Girls are what the state and the church and the law and the press and the medical profession endorse and command me to desire. My mother endorses them too. She is silently brutishly willing me to get married and breed grandchildren for her. Her will is the will of Nearly Everybody, and in their will is my death. . . . If boys didn't exist, I would have to invent them [pp. 11–12].

The passion in these statements suggests that conflict is not really resolved. Isherwood has said about these remarks, "Psychologists might find Christopher's admission highly damaging to his case, and his

violence highly suspicious. They might accuse him of repressed heterosexuality" (p. 12). Perhaps we might better say that his protracted self-
examination, which continued for more than half a century, represents
courageous truth-seeking, but that it remains incomplete.

Isherwood was not alone in being personally affected by World War
I. An entire generation of fathers and older brothers was wiped out on
both sides of the channel, bringing into reality the worst unconscious
wishes and fears of a generation of boys (Wangh, 1968). The sons of the
heroic dead and living victors, the English, were as affected as the sons
of the humiliated dead and living defeated, the Germans. It would be
simplistic to attribute the disaffected, bisexual, lost generation on both
sides of the channel to the rebellion against the generation of heroic
and humiliated, but, above all, absent fathers and their hated, desired,
feared, martyred mothers. Nevertheless, this was a factor not limited
to the few famous literary figures that we have been considering. After
all, their literature spoke to a sizable population, who bought and read
their books.

DISCUSSION: INTEGRATION OF THEMES

Toward the end of *Cabaret,* a scene provides a point of contact for
the interrelated themes that have been considered so far: cultural and
social history, individual history (Christopher Isherwood), form and
content of the texts, novel and film. Fritz and Natalia, the Jewish
couple, have just been married. Brian and the pregnant Sally are
picnicking in a park. Sally is in a romantic frame of mind; Brian looks
sulky. Bubbling with enthusiasm, Sally says, "Oh Brian. It's fantastic
isn't it? Just—your life and mine solved in one fell swoop and all by the
baby. I guess it's just about the most significant baby the world has
even known—since Jesus. He'll be a most strange and extraordinary
baby." In the background a song is being sung, "Heirat" ("Marriage"). Brian does not, can not respond to her. Without further ado,
Sally decides on an abortion.

From the moment the affair with Brian was consummated, despite
wild vicissitudes—her promiscuity, the ménage with Maximillian and
Brian—Brian represented conventional stability for Sally. He would be
there for her as her father was not. When she first found herself to be
pregnant, without knowing by whom, Brian did say, "I'd like to marry
you." When they argue following the abortion, a scene in which Brian
is more than a little self-righteous, it is Sally who says, "Brian, I really
do love you." He can merely respond, "I think you do love me. Are
you all right? Is there anything I can do for you?" He can not commit

himself. When Brian leaves the room, Sally says, miserably, "Aw, shit!" The leave taking follows.

As "wild" as she may be, Sally (like Germany?) has been asking for "conventional" stability. As conventional as he may seem, Brian can not, will not offer that. His response is not the open fury of Isherwood to his mother, but it can be seen as vengeful. He shows that he has the means to satisfy her—to impregnate her and to marry her—but in the end he withdraws and withholds.

As has been indicated, an important element of Isherwood's life and work has been a relentless campaign against "The Others" and all traditional values. These values embody what mother wanted, duty to the Hero-Father and an heir. The sudden killing of his father in battle had left him alone with his mother and with the potential to please her. But he did not. His solution was to invent an Anti-Heroic Hero, who only appeared to be a soldier but whose aim in life was to ridicule the military establishment by getting killed in battle. Christopher could then identify with this revisionist version of his father, Frank, doing his "bidding" by defying his mother and tradition—including, of course, through homosexuality—thereby remaining his father's "good boy," mollifying his spirit through rebellion and masochistic sexual submission and denying his oedipal satisfaction and guilt.

When the authors of Cabaret created the centrally important character of the Master of Ceremonies, they responded to the unconscious fantasies embedded in the text of the novel; they unwittingly brought the off-stage and silent author of Goodbye to Berlin onstage. In so doing they intuitively presented not only the author, but also his imagined absurdist fantasy figure in an "anti-military masquerade"; they preserved the revisionist Frank. They powerfully evoked the plight of post-World War I British and German youth, the political and cultural revolution that the Weimar Republic signified, and the radical changes that were taking place in the historically deeply held English class distinctions.

When Cabaret first appeared, it was to somewhat mixed critical reviews, but there was agreement that it was unconventional. For example, Kael (1972) wrote, "After Cabaret it should be a while before performers once again climb hills singing or a chorus breaks into song on a hayride; it is not merely that Cabaret violates the wholesome approach of big musicals but that it violates the pseudo-naturalistic tradition . . ." (p. 84). Again, the feeling evoked is of rebellion against established values.

There is another formal element in the presentation of these works that is noteworthy: concealment and revelation. Maximillian's heterosexuality conceals his homosexuality; Brian's homosexuality conceals his heterosexuality; Fritz, the gentile impostor, conceals his Jewishness; the prim and proper Natalia conceals her passionate sexuality. Isherwood's writing begins with concealment (fiction) and ends with stark revelation (autobiography). The concealment seems to be, in Isherwood's terms, "playing to the gallery" (1976, p. 52)—again the metaphor of a primal scene—ideally suited for theatrical or cinematic presentation, the "disguised" Master of Ceremonies.

All of this fits the idea of a masquerade, that which is being presented as both concealing *and* revealing the truth. We might suppose that the concealed truths include observation of the primal scene, the unconscious fantasy of having committed an oedipal crime (unconscious parricidal fantasies) and the unconscious fantasy of having been given to the mother by an abandoning father. At the cultural level, the overt rebellion against established values (modernism, expressionism, Dada, decadence) concealed a wish to submit slavishly to absolute authority, to, ultimately, Hitler and the Nazis. What is revealed to us in these works, particularly dramatic in *Cabaret,* is the defensive masquerade. Such public display might also be seen as rebellious.

CONCLUSIONS

The human response to overwhelming trauma is often denial, dissociation, or both. Children often do not believe that a parent or a beloved grandparent has died, or else seem to behave as though nothing of much moment has happened. But the sudden death of a parent, especially during the oedipal phase or early adolescence, will have lasting effects on the person, in particular on those intrapsychic structures that result from the resolution of the oedipus complex: the superego and the ego ideal. When a generation of fathers is suddenly slain, the cultural response will also be massive (Wangh, 1968). There will be individual vicissitudes—Isherwood presents for us his own—but the entire society will be affected. Isherwood's fiction and life can be seen, from one point of view, as representing a protracted working through of a catastrophe.

In this connection, Brenner (1976) has pointed out that:

. . . what one observes in adult analytic patients and what one can construct and observe, both directly and through analysis of childhood mental life, is that intense unpleasure associated with libidinal and aggressive wishes is not limited to danger situations, i.e., it is not present only as anxiety. It occurs also when one is convinced, whether consciously or unconsciously, whether by fact or by fantasy, that what is at other times only feared has actually happened [pp. 99–100].

Freud (1926) postulated four major calamities (real or fantasied) as the sources of traumatic situations: object loss, loss of love of the object, genital loss or injury, and superego condemnation. Brenner suggests that there are two major affective responses to these situations: anxiety (something terrible may happen) or depression (something terrible has already happened).

Goodbye to Berlin has undergone at least four theatrical revisions (none by Isherwood himself) and has at least six related autobiographies and semi-autobiographical novels. It is not surprising to note the emergence of the Isherwood stories and their revisions by other artists, at the times they have occurred: *Goodbye to Berlin,* 1939, just at the outbreak of World War II; *I am a Camera,* 1951, during the McCarthy era and the Korean Conflict; *Cabaret* (musical play), 1966, and *Cabaret* (film), 1972, at the beginning and the end of the Vietnam War. Through his early novel and the later novels and autobiographies, Isherwood has presented his efforts at working through a life situation. In his instance, universal conflict (the oedipus) is brought into apposition with catastrophic trauma. The presentation of the Berlin stories in other forms by other artists took place during strategic historical moments. Thinking along the lines suggested by Brenner, we may say that these artistic works can be taken as cautionary: something terrible may happen again. Audience reaction, however, tends to be depressive and pessimistic: something terrible has already happened and it's being done to us again. This latter response seems to have reached its acme (of the constellation of works based on *Goodbye to Berlin*) with the movie *Cabaret*.

We might say that the film *Cabaret* is for the movie audience what the Master of Ceremonies is for Brian and Sally in the film, what the author Isherwood is for the character Christopher in the novel, and what the fantasied Anti-Heroic Hero (the disguised Frank) was for Isherwood: a device that selects and records for us what we can know and are defended against. That is, it is a mechanism by which we become engaged in the affects and conflicts against which we defend by denial, repression, and dissociation, tending to repeat neurotic patterns rather than remembering events.

A study of Isherwood's own writings strongly suggests that his own rebellious "masquerade" has something to do with an unconscious fantasy of having committed an oedipal crime; it is the fantasy life of a "young man living at a certain period in a certain European country, ... subjected to a certain kind of environment, certain stimuli, certain influences" (Isherwood, 1938, Preface). I would add: following a great world catastrophe with another one impending. In itself that most elemental act of human rebellion (the fantasied oedipal crime) embedded in these works probably has something to do with their power.

The oedipal vicissitudes discussed herein thus take on specific meaning in the context of the cultural and historical currents described, and those same societal events take on additional meaning in the context of the oedipal vicissitudes of its members.

Although applied psychoanalysis presents vexing problems, it offers an additional means of enriching the study of related disciplines, in this instance, literary and film criticism and cultural history. The repeated reinterpretation of a literary text in other forms (theater, film) over a number of decades may be conceptualized along the lines of Freud's compulsion to repeat. Such repetition suggests that embedded in the original work are universal factors (organizing fantasies) that can be discerned in the different but related reinterpretations of the original by successive generations of artists. Furthermore, it is suggested that these reinterpretations, when presented in the theater arts, specifically meet cultural needs of the moment—the needs of an audience—and that the study of these events is assisted by psychoanalytic knowledge. That is, the text and its contexts will show a consistency of relationship. In that sense, "the text is not all."

BIBLIOGRAPHY

ARLOW, J. A. (1961). Ego psychology and the study of mythology. *J. Amer. Psychoanal. Assn.*, 9:371–393.

BALTER, L. (1981). Discussion of *Cabaret*. North Shore University Hospital, Department of Psychiatry Grand Rounds.

BRENNER, C. (1976). *Psychoanalytic Technique and Psychic Conflict.* New York: International Universities Press.

CABARET (1972). A movie musical produced by Feuer and Martin, directed by Bob Fosse. Music and Lyrics by John Kander and Fred Ebb. Script by Jay Allen and Hugh Wheeler. Based on *Goodbye to Berlin* by Christopher Isherwood.

DRUTEN, J. van (1951). *I am a Camera.* Play based on *Goodbye to Berlin* by Christopher Isherwood.

ERIKSON, E. H. (1950). *Childhood and Society.* New York: W. W. Norton.

FINNEY, B. (1979). *Christopher Isherwood, A Critical Biography.* New York: Oxford University Press.

FREUD, S. (1914). Remembering, repeating and working through. *Standard Edition,* 12:145–156. London: Hogarth Press, 1958.

———(1920). Beyond the pleasure principle. *Standard Edition,* 18:1–64. London: Hogarth Press, 1955.

————(1926). Inhibitions, symptoms and anxiety. *Standard Edition,* 20:75–172. London: Hogarth Press, 1959.

GAY, P. (1968). *Weimar Culture.* New York: Harper Torchbooks.

HIRSCHFELD, S. B. (1980). *Expressionism, A German Intuition 1905–1920.* New York: Solomon R. Guggenheim Foundation.

HYNES, S. (1977). *The Auden Generation.* New York: Viking Press.

ISHERWOOD, C. (1937). *Sally Bowles.* London: Hogarth Press.

————(1938). *Lions and Shadows.* New York: New Directions, 1977.

————(1939). Goodbye to Berlin. *The Berlin Stories.* New York: New Directions, 1954.

————(1971). *Kathleen and Frank.* New York: Curtis Books.

————(1976). *Christopher and His Kind.* New York: Discus.

KAEL, P. (1972). Grinning. *The New Yorker.* Feb. 19, 1972, pp. 84–88.

REED, G. S. (1982). Toward a method for applying psychoanalysis to literature. *Psychoanal. Quar.,* 51:19–42.

SPENDER, S. (1951). *World Within World.* New York: Harcourt, Brace.

————(1980). *Letters to Christopher.* Santa Barbara, CA: Black Sparrow Press.

WANGH, M. (1968). A psychogenic factor in the recurrence of war. *Internat. J. Psycho-Anal.,* 49:319–323.

Author Index

Subject Index